Birth on the Threshold

Birth on the Threshold

Childbirth and Modernity in South India

Cecilia Van Hollen

UNIVERSITY OF CALIFORNIA PRESS
Berkeley · Los Angeles · London

University of California Press
Berkeley and Los Angeles, California

University of California Press, Ltd.
London, England

Chapter Four was published in different form as "Invoking *Vali:* Painful Technologies of Modern Birth in South India," *Medical Anthropology Quarterly* 17, no. 1 (March 2003). Chapter Five was published in an earlier form as "Moving Targets: Routine IUD Insertion in Maternity Wards in Tamil Nadu, India," *Reproductive Health Matters* 6, no. 11 (May 1997); and Chapter Six was published in different form in Santi Rozario and Geoffrey Samuel London, eds., *The Daughters of Hariti: Birth and Female Healers in South and Southeast Asia* (London: Routledge, 2002). All are reprinted here by permission.

Library of Congress Cataloging-in-Publication Data

Van Hollen, Cecilia Coale
Birth on the threshold : childbirth and modernity in South India / Cecilia Van Hollen.
p. cm.
Includes bibliographical references and index.
ISBN 0-520-22358-6 (cloth : alk. paper)—
ISBN 0-520-22359-4 (pbk. : alk. paper)
1. Childbirth—India, South. I. Title.
RG530.3.I42 I583 2003
618.2'00954—dc21

2003003890

Manufactured in the United States of America

12 11 10 09 08 07 06 05 04 03
10 9 8 7 6 5 4 3 2 1

The paper used in this publication is both acid-free and totally chlorine-free (TCF). It meets the minimum requirements of ANSI/NISO Z39.48–1992 (R 1997). ♾

For Christopher and Eliza Van Hollen,
who gave birth to my life in South Asia,
and for Jeffrey and Lila Rodgers,
who let me share that life with them.
And in loving memory of baby Charlotte.

Contents

Acknowledgments

Had my parents not taken me as a child to live in South Asia, this study and the book would, most likely, have never come to be. First and foremost, I thank them for teaching me the importance of embracing the world.

In India, so many have helped so graciously that I cannot mention them all. My deepest gratitude is to all the women and men who participated in this study, sharing their stories of joy and pain, of frustration and accomplishment, and including me in their celebrations. My research assistants—Annette Mathews and Haripriya Narasimhan—were true collaborators on this project; without their knowledge, sensitivity, and friendship none of this would have been possible. I am particularly indebted to Annette Mathews, who worked with me the entire year of 1995, assisting with interviews and with the painstaking work of translation and transcription, as well as with the collection of materials from numerous government offices. With a background in social work and a familiarity with medical establishments in Tamil Nadu, Annette was also an invaluable asset in the process of analyzing the underlying meanings and motives behind people's comments in interviews, and she often suggested avenues of inquiry which would not have occurred to me. Perhaps most important, Annette's lively and humorous personality helped to both put people at ease and inspire animated discussions. Haripriya Narasimhan's assistance with the same kind of work toward the end of 1995 and again in 1997 also proved invaluable. I am particularly grateful that Haripriya was able and eager to travel with me on my visits to regions of Tamil Nadu beyond Madras and Kaanathur-Reddikuppam. Haripriya's background in anthropology and, particularly, in different cultural ideologies and practices within Tamil Nadu led me to think about my research materials in a new light. Finally, Rajeswari Prabhakaran devoted much time and energy to helping with transcriptions and translations and made arrangements for me to witness an elaborate Brahmin *cīmantam* ritual. Much of this research was facilitated by my long-standing affiliation with the Working Women's Forum in Madras. I am greatly indebted to the forum's president, Jaya Aranachalam, and to all of the women involved in the Reproductive Health program for their insights and organizational skills. I am also appreciative of the staff at the IPP-V Santhome zonal hospital in Madras for facilitating my ongoing research in that hospital. And Padmini Swaminathan, my mentor at the Madras Institute for Development Studies, provided suggestions and encouragement throughout the project.

My greatest intellectual debt is to my mentor and friend Lawrence Cohen, who gave generously of his time, and who guided, challenged, and encouraged me at every stage of this project. Arjun Appadurai, Peter van der Veer, and David Ludden all helped with the initial formulation of this project. Nancy Scheper-Hughes, Judith Justice, Eugene Irschick, Patricia Jeffery, Pauline Kolenda, Akhil Gupta, Barbara Ramusack, Susan Wadley, Kathleen Erwin, Sandra Cate, and the anonymous reviewers for the University of California Press have all provided invaluable comments at various stages throughout the process of writing the book. I am also extremely grateful to Kausalya Hart for her careful assistance with translating tape-recorded interviews, and to V. A. Vidya for her help with the use of diacritics in the book.

This book has benefited from the material support of many institutions. Grants from the University of Pennsylvania enabled me to carry out two preliminary fieldwork studies in 1991 and 1993 to set the groundwork for this project. The bulk of the research was carried out in 1995 with the generous support of a Fulbright-Hayes Doctoral Dissertation Research Abroad grant. A Lowie grant from the University of California, Berkeley, allowed me to do a follow-up study in 1997. A Woodrow Wilson Dissertation Grant in Women's Studies provided support while I was writing the manuscript for this book. Finally, the Institute for Scholarship in the Liberal Arts at the University of Notre Dame provided financial assistance with the final production of the manuscript. Thank you also to Naomi Schneider, Caralyn Bialo, and Dore Brown at the University of California Press for their enthusiasm and editorial insights.

Finally, my heartfelt thanks to Jeffrey Rodgers, who has provided every kind of support imaginable, not only during the processes of researching, writing, and editing this book, but throughout my long, itinerant, and sometimes arduous journey as an anthropologist. Our children, Lila and Jasper, have taught me that the fruit of birth is certainly worth the pain! I hope others will feel the same about this book.

Note on Transliteration

VOWELS

Tamil vowels can be either long or short; short vowels are unstressed and long vowels are stressed. Long vowels are indicated with a dash over the letter.

SHORT VOWELS

a	as in c*u*p
i	as in s*i*t
e	as in n*e*t
u	as in p*u*t
o	as in *o*ld

LONG VOWELS

ā	as in f*a*ther
ī	as in n*ee*d
ē	as in l*a*ke
ū	as in m*oo*d
ō	as in r*o*pe

There are also two diphthongs:

ai	as in m*i*ght
ow	as in c*ow*

CONSONANTS

Consonants are also short and long; short consonants are unstressed, long consonants are stressed. Long consonants are indicated by doubling the letter.

The sounds "b," "j," and "g" are represented by *p, c,* and *k*. Whether or not they are voiced depends on their position.

Consonants are also differentiated by stops, nasals, and medials. There are six different points of articulation of consonants (velar, palatal, retroflex, dental, labial, and alveolar).

STOPS

Single

velar	k	as in *g*et or *h*ard
palatal	c	as in *s*ing
retroflex	ḍ	similar to i*d*le (but retroflexed)
dental	t	similar to *th*e
labial	p	as in *p*ut or am*b*er
alveolar	ṟ	pronounced like a slightly trilled English *r*

Double

velar	kk	as in sti*ck*y
palatal	cc	as in *ch*ick
retroflex	ḍḍ	similar to la*dd*er (but longer and retroflexed)
dental	tt	as in *t*ape
labial	pp	as in sta*p*le
alveolar	ṟṟ	similar to *tr*ain

NASAL CONSONANTS

velar	ṅ	as in i*n*k
palatal	ñ	as in lou*n*ge
retroflex	ṇ	similar to u*n*der (but retroflexed)
dental	n	as in a*n*them
labial	m	as in *m*y
alveolar	ṉ	as in ma*n*

MEDIAL CONSONANTS

palatal	y	as in pa*y*
flap	r	as in fa*r*
lateral	l	as in ca*ll*

labial	v	as in *v*an or *w*ander
retroflex flap	ṛ	similar to si*r*
retroflex lateral	ḷ	similar to o*l*den

SANSKRIT-DERIVED SOUNDS AND WORDS

In Sanskrit-derived words, ṣ indicates the sound "sh," as in *sh*ut; and in some Sanskrit-derived words, *s* indicates the sound "s" as in *S*am.

NAMES

Names of people, places, deities, and castes are spelled in the book without diacritical marks.

PROLOGUE

Birth on the Threshold

Mumtaz was nineteen years old when I first met her in her home in Nochikuppam, Madras (now called Chennai), the capital of Tamil Nadu, in 1993.[1] *She lived in a one-room thatched house that looked out onto a sandy beach dotted with fishing catamarans and then onto the Indian Ocean beyond. I entered her house with a group of four other women, all of whom worked for the Working Women's Forum (WWF), a women's organization based in Madras. Kasthuri and Komala were both health workers for WWF; Durga was a health supervisor; and Mary was a coordinator who came along to help with translations. We all stooped our backs to pass through the doorway into the house and sat in a circle with Mumtaz and her one-year-old son. Mumtaz's son had been born right in this house, and we came to talk with her about his birth. It was increasingly difficult to find women in this city who had their deliveries at home, so I was interested to know more about the events of the birth.*

Mumtaz was the seventh daughter born into a Muslim family. Her eldest sister was educated through high school,[2] *but Mumtaz and her other sisters did not receive any formal education. She was married when she was seventeen and had her first baby when she was eighteen. Her mother-in-law lived in Royapettah, an area of Madras north of Nochikuppam. Her husband spent most of his time in that house in Roy-*

apettah with his first wife and their three children but would come to see Mumtaz once or twice a week. When she married him, Mumtaz did not know that her husband already had a wife. When he came to visit her he would bring her enough money for food. He refused to let her work outside of the home since he said she did not need to work as long as he was providing her with money. Mumtaz's own mother and one of her sisters lived in Nochikuppam, close to Mumtaz.

Mumtaz had been planning to have her delivery in Kasthurba Gandhi Hospital, one of the largest public hospitals in Madras, where most women from Nochikuppam went for their deliveries. Her mother had told her that she should go to the hospital because it was considered unlucky (rāci illai) *to have the baby at home and because in the hospital there were many people to take care of everything and to clean the mother and baby.*

Mumtaz's labor pains began in the middle of the night. She tried to bear the pain alone for a while by whispering "Allah, Allah, Amman" to herself. But when the pains became too severe she called for her mother. Her mother sent a neighbor off to summon an auto-rickshaw to take her daughter to the hospital, and then she came quickly to Mumtaz's house and prepared an herbal medicine (kaṣāyam) *to help speed up the labor. The baby was born before the man returned from getting the rickshaw. Mumtaz explained that she had delivered the baby right in the doorway* (vācal) *of the house. As soon as the baby was born, even before the placenta had come out, Mumtaz's mother ran to summon Komala, who came immediately and helped with the delivery. Although Komala was not mandated to conduct deliveries in her capacity as a WWF health worker, she had some basic knowledge of the procedures involved because she had received training in maternal and child health care in order to become a health worker for WWF and she frequently accompanied women to the hospital for their deliveries.*

Komala boiled some water to wash her hands and a razor blade and then helped deliver the placenta while Mumtaz was still on the doorstep. Komala cut the umbilical cord and tied it with a piece of household thread. She put the placenta in a pot and buried it on the beach in a hole which was deep enough that the stray dogs roaming on the beach would not be able to dig it up. Komala then washed and wiped Mumtaz and her baby, changed Mumtaz's clothes, and took them inside the house to lie down and rest. After three days, Komala took Mumtaz to the hospital to register the birth. Since the baby had been born at home, the hospital staff gave Mumtaz and the baby a tetanus shot and dressed the baby's umbilical cord.

• • •

I met a number of other women throughout Tamil Nadu who, like Mumtaz, had been planning to deliver their babies in a hospital but in the end suddenly found themselves delivering at home. What struck me was the fact that several of these women told me that they had delivered their babies *right* in the doorway *(vācal),* the threshold between the home and the world. In Tamil Nadu this is considered to be a vulnerable space through which evil influences can pass, and a fierce mask or a scarecrowlike image is often posted above the doorway on the outside of the house to ward off evil spirits.[3] It is also considered to be a sacred space, one which Tamil women decorate every day at dawn with geometric designs made of rice flour known as *kōlams.* These *kōlams* bring blessings to all sentient and nonsentient beings who pass in and out of the house throughout the day.[4] The *vācal* is considered to be both vulnerable and sacred because of its association with the movement back and forth between a private, protected space and a public arena. When women say that they delivered their babies "right on the *vācal,*" it can be understood as a metaphor for the transition from the private space of the home to the public domain of the hospital.[5] Because these are women from poor communities in Tamil Nadu, the hospitals in which they are increasingly giving birth are government-subsidized public hospitals.

The saying that one has given birth right on the *vācal* is not simply a metaphor for a shift from one *institutional* site (i.e., the family and the midwife) to another institutional site (i.e., the public hospital as a site of both the state and biomedicine), but also symbolizes a shift in systems of knowledge about the body in general and women's reproductive bodies in particular. Women like Mumtaz, who report having given birth right on the thresholds of their houses, are quite literally straddling divergent systems of meaning. And the vulnerability attributed to the *vācal* mirrors the tension experienced by women and by communities as they negotiate multiple understandings of the bodies they inhabit.

This is a book about birth on the threshold, about movement and change in the conceptualization and experience of childbirth. (I use the term "childbirth" in an inclusive way to refer to processes of pregnancy, delivery, and the postpartum period, as well as to practices of birth control as they affect the experience of childbirth.) More specifically, this is an ethnographic study of how modernity was impacting the experiences of poor women during childbirth in the South Indian state of Tamil Nadu at the end of the twentieth century, and of the transformations of the cultural constructions of gender—particularly of maternity—produced in this process. Like Margaret Jolly, I am interested in how the relationship between maternity and modernity is experienced, understood, and represented.[6]

One of the key points I want to make is that to speak of "how modernity impacts childbirth" is *not* to imply that there is one monolithic thing that we can call "modern birth" in the contemporary global order. Although the modernizing project, including the interest in promoting biomedical systems of knowledge, is global in scope, it is interpreted and acted upon in unique ways at the microphysical level by individual actors, collectivities, and institutions. In this book I examine the ways in which particular aspects of the modernizing process are localized to create a unique, or vernacular, form and experience of modern birth among lower-class women in Tamil Nadu. Here "local" refers not only to specific national, regional, and community contexts, but also to class and gender categories, namely lower class and female.[7] This is a crucial point, since women whom I met were critical of the class- and, to some extent, caste-based forms of discrimination which they faced in public hospitals, and they were acutely aware of how their class and gender status constrained the choices they could make about their reproductive health.

During the 1995 United Nations' Fourth World Conference on Women, in Beijing, debates were waged over two opposing (or so they were constructed) agendas for the international women's movement—the fight for reproductive rights and the struggle against the feminization of poverty. For poor women in Tamil Nadu who were making decisions about what kind of care to seek in childbirth, reproductive rights and the feminization of poverty were always inextricably linked.

INTRODUCTION

Childbirth and Modernity in Tamil Nadu

Modern Birth and the Transformation of Gender

Whereas earlier anthropological approaches to reproduction tended to focus on how reproductive practices and beliefs *reflected* social and cultural systems,[1] scholars now argue that anthropology can benefit from viewing reproduction itself as a key site for understanding the ways in which people *re*-conceptualize and *re*-organize the world in which they live.[2] This book also takes this *processual* view of culture-in-the-making.

What then is reconceptualized and reconfigured in the process of the modernization of birth for poor women in Tamil Nadu? This book does not make one, overarching point about the transformation of ideas and practices relating to childbirth in Tamil Nadu at the end of the millennium. It does not provide the reader with some neatly packaged before-and-after scenario of modernity as the grand makeover. Instead, like the intricate patterns of *kōlams* which adorn the thresholds of houses in Tamil Nadu, this book loops and swirls around several key points of reference, each of which is given equal valence. Each point in the *kōlam* maintains its independence, suspended in space in the interstices of the looping lines which pull the individual points together into one web of interlocking boomerangs flying in different directions. Unlike the elaborate *kōlams* drawn for the festivals of Pongal or Dipavali, with hundreds of individual points, mine is a very humble *kōlam*. I do not begin to touch on *all* the ways in which childbirth and reproduction are being transformed. I have tried to highlight those aspects of change which seemed to be of greatest concern to the women whom I met and which had the greatest impact on their decisions about where to go for prenatal, delivery, and postnatal care. Also, out of my interest in underlining unique aspects of modernized birth in Tamil Nadu, I have highlighted those transformations which are different from those noted in similar studies of the biomedicalization of birth in Europe and the United States.

My *kōlam* twists around five primary processes of change, five aspects of the modernizing process which impact childbirth in Tamil Nadu: 1) the professionalization and institutionalization of obstetrics, 2) transformations in the relationship between consumption patterns and reproductive rituals, 3) the emergence of new technologies for managing the pain of birth, 4) the international mandate to reduce population in India, and, 5) development agencies' agenda to spread biomedical conceptions of reproductive health for mothers and children. These processes, taken together, have transformed cultural constructions of reproduction and social relations of reproduction in myriad ways.

In the process, constructions of *gender* are reconfigured. First, women's reproductive bodies have become irrevocably linked to colonial and postcolonial state interests as well as to the interests of transnational development projects. This is particularly evident in the context of international fears of India's "population explosion." Women in India have thus come to be viewed as the bearers of bodies to be counted. The state of Tamil Nadu prides itself on being a "success" in the area of modern population control. For women in Tamil Nadu, being sterilized or having an IUD is a sign of being "modern." But women have mixed feelings about this embodied modernity.

Second, new forms of ritual and patterns of consumption and exchange, along with new drugs for pain, have radically altered the cultural construction of women's power, or *sakti,* such that in some respects women are said to have more *sakti* than in the past, while in other respects they are said to have less. But to culturally ascribe women with more or less *sakti* can have unexpected effects on women's social power.

And, finally, new concepts of nutrition and disease are transforming understandings of the mother's body, the baby's body, and the relationship between the two. Some of these new concepts have the potential to save lives. But when this transformation is occurring in the context of a developmentalist discourse, which reinforces *social* differences by equating poverty and non-biomedical practices with "underdevelopment," new concepts of the body are unevenly conveyed and may be resisted because of the condescending way in which they are imparted. Whereas non-biomedical understandings in Tamil Nadu tend to view the mother-child body as one, this entity is coming to be viewed as two distinct bodies, in the context of not only biomedical praxis but also policy, where the emphasis has shifted from maternal-child health care to a focus on the child as a separate entity. In Tamil Nadu, where female infanticide is reported to be on the rise in *some* poor communities, poor mothers in general are increasingly viewed as potential criminals, and non-biomedical practices are sometimes associated with this criminality. Clearly, then, new constructions of gender, and particularly of motherhood, are class-specific. That is, they are reconstructions of *lower-class* mothers.

My *kōlam* then turns around a sixth point. I try to assess how the five processes of modernity mentioned above, in relation to other factors, influence the "choices" poor women and their families make about the kind of care to seek for childbirth-related needs. "Choice" here is in quotation marks simply to remind us that the decision-making process is never a matter of the free will of rational, value-maximizing individuals, but, rather, it is always enacted in political-economic contexts and shaped by socio-cultural factors such as gender, class, caste, and age. As Linda Garro points out, however, an awareness of the contextualized nature of "choice" does *not* negate the relevance of applying a decision-making perspective.[3]

In her work on decisions regarding obstetrical care among the Bariba of Benin, Carolyn Sargent suggests that we anthropologists should differentiate between aspects of the decision-making process in which an individual "believes herself/himself to be engaged," on the one hand, and the macro-social forces which may be more evident to an external analyst, on the other hand. Thus, she argues, women have a definite *sense* of making rational choices.[4] In my own research in Tamil Nadu, I found women to be not only aware of but extremely articulate about what we might call the "macro" factors impinging on their reproductive decisions. In fact, I do not feel that it is useful to make a distinction between the "macro" and the "local" in discussions of decision making. As the reflexive turn in anthropology reminds us, even the "macro" of the analyst is always locally constructed.[5]

Like most complex societies within which medical anthropologists work today, India contains a plurality of medical systems of knowledge and practice, including multiple forms of biomedicine; "indigenous" systems of medicine such as Ayurveda, Unani, and Siddha; homeopathy; and a wide variety of medical knowledge tied to religious practice and astrology.[6] These all become part of the decision-making process for women during childbirth.

In India biomedicine is most commonly referred to as "allopathy." The other term most frequently used by informants is "English medicine." In the medical anthropological literature terms such as "Western medicine," "modern medicine," and "cosmopolitan medicine" are often used interchangeably with "biomedicine." In this book, when referring specifically to the Indian context I use the term "allopathy" or "allopathic medicine," since my aim is to stay within the specific ethnographic field of my research and to underscore my point that biomedicine always takes on a unique form at the local level. When referring to the global context, I use the term "biomedicine."

There has been very little anthropological or sociological attention given to the use of allopathic services for childbirth in the context of India's medical pluralism in the postcolonial period; although Kalpana Ram's work on the management of birth among the Mukkuvar fishing community in southern Tamil Nadu is an important exception.[7] Most of the studies dealing with these questions were carried out by colonial historians (as I discuss in Chapter One). Most anthropological and sociological research on childbirth in India in the postcolonial era has focused on rural areas and has tended to depict childbirth practices as relatively untouched by allopathic institutions.[8] Yet allopathy has had a major impact on childbirth in urban and semirural areas throughout India, though the impact has been uneven. By focusing on the major metropolitan city of Madras and a semirural town on the outskirts of Madras, my study looks at the central role which allopathy plays in women's decisions regarding childbirth and considers how women choose from among different allopathic options as well as non-allopathic practices.

According to Linda Garro, anthropologists interested in decision-making processes can be loosely grouped into two camps: those who are primarily concerned with policymaking issues and those who are interested in the cultural underpinnings of the cognitive processes that go into decision making. While still others, she writes, "see cognition and policy as intertwined, but they discernibly foreground the policy implications."[9] As far as my work addresses questions of decision making, I would place myself in this third group. Although I am interested in the wide range of social and cultural processes which go into decisions about where to go for prenatal care, whom to see during a delivery, and whose advice to seek in the postpartum period, I must make my own "choices" about which of these processes to foreground. In my own selection process, I try to attend to the voices of the women whom I met, to hear what they considered to matter most to them, and to convey as forcefully as possible their concerns, their criticisms, and the problems they faced in pursuit of reproductive health care during their childbearing years.

As a result, this book may at times seem like a litany of complaints and an unsolicited condemnation of the reproductive health services provided in Tamil Nadu, a state which is usually viewed as a success story in maternal-child health vis-à-vis India as a whole. My intent is not to criticize from afar the work of so many hardworking and dedicated health care providers and policymakers. In fact, I am keenly aware of the historical legacy of the damning depiction of maternal and child health care in India used by colonial discourse to legitimize colonial rule. So I present these criticisms with a certain amount of discomfort about my role in perpetuating this discourse in the postcolonial era, despite the fact that I strive to show how international and globalizing forces are intricately implicated in women's critiques. But as a critical medical anthropologist, my work is first and foremost concerned with issues of social justice. And so, although I hope my ethnography provides what Clifford Geertz has called a "thick description" of the world through the eyes, and indeed through the bodies, of the working-class women whom I met in Tamil Nadu, the "thickness" is not evenly distributed, but, rather, tends to bunch up around those sites where women sense discrimination and desire change.[10]

In his book about aging in India—the stage both farthest from and closest to birthing in the Indian life cycle—Lawrence Cohen continuously pushes us to ask, "What is at stake" in the social, cultural, and medical transformations of the conceptualization of and practices surrounding old age in India?[11] He insists that our conclusions not be simplistically spawned by false dichotomies which force us to take sides, for example, "with medical rationality *or* its holistic or feminist critics, with cultural autonomy and distinctiveness *or* world systems theory and the deserving poor, with medicine as a resource *or* as an ideology."[12] The same question of what is at stake could be asked of my study, substituting "childbirth" for "old age." And, as mentioned above, my response lies in the multiple and complex ways in which gender, as it intersects with class, is being reconstituted.

In my head, I constantly find myself returning to a simpler, perhaps somewhat simplistic response to the question of what is at stake: lives and the potential for suffering. I know from my research and from my own personal experience that the lives of babies and of mothers can never be guaranteed, regardless of what kind of medical care is given and what kind of material resources are available. And I agree with Ivan Illich when he poignantly argues that we must not lose sight of the art of suffering in the wake of modern medicine's determination "to kill pain, to eliminate sickness, and to abolish the need for an art of suffering and of dying." [13] But when discriminatory practices based on things like class and gender have the potential to deny women easy access to biomedical reproductive health care and thus to precipitate loss of life and suffering, action must be taken. This action, however, must not entail falling into the trap of representing others simply as victims, a pitfall that Chandra Mohanty and Arthur and Joan Kleinman have helped me to see and, hopefully, avoid.[14] This book, then, is my enactment of the action taken by those women who shared part of their lives with me.

THE ANTHROPOLOGY OF REPRODUCTION AND MODERNITY

Because I am interested in emphasizing the specificity of modern birth in this particular ethnographic setting, there is a constant comparative vein which runs through the book. This is, however, an ethnographic tale, not a cross-cultural study. The comparative element hovers in the background as a constant reminder of difference, rather than taking center stage. The scenario with which I contrast my study is the biomedicalization of childbirth in Europe and the United States, not because these are the only valid sites of comparison, but because these are the stories that dominate social and cultural studies of the relationship between reproduction and modernity in medical anthropology, medical sociology, and the history of medicine.

During the first decades of the twentieth century, anthropologists paid very little attention to the study of reproduction in diverse cultural contexts; this is usually attributed to the dearth of female anthropologists at the time and, therefore, to the lack of interest in or access to what was considered an exclusively female domain. It may also be due to the fact that social and cultural anthropologists shied away from studying those aspects of human practice which were so intricately linked to biology.[15] To the extent that anthropologists during this period did concern themselves with the study of reproduction, it was within the context of very broad ethnographic accounts and was given only passing mention which was descriptive rather than analytical.[16]

Anthropologists began to focus explicitly on the study of reproduction within the framework of cross-cultural analyses, around the middle of the twentieth century. These comparative studies sought to discover which aspects of human thought and behavior relating to reproduction are universal and which are culturally specific.[17] These anthropologists paid particular attention to how pregnancy, labor, and the postpartum period are managed both physically and socially and to the degree to which these practices are symbolic or biologically based. In short, they established the central tenet of the anthropology of reproduction: reproduction and the management of reproductive processes are not simply biological; they are also always culturally constructed in unique ways in diverse historical contexts.

The study by Margaret Mead and Niles Newton titled "Cultural Patterning of Perinatal Behavior" was particularly noteworthy for the way it used a cross-cultural approach to critique the social and cultural patterning of birth in American society. Though Mead and Newton did not use the term "medicalization," their analysis of the problems which can arise from defining birth as an illness and from the increasing use of hospitalization and pharmaceuticals during the birth process was a harbinger of later studies which explicitly addressed the issue of the medicalization of birth.[18]

Medicalization is a key theme which permeates much of this book. What, then, do I mean by "medicalization" in the context of this study? The medicalization of everyday life is the process by which medical expertise "becomes the relevant basis of decision making in more and more settings"[19] and has become a key component of the modernizing process throughout the world.[20] The medicalization of childbirth is thus the process whereby the medical establishment, as an institution with standardized professional guidelines, incorporates birth in the category of disease and requires that a medical professional oversee the birth process and determine treatment.

The term "medicalization" is often used to refer to a process of "mystification" of social inequities. As Scheper-Hughes and Lock say, "Medicalization inevitably entails a missed identification between the individual and the social bodies and a tendency to transform the social into biological."[21] Thus, such things as hunger, alcoholism, and attention deficit disorder come to be viewed as purely biological disorders and treated with biomedical interventions on individual bodies rather than with attempts to transform the *social* structure and causes which gave rise to such problems. Like this process of mystification, the medicalization of childbirth is an extension of the power of professionalized medical institutions.[22] Yet the process of the medicalization of childbirth is different because "non-medicalized" birth is not necessarily a symptom of inequality. Rather, the medicalization of birth entails a pathologizing of the "normal" by placing birth under the domain of the professional doctor. State-regulated institutions have gained a foothold in the domain of birth through this pathologizing process. From a Foucauldian perspective, however, Margaret Lock and Patricia Kaufert point out, "an account limited to the interests of the medical profession and of the state is inadequate because medicalization cannot proceed unless a cooperative population of patients exists on whom techniques can be performed."[23] Yet, to speak of a "cooperative population" does not negate the possibility of resistance. Furthermore, the medicalization of childbirth *can* be viewed as a mystification of social ills when it comes to be touted as the only and most essential means of reducing risks of infant and maternal mortality and morbidity, thereby erasing the critical role that malnutrition and a wide range of other diseases associated with poverty may have on maternal and infant health.[24]

A "non-medicalized" birth does not mean that no medical care or treatment is given if by "medicine" we mean all forms of healing, of promoting and maintaining a healthy, "mindful body."[25] In many communities throughout the world, and certainly in India, there are a wide variety of non-biomedical practices used to attempt to ensure a risk-free delivery and the birth of a healthy baby. And in India, as in many other parts of the world, there are "indigenous" midwives with specialized knowledge regarding childbirth. Therefore, rather than using the term "medicalization," I use the more specific term "biomedicalization" to refer to this process.

Since the 1970s, feminist-inspired anthropological and sociological studies of birth have critically examined the cultural and political underpinnings of modern biomedical approaches to birth in the United States and Europe. This literature is vast, and I do not intend to review the field here.[26] I elaborate more on these various scholars' approaches in the context of specific debates and discussions in the following chapters. In a nutshell, however, most of these studies argue that the roots of modern, biomedical approaches to birth in Europe and the United States lie in Enlightenment thinking. According to these scholars, the modernization of medicine has entailed a shift from viewing reproductive processes, such as childbirth, as tied to natural and cosmological processes, which could be facilitated through some degree of human intervention but which ultimately lay beyond human control, to viewing childbirth as something which can and should be improved upon through the application of new, scientific practices based on the study of the *laws* of nature.[27] This Enlightenment thinking and the drive to control and harness nature for human, capitalist interests laid the groundwork for the Industrial Revolution. The Industrial Revolution brought with it an increasing reliance on machine-driven production and placed a premium on efficiency for the sake of enhanced capitalist profits. Scholars have pointed out that in the context of the Industrial Revolution, women's reproductive bodies came to be viewed as machines which should operate in uniform and "efficient" ways to facilitate (re)productivity.[28] These studies have focused on the shift from home births attended by female midwives to hospitalized births overseen by a cadre of biomedical professionals with male obstetricians in charge, and have demonstrated how women's reproductive bodies became the object of the "medical gaze."[29] Many have emphasized the ways in which birthing women and female midwives have been disempowered by the rise of the male biomedical establishment. And they demonstrate that this control is legitimized and naturalized by the "authoritative knowledge" of the biomedical establishment, which puts its faith in and derives authority from increasingly complex and costly technological interventions during conception, pregnancy, and delivery.[30] Some scholars, however, have highlighted the ways that women were themselves active agents in shaping the development of obstetrics, and reproductive technologies more generally, and have shown how women have both gained and lost control in this process.[31]

A cadre of feminist activists who have resisted the biomedicalization of childbirth in the United States and Europe have advocated for a return to "natural childbirth" and to "woman-centered" home births attended by female midwives with as little technological intervention as possible, unless intervention is deemed medically necessary.[32] Some anthropologists have become advocates for midwifery and the natural childbirth movement.[33] And ever since the early work of Mead and Newton in 1967, anthropologists have found it useful to study childbirth practices in non-biomedical contexts in other parts of the world in order to learn alternative birthing techniques which can be applied to birthing practices in the West.[34]

Anthropologists have not only been interested in considering how non-Western approaches could be applied in the West; they have also studied the impact of Western obstetrics on childbirth practices and therapeutic selection in non-Western societies.[35] Such studies often focus on the social, political, and cultural barriers to the acceptance of Western obstetrics in non-Western societies and make recommendations for changes in the manner in which Western obstetrics are delivered in such settings. Conjoining both these approaches in her seminal book, *Birth in Four Cultures* (1978), Brigitte Jordan calls for "mutual accommodation" between non-biomedical, in her case Mayan, and biomedical, in this case American, practices.[36]

One of the important contributions of Jordan's original work was the fact that she not only looked at differences between highly biomedicalized and non-biomedicalized birth practices, but she also revealed variation *among biomedical models of birth* in three different countries: the United States, Sweden, and Holland. Some anthropologists and sociologists have continued to reveal variations in how biomedical models of birth are constructed and acted upon across class, ethnicity, and race within the United States and among different Western nations.[37] And historians have often focused on the history of childbirth in one country or on one continent, thereby pointing to national or regional specificities in the modernization of birth.[38]

In the most recent edition of Jordan's *Birth in Four Cultures,* published in 1993, however, she tends to depict a modern biomedical model of birth as a kind of monolithic structure which she refers to as "cosmopolitical obstetrics" and defines as "a system that enforces a particular distribution of power across cultural and social divisions."[39] Jordan argues that the export of this "cosmopolitical" model to the Third World is a form of "biomedical colonization" and "imperialism."[40] She depicts a scenario in which modernity, and biomedicine in particular, does not emerge locally throughout the globe, but is transplanted around the globe. But biomedicine is *not* a monolithic entity.[41] And the biomedicalization of reproduction is *not* a uniform process either within or across national boundaries.

Somewhat like Jordan, Faye Ginsburg and Rayna Rapp are also concerned with how unequal power relations manifested in the globalization process impact control over reproduction and lead to what they describe as the "stratification of reproduction on a global scale."[42] Yet at the same time, they caution against unidirectional models of the relationship between power and knowledge in the context of globalization. They write, "While our work calls attention to the impact of global processes on everyday reproductive experiences, it does not assume that the power to define reproduction is unidirectional. People everywhere actively use their local cultural logics and social relations to incorporate, revise, or resist the influence of seemingly distant political and economic forces."[43] In addition to the contributors to Ginsburg and Rapp's (1995) edited volume, other anthropologists have begun to examine the *diverse* and uneven ways that childbirth is being biomedicalized throughout the world.[44]

This perspective can help dispel the misconceptions embedded in those feminist studies that view all the controlling aspects of biomedicalized births as derived from a Western historical legacy of the Enlightenment and Industrial Revolution and that present a romanticized vision of holistic "indigenous" birth, or "ethno-obstetrics," as egalitarian, "woman-centered," and noninterventionist. Janice Boddy's study of childbirth in postcolonial Sudan, for example, shows that due to the practice of infibulation and the need to open and restitch the scars from infibulation during delivery, midwifery there can hardly be viewed as noninterventionist.[45] In this book, I am not engaging in a debate about whether hospital deliveries are fundamentally controlling or liberating. They may of course be both, just as home deliveries may be experienced as repressive, comforting, or both. Rather, my interest is in demonstrating the historical and cultural specificity of the transformations in the experience of childbirth for working-class women of Tamil Nadu in the late twentieth century.

It is important to underscore the fact that just as the nature of modern birth is unique, forms of resistance will, of course, also be distinct. Due to international and local political-economic structures and cultural processes, biomedical births have not become hegemonic in Tamil Nadu, even in urban areas such as Madras, where almost all births take place in the hospital. And obstetrics has never been the domain of medical *men* in India as it is in the United States. Following Jean and John Comaroff's interpretation of Gramsci, I use the term "hegemony" to mean those systems of knowledge, symbols, and practices which are culturally constructed in the context of relations of power and which "come to be taken for granted as the natural and received shape of the world and everything that inhabits it."[46] It is the apparent "natural" quality of hegemony which gives it its profound power. Although allopathy may indeed be the dominant form of maternal and child health care in urban India, it is not taken for granted as the *only* naturally legitimate form of care. Its apparent superiority must still be publicly articulated. It, therefore, cannot be viewed as hegemonic. Unlike the woman-centered, natural, home-birth movement in America, resistance to biomedical birth in Tamil Nadu is not counterhegemonic; it is based on a critique of the discriminatory ways in which allopathic services are (or are not) provided rather than on a critique of allopathy itself. Resistance to the biomedicalization of birth among the poor of Tamil Nadu, therefore, reflects an effort at bricolage rather than an effort to replace one system of birth with another, wholesale.

Recalling the opening story of Mumtaz, who says she gave birth to her child *right* on the threshold of her home, we can, following James Scott, view her action and inaction as one of those partial, everyday forms of resistance that are the "weapons of the weak."[47] But a far more interesting and significant form of resistance is taking shape in Tamil Nadu today. Some women *want* new technologies offered by allopathy but they want to avoid forms of discrimination which they face in public hospitals. Increasingly, these women are opting to bring allopathy and allopathic practitioners back across the threshold into their homes. In some ways, this appears to be a creative and positive solution to their predicament. But, as we see in the coming chapters, there are also potentially serious health risks involved in partially administering biomedical technologies at home without immediate access to full-fledged biomedical emergency care.

TAMIL NADU: URBAN AND SEMIRURAL FIELD SITES

The state of Tamil Nadu, in the southeast corner of India (see Map 1), is often considered one of India's model states with respect to the provision and use of allopathic maternal-child health (MCH) care. A 1994 government of Tamil Nadu publication showed that 60.6 percent of all reported deliveries in the state were institutionalized; the remainder took place in homes.[48] A separate 1993 government of Tamil Nadu report stated that hospital deliveries accounted for "more than 90 percent" of all deliveries in urban areas and "about 50 percent" of all deliveries in rural areas.[49] In 1993 the World Bank reported that in the capital city of Madras 99 percent of all deliveries were in hospitals.[50] And, by the beginning of 1995, the director of the World Bank–funded India Population Project-V (IPP-V) for Madras reported that 99.9 percent of all deliveries in Madras were conducted in hospitals.[51] Because a number of home deliveries go unreported, these figures reflect a somewhat unrealistically high percentage of hospital deliveries. Nevertheless, they demonstrate that the rates of hospital deliveries in Tamil Nadu are significantly greater than those for India as a whole, for which it was

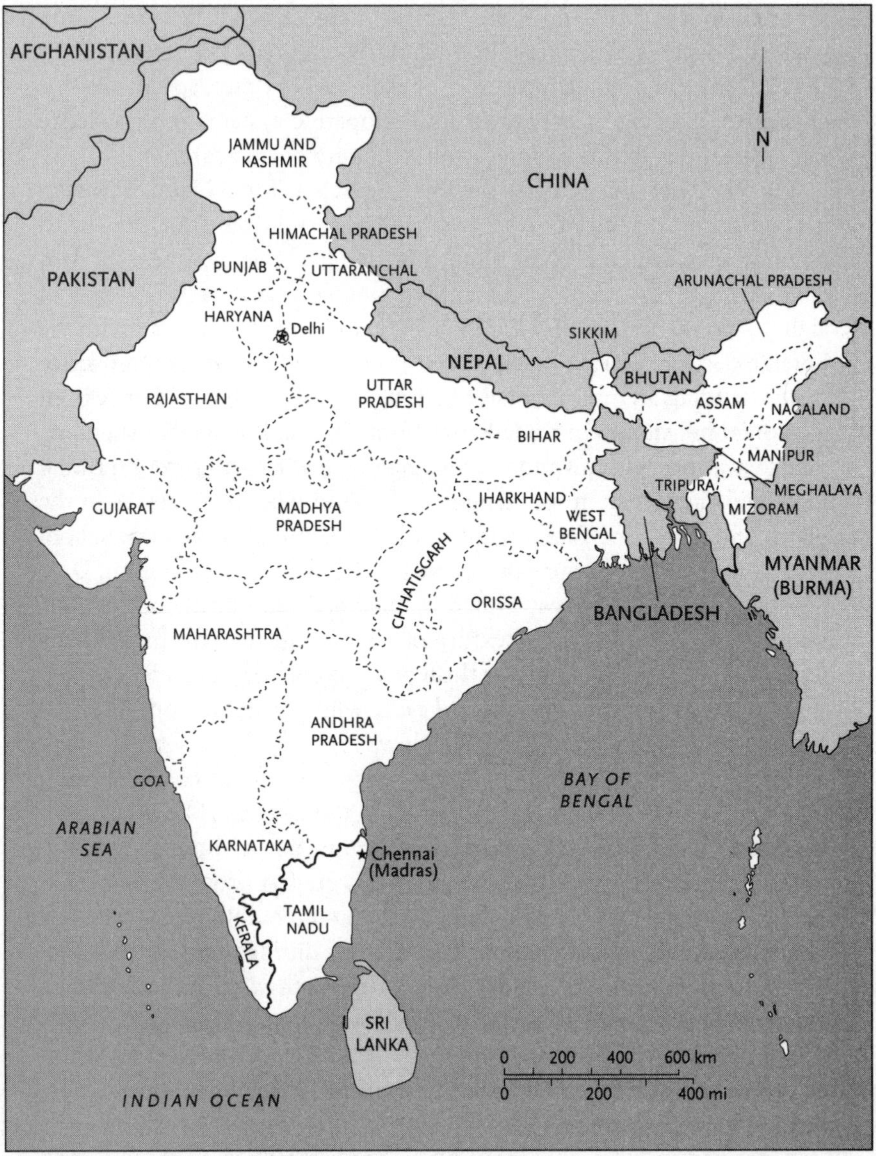

Map 1. The states of India, 2001.

reported in 1995 that no more than 20 percent of all deliveries took place in hospitals.[52] Yet very little scholarly attention has been given to the cultural and political processes by which MCH care, specifically for childbirth, is being incorporated into allopathic systems of knowledge and institutions in this region or to the quality of that care.[53]

My initial decision to carry out this research in Tamil Nadu, however, had more to do with my own personal history in the state than with a purely scholarly interest in filling a lacuna in academic research. As a child, I spent three and a half impressionable years, from the ages of eight to twelve, living in Sri Lanka, where my father was posted with the Foreign Service. During much of that time, my older brother and sister were attending an international boarding school in what had once been a colonial hill station in Kodaikanal, Tamil Nadu. I remember spending many vacations with my mother visiting my brother and sister on Kodai Lake and sightseeing in the temple towns and wildlife preserves in the plains and jungles of Tamil Nadu. And I, too, attended the same school briefly in 1976 before our family was posted back to Washington, D.C. During that time, I was captivated by the hustle and bustle of even this small bazaar, by the crispy texture of *dosais* and the sweetness of the sesame seed candies, and by the thrill of sneaking off to the mist-covered slope of Coaker's Walk to smoke *beedis* while contemplating the vast spread of the plains, barely visible below.

Ten years later, I found myself returning to the plains of Tamil Nadu in 1986 as a college senior participating in the University of Wisconsin, Madison, Year in India Program in Madurai, one of India's most important centers of Hindu pilgrimage. It was on that program that I first began to struggle with and delight in the innumerable retroflexes and alliterations in the Tamil language. And it was during that year that I began to explore issues of gender in India through visits to a Gandhian women's development project in nearby Gandhigram, through the practice of Bharatanatyam dance, and through a fieldwork project on women's roles in my own neighborhood's nocturnal festival for Mariamman, the goddess of smallpox.

I returned to India and Tamil Nadu again briefly in 1991 and 1993 as an anthropology graduate student trying to formulate a dissertation project which would combine my interest in issues of gender and class and which I felt would have social relevance to people involved in the Indian women's movement.[54] It was during these visits that I was drawn into the field of maternal and child health care and decided to focus on childbirth. And it was this topic which led me to become a medical anthropologist. Once again personal experience was influencing my intellectual agenda. In this case, my own stage in the life cycle was a motivating factor, since I was recently married and contemplating having a child myself.

Finally, in January 1995 I returned to Tamil Nadu with my husband and our six-month-old daughter to begin my dissertation fieldwork.[55] We set up home in Besant Nagar, a quiet, newly developed residential neighborhood on the southern edge of Madras. This location enabled me to split my research time between the city of Madras and the semirural community of Kaanathur-Reddikuppam, which lies directly south of Madras, one hour away by bus. Since most of the studies on childbirth in India had been conducted in rural areas, I wanted to look at an urban situation and a semirural community like Kaanathur-Reddikuppam, which was going through a rapid transition in the availability and use of modern MCH services. I spent the year of 1995 in Tamil Nadu, and we all returned to the United States in January of 1996. I then returned to India for a one-month follow-up research trip in May of 1997.[56]

Urban Landscapes: Nochikuppam, Madras

My research in Madras (now officially called Chennai) was greatly facilitated by my affiliation with the Working Women's Forum (WWF), a women's NGO based in Mylapore, Madras, which has branches throughout Tamil Nadu and beyond. It was through the WWF health supervisors and health workers that I was introduced to the residents of Nochikuppam and Bapu Mastan Dargha (BM Dargha), low-income neighborhoods in south and central Madras, respectively. I decided to focus much of my research on the predominantly Hindu neighborhood of Nochikuppam since I felt an immediate rapport with the two WWF health workers who lived and worked there. Therefore the descriptions of Madras field sites which follow will focus on Nochikuppam. My work in BM Dargha was less comprehensive but important for my study since the majority of the residents in this neighborhood were Muslims, and I wanted to be sure to meet women from all three major religious groups in Tamil Nadu, namely Hindu, Muslim, and Christian. Both Nochikuppam and BM Dargha had small populations of Christians as well.

A fishing community, Nochikuppam lies on the southern end of Madras's Marina Beach, the second longest urban beach in the world. Like other beaches around Madras, Marina Beach remained virtually empty all day, scorched by the hot sun. But in the coolness of the evening, it became a fairground. Parents brought their children to play on the slides. Lovers sat together quietly in the secrecy of dusk. And groups of young men met to smoke cigarettes and cool their feet at the water's edge. For the residents of Nochikuppam, Marina Beach was practically an extension of their own beach front, and many set forth in the evening to try to sell snacks to the revelers. The stretch of beach directly in front of Nochikuppam, along its eastern border, was used as a staging ground for all the activities surrounding the arrival and departure of the fishing boats.

The temple of Ellaiamman, a Hindu goddess whose temples reside on the edges of many Tamil villages and towns, lay on the western edge of Nochikuppam.[57] Ellaiamman both defines the spatial parameters of the community and protects those inside the boundary from the dangers which lurk outside of it. She was a special goddess for the fisherpeople of Nochikuppam. Fishermen worshiped Ellaiamman before they set out in their boats; and as their boats pushed out to sea, they sometimes stood to look upon the tower *(kōpuram)* of the temple and pray. Some fisherwomen took pots of milk out to the beach on Fridays and prayed to Ellaiamman from there. They then entered her temple and poured the milk onto the statue of the goddess as a form of worship *(abishekam)*.

As a community grows, it tends to extend beyond the boundary on which Ellaiamman sits. But in Nochikuppam her temple remained the geographic marker of the community since a paved thoroughfare ran along the backside of the temple. The residential and commercial areas which lay on the other side of this main road were connected by paved roads, whereas the government-subsidized high-rise cement buildings and thatched huts of Nochikuppam were connected by footpaths which were dusty in the summer months and muddy and slippery during the monsoon season. Above these narrow footpaths brightly colored saris hung flapping in the sea breeze, drying on poles which connected one high-rise building to another.

With no public roads running through the neighborhood, Nochikuppam remained somewhat secret and closed off from nonresidents. And many people from Madras, particularly from the middle and upper classes, had never even heard of this neighborhood. Those who had knew it for its reputation as one of the poorest and most crime-ridden sections of the city. It was in part because of this geographic boundedness that residents of Nochikuppam would often say their neighborhood was like a village *(iṅka namma kirāmam mātiri)*. This self-definition also referred to the social boundedness of this community, since most of the people living here belonged to the Pattinavar caste. The Pattinavar caste was divided into two subcastes, the Periya Pattinavars ("Big Pattinavars"), said to be the "higher" of the two groups according to caste hierarchy, and the Chinna Pattinavars ("Small Pattinavars"), said to be the "lower." These subcastes were endogamous and their members often married others from the same subcaste within Nochikuppam or from other fishing communities up and down the coast of Tamil Nadu. In the past, this neighborhood was comprised exclusively of Pattinavars. Now, members of other low, "scheduled caste" (SC), or *harijan,* communities have also taken up residence here.[58] While most members of the Pattinavar caste worked in the fishing industry, members of the other caste communities from Nochikuppam were involved in various types of employment, working as fruit and vegetable sellers, snack vendors, auto-rickshaw drivers, or in factories (particularly leather factories). Residents of Nochikuppam likened their community to a village also because of the existence of a kind of informal *panchayat*—a body of local government (traditionally comprised of five members) which made important decisions for the community.

Nochikuppam got its name from the fact that the land used to be covered by a forest of *nochi* trees. The forest was gradually cleared as members of the fishing community began to build huts right along the beach. It was not until 1973 that the cement, three-story "housing board" complexes were constructed on this land by the Tamil Nadu Slum Clearance Board, while Dr. M. Karunanidhi, of the Dravida Munnetra Kazhagam (DMK) party, was Tamil Nadu's chief minister. After the housing board complexes were constructed, the government assigned flats to families based on a lottery system. Each flat consisted of one all-purpose room (used as living room, bedroom, and dining room), one small kitchen, and a bathroom. Often an extended family of six or more lived in one such flat. Initially each family was required to pay the government Rs. 12 per month per flat. In a later power struggle between the DMK and the AIADMK (All India Anna Dravida Kazhagam) parties, however, promises were made to do away with the rent altogether, and that remained the policy in 1995.

Electricity was installed in all the flats at the time of construction, and it was paid for by the flat owners. The supply of water, however, remained the greatest problem in many people's minds. City water was not provided in the flats. Some residents had their own pumps which drew water from the community well, but that water was salty. Most residents got their water from the large water tanks which dotted the road that ran along the eastern edge of Nochikuppam, separating the houses from the beach. These water tanks, which brought in water daily, were provided by the Madras city government, which is called the Madras Corporation. Each nuclear family was entitled to three large pots of water per day. Although the water was supposed to be free of charge, the truck drivers demanded bribes for delivering the water, so each family gave a small fee (approximately 50 paise/day) to the *panchayat,* which used some of that money to pay off the truck drivers. As in most parts of India, in Nochikuppam the women were responsible for the daily collection of water. This was strenuous labor and often entailed waiting in lines under the hot sun for the water trucks to come.

For most residents of Nochikuppam, life centered around fishing. Fishing set a daily routine as well as created a daily state of unpredictability. Sometimes a fisherman might earn as much as Rs. 2,000 in one day; at other times he might go for weeks with no daily income at all. On average, the fishermen of Nochikuppam earned Rs. 500 (approximately US $14) per month, which came to approximately Rs. 6,000 (US $167) per year. The amount a fisherman could earn depended in part on a combination of skill and fate, and in part on the equipment he could afford. With a motor it was possible to earn up to Rs. 2,000 per day. Without a motor one could only earn up to Rs. 300 per day. The deep-sea fish brought in better profits, and it was only the boats with motors which could go far enough out to sea to catch such fish. The cost of buying and attaching a motor to a catamaran was, however, exorbitant, somewhere in the order of Rs. 26,000. So, despite the fact that there were government schemes and the local Fisherman's Cooperative Society to help purchase motors, for most this remained an elusive dream.

As in most parts of the world, in Tamil Nadu fishing is a highly gendered occupation; only men go out to sea and women are largely responsible for selling the fish. Men would push the boats out to sea around four o'clock in the afternoon. Those boats which went out for shallow-water fishing would return in the evening around nine o'clock; those which ventured out to deeper waters would not return until the following morning. When the boats came onto shore the women from Nochikuppam were there, ready to collect the catch of the day and take it to the market to sell. Some fish were sold directly to buyers who came to the beach when the boats arrived or were sold on the roadside in front of Nochikuppam. The women from Nochikuppam took most of the fish to government-designated open-air fishing markets throughout Madras. Fish which were ear-marked for export were sold to middlemen who took them to an ice house in Chindaraipet near the Madras harbor. And, finally, some fish were kept for family consumption. The seafood included in the daily diets of most residents of Nochikuppam was nutritionally beneficial to pregnant women and breastfeeding mothers.

Although before marriage many women in Nochikuppam actively engaged in work which brought in cash, such as fish sales or other work in the informal sector or in factories, they often stopped this work after marriage and during their reproductive years. They would then resume such work once their last child was weaned. During their reproductive years, however, women did continue to do non-cash-earning work, such as cleaning fish and prawns and repairing nets, in addition to their heavy workload looking after the household. And some had no choice but to continue to sell fish in the markets even during their reproductive years.

Semirural Landscape: Kaanathur-Reddikuppam

I was first introduced to the Kaanathur-Reddikuppam area by Dr. Vijaya Srinivasan,[59] who had set up a small outpatient clinic in a new retirement community in Muttukaadu, just south of Kaanathur-Reddikuppam. A couple of the health workers at this clinic also worked for the Voluntary Health Services (VHS) in Kaanathur-Reddikuppam, so they became my first contacts in this small town.

The area referred to as "Kaanathur-Reddikuppam" consisted of a cluster of three communities which were adjacent to one another: Kaanathur, Reddikuppam, and Bilal Nagar. In 1995 a main road separated Kaanathur on the west side of the road from Reddikuppam and Bilal Nagar on the east side. Kaanathur and Reddikuppam were the two original communities in this area. Kaanathur was a community made up primarily of "scheduled caste" Hindus and some Christians, many of whom worked as agricultural laborers in the fields away from the coast or as wage laborers on construction projects. According to the Integrated Child Development Services' (ICDS) *balwadi* workers who kept census-type records for the area, agricultural laborers here earned approximately Rs. 4,000 (US $111) per year, and other wage laborers earned approximately Rs. 3,000 (US $83) per year. Generally, men earned more than women engaged in the same kind of work. For example, female agricultural laborers sometimes earned Rs. 15 per day, whereas male agricultural laborers often earned Rs. 30 or more per day.[60]

Reddikuppam was primarily a Hindu Pattinavar fishing community settled close to the beach. As did their counterparts in Nochikuppam, these fishermen earned an average of approximately Rs. 6,000 (US $167) per year, but their income varied greatly depending on equipment and the vagaries of nature. Prior to the 1980s all the residents of Reddikuppam were living in thatched huts. Over the years, these huts were repeatedly destroyed in fires and then rebuilt over and over again. Finally, during the 1980s, the Tamil Nadu government began building individual cement-block houses for the residents of Reddikuppam. The government requested payment for these houses, but most residents moved into the houses without paying for them. All the utilities and facilities, such as electricity and the water pumps connected to bore wells, had to be installed and paid for by the residents themselves.

All the land occupied by residents of these two communities was owned by one Telegu landowner whose last name was Reddi. Much of the land that was not cultivated and that was not right on the coast was covered with *casurina* trees, which were sold in Madras as firewood. When Mr. Reddi decided to sell off his land, the people from Kaanathur and Reddikuppam joined together and asked for twenty acres. Ten acres went to Kaanathur and ten acres to Reddikuppam. An adjacent ten acres were sold to a Muslim man named Ahmet Khan. Bilal Nagar was a newer Muslim community which was established in the early 1980s when Ahmet Khan practically gave away plots of land at a very low price (Rs. 25/plot) to poor Muslim families. In 1995 these plots were selling for Rs. 10,000–60,000 and being bought by more wealthy Muslim merchant families who were relocating from but maintaining business connections in Madras.

There was a general consensus that the most significant change in this area in people's memory was the laying of the main road from Madras. This project began in the mid-1960s, and originally the road only went as far as Uthandhi, a small town about 1 km. north of Kaanathur-Reddikuppam. Residents of Kaanathur-Reddikuppam then had to walk to Uthandhi to catch the bus. This distance was difficult not only for women carrying basketloads of fish to sell in distant markets or bringing back vegetables newly available from Madras, but also for women in labor who wished to deliver their babies in Madras. The road was extended through Kaanathur-Reddikuppam south to Kovalam a few years later. The bridge which crosses the lagoon in Kovalam, south of Kaanathur-Reddikuppam, was finally built in 1987, enabling the road to stretch beyond Kovalam all the way to Mamallapuram,[61] home of the famous seventh-century shore temples from the Tamil Pallava dynasty. Mamallapuram has long been a pilgrimage destination for Hindu worshipers; with the completion of this road it also became a popular tourist destination and a weekend outing spot for Madrasis. Buses passed through Kaanathur-Reddikuppam regularly on their way between Mamallapuram and Madras.

There was a bus stop in the middle of Kaanathur right at the point where the dirt road led down to Reddikuppam and to the sea. In the mid-1960s there was only one tea stall in this zone between Kaanathur and the road leading out to the sea. In 1995, however, passengers getting down from the bus faced a long row of small shops which ran along the side of Kaanathur parallel to the new road, giving Kaanathur the air of a very small town.

The new road not only enabled people from Kaanathur-Reddikuppam to travel farther for such things as trade and medical care but also provided a direct conduit for the flow of people, goods, and ideas from the metropolis into Kaanathur-Reddikuppam and its surroundings. In fact, ever since the road was built to connect Madras with Mamallapuram, the entire stretch of land between these two destinations had been changing rapidly, transforming from a rural agricultural and fishing area into a major resort area. Amusement parks, health spas, an upscale drive-in theater, new homes for the elderly, hotels, and numerous privately owned vacation homes, also known as "farms" (many of which are owned by nonresident Indians), now dotted the landscape on both sides of this road. One major effect which this development had on residents of Kaanathur-Reddikuppam was that landowners were selling off their plots to these new enterprises, so agricultural laborers from Kaanathur were increasingly turning to employment as construction workers and servants for these resorts and vacation homes. And laborers who previously also owned and cultivated small plots of their own land were selling these off as well, leaving them increasingly dependent on wages from the new developments. Some people commented that this loss of ownership had created a sense of helplessness and depression within the community and that alcoholism was on the rise as a result. Some turned from agricultural work to working in an illicit liquor trade.

The emergence of these new resorts did not have the same kind of immediate impact on the work of the fishing community in Reddikuppam. The fishing industry was, however, significantly affected by the increasing use of new technologies, especially new motors. As in Nochikuppam, some residents of Reddikuppam joined the fisherman's cooperative and could purchase motors at discount rates. People in Reddikuppam were somewhat ambivalent about the merits of these new motors. Although a motor could indeed bring in a much more profitable catch, the investments required to purchase the motor, the diesel, and repairs to the motors were very substantial, so that anyone who made these investments and yet still did not have a good catch could suffer extreme financial losses. Another significant change in Reddikuppam was the recent arrival of private companies that used aquaculture technology to farm prawns. These companies created competition in the prawn trade and perpetuated the loss of land in Reddikuppam by buying land from poor fishing families who resorted to selling it. These companies, however, did not employ Reddikuppam residents in their operations.

The new road not only ushered in the leisure establishments which catered to the whims of middle- and upper-class Madrasis and other outsiders, but it also brought new institutions (such as schools and medical facilities) and new forms of media (particularly via televisions and VCRs) which were used by the local population. In addition, the road linking local residents more directly to institutions and markets in Madras resulted in dramatic changes in the provision of maternal and child health services in the Kaanathur-Reddikuppam area. The changes in childbirth practices which will be discussed in the remainder of this book need to be seen in the context of these more general changes brought in by the construction of the main road. The following story of Murugesan provides an example of the availability and accessibility of MCH services for birth prior to the building of this road.

When I met him, Murugesan was sixty-five years old and the president of the Kaanathur-Reddikuppam *panchayat.* He lived in one of the largest houses in Kaanathur, a light blue, cement house in a walled-in compound at the far end of the main road. Murugesan was born in Kaanathur and had lived there for most of his life. He told me about changes in childbirth practices which he had witnessed during his lifetime.

• • •

When Murugesan himself was born, a maruttuvacci *(midwife) from the nearby village of Navallur assisted with his mother's delivery and continued to come to their house to help his mother for fifteen days following the delivery. Murugesan explained that the* maruttuvaccis *in those days were very knowledgeable about children's diseases like* māntam *(infant indigestion) and* iṛuppu *(fits) and that they prepared their own medicines with herbs* (mūlikaikal) *to treat these diseases.*

Murugesan himself had had nine children, of which only three had survived. His first wife had had two children but only one survived, and that wife died in childbirth. The second wife, who was his first wife's younger sister, had had seven children and only two of those children survived. All of the children had died before they reached the age of three, and most died within one year. The first child of the first wife was born at home with a maruttuvacci *and died after 28 days. The second baby was also born at home and six days later his wife got* janni *(fits with a fever; in childbirth this often refers to tetanus). The people in the community thought that she was possessed by some spirits and they called the* maruttuvacci *to provide a cure. The* maruttuvacci *gave his wife a* janni *tablet along with* cukku *(dried ginger). But this did not cure his wife and her condition was deteriorating rapidly. It was decided that since the situation was so dire it was necessary to take his wife to Kasthurba Gandhi Hospital in Madras.*

There was no main road to Madras in those days and therefore no buses. The journey was long and arduous so people did not consider going to the Madras hospitals when a woman's labor began. Only if an emergency arose would they make the voyage as they did with Murugesan's wife. It was 9 P.M. when they strapped her onto a board and transported her by bullock-cart to the canal. It was December and the night was cold. At the canal they boarded a small sailboat and sailed to Thiruvanmiyur. It took seven hours to reach Thiruvanmiyur from Kaanathur. From Thiruvanmiyur they went by horse-cart to Adyar. And from Adyar they could take a bus to Kasthurba Gandhi Hospital. They reached the hospital at 7:30 A.M. There was a doctor there who attended to them. The baby survived but his wife died in the hospital two days later. That was in 1952. It had taken them ten and a half hours to reach Kasthurba Gandhi Hospital from Kaanathur. In 1995 they could travel that distance within an hour.

His second wife's first child was born in the Andhra Sabha Hospital near the Adyar bridge in Madras. They had gone to the hospital in advance to avoid the complications which his first wife faced. That baby died from diarrhea after ten days at home where they were treating him with nāḍḍu maruntu *(country medicines).*[62] *The next four babies were all born at home and all died. They were growing concerned, so for the next delivery they went to Kasthurba Gandhi Hospital in advance. That child was healthy until he was nine months old and got severe diarrhea. They took him to the hospital and the doctors said there was no hope to save him. So they brought him home and called the* maruttuvacci, *who gave the child* nāḍḍu maruntu *made out of nutmeg* (jātikkāy), *clarified butter (ghee), and honey, and the child was revived within fifteen days. The seventh child was also born in the hospital and never had any serious illnesses.*

• • •

Murugesan and others of his generation all told me that before the bus route had been established in the 1960s almost all deliveries in the area took place in the home and were assisted by a *maruttuvacci.* Only in extreme emergencies were women, like Murugesan's first wife, transported to Madras for hospital attention. It was because of the death of his first wife and the deaths of so many of his children born by his second wife that they had taken the trouble to have three of her deliveries in the hospital in Madras. Murugesan came from one of the wealthier families in Reddikuppam and had received more education than others in the community at the time. He said that his wives' visits to the hospitals in Madras were unusual within the community, where most could not afford the time and money required for these trips.

Everyone told me that since the road had been laid and the buses had begun to ply this route, women were all "running to the hospital for deliveries." In fact this was not quite true. What was no doubt true was that there had been a marked increase in the number of women traveling to hospitals for deliveries. But many women I met in 1995 had had their deliveries at home. I decided to gather some statistics on the delivery sites for women in this area during the time of my research.

Based on the records of the Kaanathur Voluntary Health Services mini-health-center and the ICDS *balwadis* in both Kaanathur and Reddikuppam for the period from November 1994 to November 1995, I found that the total number of deliveries during this time period for the whole Kaanathur-Reddikuppam area (including Bilal Nagar) was sixty-one. Of these, twenty-nine were home deliveries, thirty-one were hospital deliveries, and one was unknown. As these records indicate, slightly less than 50 percent of the deliveries took place at home, and slightly more than 50 percent occurred in a hospital. These numbers clearly represent a region going through a transition with regard to maternal health care. In Nochikuppam, Madras, on the other hand, there were no home deliveries at all during 1995.

These two communities—Nochikuppam and Kaanathur-Reddikuppam—are similar and different in ways that are important for understanding women's experiences during childbirth. Both were, for the most part, poor communities which relied heavily on government-subsidized support for many aspects of life, including maternal and child health care. Both also received NGO support for MCH services. Both were comprised primarily of a combination of Hindu Pattinavars engaged in fishing and "scheduled caste" Hindus engaged in wage labor in the informal sector.

The major differences between these two communities as far as this study is concerned was that Nochikuppam was located right in the city of Madras and women had had easy access to government-subsidized MCH care in the city for a few generations. Furthermore, the government had been actively working to prevent home births from occurring in urban centers. For women in Kaanathur-Reddikuppam, however, this access had been greatly restricted until the 1960s, and there had not been such an active effort on the part of the government to prevent home births in the rural regions.

Because of their similar class and caste backgrounds, women from both these communities faced many of the same difficulties and forms of discrimination in government maternity wards during childbirth, which will be discussed. The women from Nochikuppam had few means of circumventing this discrimination, since home birth was no longer considered a viable option. Women in Kaanathur-Reddikuppam, however, sometimes chose to remain home for their deliveries to avoid the discrimination they faced in the government maternity wards. But they were demanding new birth practices in their homes which incorporated those elements of allopathic MCH care which they considered to be beneficial.

FIELDWORK, FRIENDS, AND FAMILY

My research consisted primarily of structured and unstructured interviews with over seventy pregnant and postpartum women and their families in their homes and in public maternity wards. Most of these interviews were tape-recorded, transcribed, and translated with the help of research assistants. Those interviews that were not tape-recorded were recorded with notes on-site. I also interviewed a range of medical practitioners, including doctors, nurses, hospital *ayahs,*[63] both governmental and nongovernmental female multipurpose health workers (MPHWs),[64] and local midwives. And I observed interactions between these workers and their patients in hospitals and homes. (See Appendix I for samples of the questionnaires used for these interviews.) In addition to observing medical procedures in hospitals and discussing childbirth in homes and hospitals, I also had the opportunity to observe, and

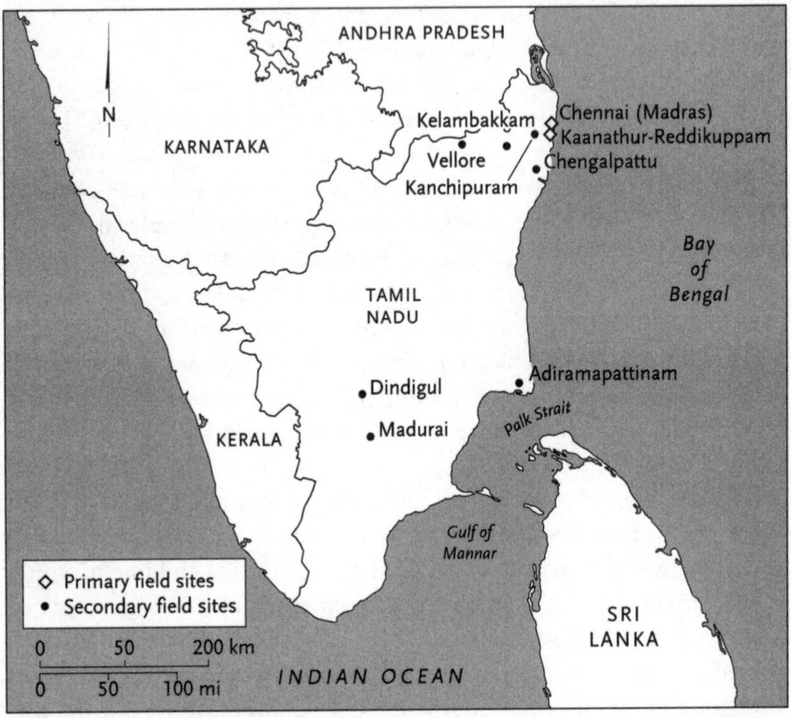

Map 2. Field sites in Tamil Nadu, Indian, 1995.

in some cases videotape, pregnancy and postpartum rituals and bathing and dietary practices in a variety of settings.[65] Finally, I interviewed governmental and nongovernmental administrators working on women's health policy issues at the state and national levels.

My research in Kaanathur-Reddikuppam and in Madras was supplemented by brief visits to low-income communities in and around several other cities and towns throughout Tamil Nadu, including Chengalpattu, Madurai, Dindigul, Vellore, Kanchipuram, and Adiramapattinam (Tanjavur District) (see Map 2). The visits to Chengalpattu were facilitated by a local organization called the Rural Women's Social Education Centre (RUWSEC). All other visits were arranged by the Working Women's Forum. In each place I met with the same range of people whom I met in my primary research sites. The purpose of these visits was to see to what extent the information I got in Madras and Kaanathur-Reddikuppam was generalizable for Tamil Nadu as a whole.

I also conducted a brief study in the maternity ward at Apollo Hospital, a prestigious private hospital in Madras catering to a wealthy clientele. Although I do not delve into the details of this research, my findings there serve as a comparative backdrop to my discussion of maternal care for lower-class women. Finally, I gathered government documents and other materials relating to the history of MCH policy in Tamil Nadu from both the Tamil Nadu State Archives and the library attached to the Tamil Nadu Department of Public Health.

Many people have asked me whether it was difficult to get women to speak with me openly about their childbirth experiences. The assumption seems to be that such a topic, which deals with women's reproductive bodies, would be too personal or embarrassing to discuss or would even be taboo in the Indian cultural context. Although it is true that women felt embarrassed to discuss these matters openly with men and that mothers and daughters often did not discuss these things, what I found was that in general this was a topic which women were very quick and even eager to discuss with me and with each other once they had already been through the process of childbirth.[66] (Women who were pregnant with their first child tended to be much more reticent.) In fact, I often found that I would begin a conversation with one woman in her home and within a half hour four or five other women in the neighborhood, who had gotten wind of the conversation, would join us, eager to add their commentary on the subject. This made for lively discussions but made it excruciatingly difficult to tease apart the diverse voices in the process of transcribing taped interviews.

One of the reasons that women seemed comfortable discussing these issues may have to do with the fact that there has been such a longstanding infrastructure of governmental and nongovernmental health workers going into people's homes to collect health data on families and to educate about and advocate in favor of family planning and MCH care. Initially many women assumed that I was in fact some kind of governmental or nongovernmental health worker. At first this was somewhat of an impediment, for I found that many women seemed to be feeding me opinions and stories which would support the family-planning and MCH propaganda they were so used to hearing. At other times, the assumption that I was a government representative had the opposite effect and women saw me as a vehicle for making demands on the government to improve MCH services in their communities. My hope is that my writings on this topic will in fact serve this purpose. The other most common initial misconception about my role was the assumption that I was a doctor, and women came to me with complaints of a variety of ailments.

When it became clear that I was neither health worker nor doctor, but rather that I was a medical anthropologist who was as interested in learning about the details of religious ritual activities surrounding birth and about the use of local herbs and dietary practices as I was in learning about women's allopathic concerns during childbirth, some women grew frustrated and felt that I was wasting their time. Others became more and more intrigued and welcomed the fact that I took a genuine interest in some of their non-allopathic practices rather than coming to condemn such practices as harmful and superstitious. And those women who were intrigued by the nature and scope of my inquiries were also curious to know about practices and beliefs surrounding childbirth in America and came to view our conversations as cross-cultural dialogues.

The fact that I had a child myself made an enormous difference in the nature of our discussions. When I talked with women about childbirth during my trip in 1993 I did not have a child of my own. And just as women were reluctant to discuss the details of their birth experiences with their daughters or daughters-in-law who had not yet had their first child, they were hesitant to speak freely with me about this subject. In part there was a sense that it was taboo to do so, and in part there was a sense that I simply would not and could not understand. When I began my research in 1995, however, and explained to women that I had a child myself and told them about my own birth experience, they were much more at ease talking with me. The difference did not only lie with their attitude toward me but also with my attitude toward them. Having been through childbirth myself I did feel as though I could understand their experiences more fully, despite the social and cultural factors which made our birth experiences vastly different. Having been through it myself, I felt I had a much better base of phenomenological, social, and biomedical knowledge from which to formulate questions and respond to inquiries.

Many anthropologists have commented that it must have been a great "in" to have had my very young daughter, Lila, with me; that it must have helped me gain acceptance in Indian society, and that this must have benefited my research immensely, especially given the topic of the research. In my more cynical moments, the implication of these comments seemed to be that having a baby must be even better than the traditional anthropological props, like cigarettes and money, for getting "informants" to take you into their homes and divulge their secrets. It was wonderful to be living in Tamil Nadu with my family and sharing with them a part of the world which has long been a central part of who I am. It was particularly significant to me that Lila was starting out her life with an experience that I hope will influence her lifelong perception of the world. The fact that her first words alternated between English and Tamil was somehow very touching. And of course having a young child did in many ways open doors to friendships as she and many of our neighbors' children played together every day. My research, however, was not focused on my immediate neighborhood but rather required me to commute all around the city, down to Kaanathur-Reddikuppam, and occasionally farther afield to other parts of Tamil Nadu. It did not make sense to drag her along with me wherever I went, into hospitals, homes, government offices, and libraries. In fact, I felt that because of the demands of her age (six months to one and a half years), having her with me during my research would have been disruptive and would have made it very difficult for me to concentrate on what others were saying or doing. Instead, most of the time Lila remained home and part-time in a local day care, and I had to contend with being a somewhat frenzied working mother in India just as in America.

OUTLINE OF THE CHAPTERS

For the most part, each chapter in this book addresses a different aspect of the modernizing process and analyzes the impact that this process is having on poor women's experiences during childbirth in Tamil Nadu. In addition to its thematic organization, the book is also organized loosely according to the chronology of the experience of childbirth itself. Thus, Chapters Three through Six emphasize pregnancy, delivery, family planning, and the postpartum period in consecutive order. Family planning is placed in between delivery and the postpartum period, since certain contraceptive methods are undertaken in hospital maternity wards before mothers return home from their deliveries. I have taken this chronological approach in the hope of conveying some sense of the flow of the experience of childbirth for the women whom I met.

Chapter One addresses the theme of the professionalization of obstetrics as one aspect of the modernizing process. Focusing on the colonial period, this chapter provides a background for understanding the historical context within which the profession of obstetrics emerged in India. As in other colonial contexts, the issues of childbirth and of the professionalization of obstetrics played a critical role in the civilizing discourse of colonialism in India.[67] Chapter Two shows how the debates and policies regarding the professionalization of obstetrics during the colonial era are reflected in official structures of maternal and child health care in the postcolonial era. This chapter also describes the maternal and child health care services available to women for childbirth in my particular field sites in Tamil Nadu in 1995. Chapter Three looks at the value placed on consumption as a central marker of modernity in the contemporary global order. In India this has become particularly apparent in the context of post-1991 liberalization policies. Increasing consumer orientation has intensified and transformed pregnancy rituals in Tamil Nadu in such a way that these rituals publicized the auspiciousness of women's fertility while simultaneously becoming an important context and conduit for the exchange of consumer goods from a pregnant woman's kin to her in-laws, resulting in the construction of poor pregnant women as, what I call, "auspicious burdens." Chapter Four examines the use of modern technologies which alter the nature of pain during delivery. Most of the women whom I met in Tamil Nadu wanted to have their labors medically induced with oxytocin drugs and were unaware of the possibility of using anesthesia and wary of this notion when presented with it for the first time. The particular use of pain medication among poor women in Tamil Nadu both draws on and transforms cultural constructions of women's reproductive bodies, and of female power, or *sakti,* and is influenced by political-economic constraints of public maternity wards in Tamil Nadu. Chapter Five takes on the theme of population-control programs in the modern era, particularly as these programs have been implemented in the context of postcolonial international development projects. The internationally driven family-planning agenda has long overshadowed all other aspects of maternal and child health care in India, and Tamil Nadu has been touted as a model state in this regard. In this chapter, I show how this impacted poor women's experiences during childbirth. Chapter Six addresses the transnational discourse of "development," in its myriad forms, as a central element in the postcolonial modernizing process. I examine the postpartum period as a key site within which such discourses of development were maneuvered in Tamil Nadu. In particular I discuss the ways in which discourses of development constructed non-allopathic practices and systems of knowledge surrounding the mother's and baby's postpartum diets and baths as "unscientific" and therefore not only dangerous but immoral.

The issue of how poor women in Tamil Nadu made decisions about what kind of care to seek during childbirth is filtered throughout the various chapters of this book. This issue of "choice" is the central theme of the conclusion. By focusing on Kaanathur-Reddikuppam as a community in transition, this chapter examines how new constructions of maternity which emerged in the context of the modernization of childbirth in Tamil Nadu simultaneously compelled women to seek and repelled them from seeking childbirth-related care in allopathic institutions. Although some women were "choosing" to remain home for deliveries, they usually claimed to do so to avoid specific class-based forms of discrimination in hospitals, rather than to rebuke allopathic obstetrics itself. Some women said they were choosing to remain home only *because* new allopathic procedures were being introduced into the home-birth context. This is a specific form of resistance to a specific form of biomedicalization. This response does not necessarily reflect greater reproductive choices for these mothers. In fact, it could, potentially, have negative consequences for their health and the health of their babies.

With improvements in quality and monitoring, however, home-birth care could provide a model for women of all socio-economic classes in rural and urban India. Such a movement should not, however, be pursued at the expense of redressing the serious problems of discrimination within the public maternity hospitals.

CHAPTER I

The Professionalization of Obstetrics in Colonial India

The "Problem" of Childbirth in Colonial Discourse

In the late nineteenth and early twentieth centuries, the management of childbirth emerged as a key issue in colonial and nationalist discourses in India, as it did in other colonial settings around the globe from Jamaica to the Sudan to Malaya and the Pacific Islands.[1] The concern with childbirth in the colonies, particularly as it related to maternal and infant mortality, echoed anxieties arising around these issues in the European metropoles. Both in the metropole and on the periphery this heightened interest in childbirth arose due to growing awareness and pronatalist fears of depopulation trends. Depopulation, particularly among proletarians, was thought to threaten capitalist interests by shrinking the labor pool. In both the metropoles and their colonial outposts the provision of maternal and child health care was thus increasingly viewed as critical to the economic interests of the state since it held the promise of arresting depopulation.

In India colonial sympathizers and nationalists alike depicted the conditions of childbirth as deplorable and used these images to legitimize their own political and economic goals in the name of protecting the "vulnerable" members of society, i.e., women and children. Differences lay in where each placed the blame for the sorry state of the birthing woman. The colonists tended to blame Indian "custom" and "tradition," while nationalists blamed the colonial government's extractive economic policies and unequal distribution of health services. Some Hindu nationalists used ancient Sanskrit texts as evidence that there had previously been an advanced tradition of obstetrics in India that had been lost through historical incursions from outsiders, namely Muslims and the British.[2] Just as Lata Mani has argued that in colonial and nationalist debates on *sati* "women are neither subjects nor objects, but rather the grounds of the discourse on *sati*,"[3] the status of women's health can also be viewed as the "grounds" rather than the subject of the discourse on the care of Indian women during childbirth in the colonial era.

In general, colonists and nationalists both considered the professionalization of obstetrics to be an antidote to the problem. Debates in the late nineteenth and early twentieth centuries revolved around the question of how and to what extent childbirth could be brought within the ambit of the emerging allopathic medical establishment in India. The focus of these debates can be viewed as part of a larger trend away from an earlier approach that emphasized coexistence and collaboration between allopathic and indigenous systems of medicine toward the late-nineteenth-century approach, which asserted the dominance of allopathy and attempted to repress indigenous medicine throughout the colonized world.[4] This shift was due in part to new scientific discoveries which rendered allopathy increasingly distinct from indigenous medicine. It was also precipitated by the growing popularity of the eugenics movement in Europe and the United States insofar as the exclusive use of Western-style medicine was deemed critical to asserting racial superiority. Furthermore, the "whiteness" of the initial allopathic doctors who served colonial administrative personnel ensured the physical separation of the "races" to a degree which was not considered necessary in the earlier phase of colonialism.[5]

This chapter examines debates regarding how to bring childbirth within the domain of the allopathic medical professions in colonial India. This is not intended as a full history of the biomedicalization of childbirth in India. Other scholars have begun to write pieces of such a history, and I draw a great deal from their findings as well as from materials I gathered in the Tamil Nadu State Archives in Madras.[6] Here I focus on how the context of colonialism as well as local cultural constructions of gender and caste combined in such a way that the professionalization of childbirth in India took on a different form than it did in the United States and Europe, and differed also from the situation in other colonial contexts. Two factors of note which differentiate the situation in the United States and Europe from that in India are, first, that from the inception of obstetrics as a profession in India, it has been largely a women's profession; and, second, hospitalized births did not become and still are not the norm in India, despite the government's conviction of the supremacy of allopathic hospital obstetric care. Combined, these factors lead us to ponder the extent to which the kinds of power relationships described by feminist scholars writing about the history of childbirth in the West are and are not replicated in the Indian situation.

Madras played a prominent role in the professionalization of obstetrics in British India. The first "lying-in" allopathic maternity hospital in British India—and in Asia as a whole—was established in Madras in 1844. The Government Hospital for Women and Children in Egmore is still one of the preeminent maternity hospitals in India. The first training school for midwives in India opened in Madras. Madras was the first city to admit women into its medical schools, and the first city with a medical school offering a post-graduate diploma in obstetrics and gynecology. It was, therefore, no surprise that in 1936 the first All India Obstetrics and Gynaecological Congress gathered in the Museum Theatre in Egmore, Madras, just down the road from the Egmore maternity hospital. Ida Scudder, an obstetrician and gynecologist—born into a missionary family in South India—who helped to found the world-renowned Christian Medical School and associated hospital in nearby Vellore, was elected the first president of this congress. In her welcoming address, the chair of the congress, Dr. A. Lakshmanaswami Mudaliar, proudly stated:

> Madras may not stand comparison in many respects with the Gateway of India or with the City of Palaces—the second largest city in the British Empire. But Madras is proud[,] and justly so, of the place it occupies in the Obstetric world of today and it is in no spirit of narrow provincialism that I venture to maintain that no other city in India could have claimed this honour with greater confidence and dignity.[7]

Prior to the 1844 opening of the Government Hospital for Women and Children, women in India had all been delivering their babies at home, usually in either their natal home or their husband's family's home. There were medical institutions for indigenous medical traditions (such as Ayurveda, Unani, and Siddha), and these traditions did have well-developed theories of reproduction and birth.[8] However, these indigenous medical institutions and practitioners were not involved in providing services to women during the actual birth. Some have suggested that this is largely due to the fact the practitioners were almost all men and it was inappropriate for a man to be present at a birth.[9]

Many of the home deliveries were overseen by senior female members of the extended family who had experience in assisting births. Other deliveries were attended by lay midwives who were called from outside the family. In South Asia these midwives are often referred to collectively as *dais* by people writing about the region as a whole. This term is most widely used in the northern regions of South Asia and is thought to be of Arabic origin.[10] Some scholars have chosen to use the term "traditional birth attendant," or "TBA," which is taken from the international development discourse, because the term "*dai*" is deemed condescending in the communities they are studying.[11] Indeed, in much of the literature on midwifery in India the primary role of the *dai* is thought to be the removal of ritual "pollution" associated with childbirth. In particular, writers mention that the cutting of the umbilical cord and the disposal of the placenta and blood are the primary tasks performed by *dais* and that these tasks are deemed defiling. In general, specialized *dais* belong to low-caste Hindu or poor Muslim communities. Many *dais* are members of the "barber" castes, which participated in an extensive network of patron-client, or *jajmani,* relationships in the precolonial era.[12] The work of the *dai* is often hereditary, passed on from mother-in-law to daughter-in-law.

Unfortunately, discussions about the deprecating connotations of the term "*dai*" have not looked carefully into the history of the *dai*'s role in South Asian societies and the extent to which colonial representations of the *dai* and the very process of the professionalization of obstetrics in South Asia may have significantly transformed these women's status. Patricia Jeffery et al. refer briefly to the possibility of a historically shifting status of *dais* when they write:

> The few historical sources that feature *dais* and women's experiences of childbearing are often written by doctors patently biased against their competitors. Thus we cannot be sure about how *dais*' skills and status might have changed, especially in the wake of the major secular changes since the mid-60s. Possibly in the face of what are probably more restricted employment opportunities for women in the poorest classes, proportionately more women are being pauperized and more women with families without traditions of *dai* practice may be resorting to an occupation that is becoming increasingly de-skilled. Further, as urban medical facilities have expanded, any ante-natal, abortion, and infertility work of *dais* may have declined, and *dais* may have become more restricted to delivery work.[13]

Yet Jeffery et al. do not pursue this line of thinking further. Such historical contextualization is critical for a more complete understanding of the *dai*'s role in India and the role of the so-called TBAs in any society. This chapter will emphasize colonial representations of *dais* and of local childbirth practices in the contexts of attempts to professionalize obstetrics in India and of the colonial civilizing process more generally.

The historical vilification of midwives in Europe and America has been well documented.[14] In Europe female healers were accused of witchcraft by the emergent elite male biomedical establishment as early as the thirteenth century, when medicine was becoming a secular science and profession. By the seventeenth and eighteenth centuries, midwives were singled out as a danger to society.[15] This clearly had an impact on colonial representations of *dais* in South Asia, and such negative representations continue to stigmatize *dais* in India today. Recently, some scholars have attempted to excavate the history of the social and cultural significance of *dais* in India, highlighting both their authority as ritual specialists and their expertise in many areas of the physical management of birth.[16]

Anthropologists working in other areas of the world have discovered that prior to colonial contact and the concomitant spread of biomedicine, lay midwives often garnered a great deal of respect and held positions of political authority. This was apparently the case for the *nanas* in Jamaica and members of the Sande society, who traditionally provided maternal and child health care, in Sierra Leone.[17] We should not, however, assume that in precolonial India lay midwives must have held similar positions of respect. To do so would be to fall into the trap of romanticizing about the "traditional other." Indeed, it may well be that in the precolonial era lay midwives in many parts of South Asia were viewed as unskilled, menial, and "polluted" members of society, as they are often considered today.[18] Both assertions need to be investigated rather than assumed. The problem is, of course, that this is an extremely difficult history to recover.

During the late nineteenth century, colonial administrators, missionaries, and medical professionals began to lump a variety of traditional midwives together under the term *"dai,"* applying it to midwives throughout colonial India (including contemporary Bangladesh and Pakistan) and to midwives of different religious communities. Stacey Pigg has pointed out that in contemporary international development projects undertaken in Nepal, the term "traditional birth attendant" is similarly used as a homogenizing gloss for a wide variety of local healers.

After this category of TBA had been created, the Nepali word chosen to translate the category was *sudeni,* which originally referred to only *one* kind of healer involved in childbirth. Consequently, the word "*sudeni*" itself has come to have new meaning in Nepali society.[19] An important and difficult task for historians of South Asia is, therefore, to begin to tease apart the regional and religious *differences* in the roles and representations of midwives prior to the colonial encounter. Remnants of these differences still exist today and must be studied more carefully by anthropologists and other social scientists.

In Tamil Nadu, for example, a hereditary Hindu midwife is most commonly referred to as a *maruttuvacci,* and a hereditary Muslim midwife is usually called a *nācuvar* or an *ampaḍḍacci.* In both cases these are generally women from "barber" caste communities, which are considered low castes and are associated with the removal of pollution. These terms may also be applied to women from other low-caste communities who are engaged in this work. For example, Nagamma, a hereditary midwife from the Pattinavar caste in Nochikuppam, is also referred to as a *maruttuvacci.* As I discuss in depth in Chapter Six, however, the removal of the "pollution" of childbirth is *not* the major concern of families I met in Tamil Nadu and is *not* considered to be the primary role of the *maruttuvacci.* Kalpana Ram has come to the same conclusion based on her research among the Mukkuvar fishing community on the southern tip of Tamil Nadu. The traditional midwives studied by myself and Ram in Tamil Nadu seem to have somewhat higher status within their communities than do those in parts of rural Uttar Pradesh, where Jeffery et al. conducted their study, or in contemporary Bangladesh, where Santi Rozario did her research.[20] Is this difference due to precolonial cultural differences between the north and south, or is it more restricted to the historical role of the midwife in fishing communities in Tamil Nadu? These issues need to be pursued further for a deeper understanding of the politics of gender in precolonial, colonial, and postcolonial South Asia.

Due to the establishment of government "*dai*-training" programs, in Tamil Nadu the term "*maruttuvacci*" has come to be associated with those who have not been officially "trained" and thus to connote a lack of scientific knowledge and state recognition. Women who go through *dai*-training programs, whether they are hereditary *maruttuvaccis* or not, tend to prefer the label "*dai*" to "*maruttuvacci,*" since they feel this gives them greater legitimacy in relation to the communities they serve and, more important, to government and nongovernmental health workers. I try, therefore, to maintain distinctions between such terms as "*maruttuvacci*" and "*dai*" in order to highlight the meanings that various terms come to have for people in different contexts. When speaking of India as a whole, I use the term "*dai*" because that is how most people refer to midwives, even, or perhaps particularly, when they are speaking English.

In colonial discourses the practices of the *dai* were repeatedly decried as "barbaric," and the *dai* herself was represented as the primary cause of high rates of infant and maternal mortality and as an obstacle to "progress," which the colonial government was promising. Once again, concerns about mortality rates were tied to anxieties about depopulation of the labor force. Two tactics were taken to rectify the situation and to bring Western medical care to Indian women during childbirth. On the one hand, efforts were made to increase the number of Western-trained doctors, nurses, and nurse-midwives who provided services to Indian women primarily in institutional settings. This effort was initiated throughout India under the Countess of Dufferin Fund in 1885. On the other hand, the Victoria Memorial Scholarship Fund was initiated in 1903 to provide training to the hereditary *dais* already working in communities throughout India.

THE COUNTESS OF DUFFERIN FUND

The first woman doctor trained in biomedicine to work in India was an American missionary named Clara Swain who arrived in India in 1869.[21] For some time following her arrival, missionary women made up the bulk of the women doctors in India. It appears that the first woman doctor to be employed by the government was Elizabeth Beilby, who began working in Lahore in 1885. It was in this year that the Countess of Dufferin Fund (known in full as the National Association for Supplying Female Medical Aid to the Women of India but generally referred to as the Dufferin Fund) was established, setting the stage for a nation-wide, nonsectarian project to employ women in the medical services. Queen Victoria herself issued a plea for the formation of this fund.[22]

The Dufferin Fund and the Victoria Memorial Scholarship Fund were initiated by then-vicereine of India, Lady Curzon. Both funds, as well as subsequent funds for women's medical care in India such as those initiated by Lady Chelmsford in 1920 and by Lady Reading in 1924, received support from the colonial government, but they were independent of the government in terms of administration and policy and had to raise much of their money from individual philanthropists. This lack of full government funding demonstrates that ultimately the government did not consider maternal health to be an issue of the state, and without full government support it was difficult for these funds to survive.

The stated purpose of the Dufferin Fund was "to bring medical knowledge and medical relief to the women of India."[23] Maneesha Lal writes that this goal was to be achieved through the provision of:

> (1) medical tuition, including the teaching and training of women as physicians, hospital assistants, nurses, and midwives, the education to be supplied first by England and America but then by India; (2) medical relief, which included establishing, under female superintendence, dispensaries and cottage hospitals for the treatment of women and children, opening female wards under female supervision in existing hospitals and dispensaries, providing female medical officers and attendants for existing female wards, and founding hospitals for women where funds were forthcoming; and (3) provision of trained female nurses and midwives to care for women and children in hospitals and private houses.[24]

It is important to note that the Dufferin Fund, unlike the Victoria Memorial Scholarship Fund, was intent on training a new cadre of midwives who were *not* hereditary *dais*. In fact, as discussed below, most of the midwives initially trained and employed through the Dufferin Fund were of European descent.

Historians writing on the Dufferin Fund have highlighted two key interrelated issues which influenced the motivation for and structure of the fund: *purdah* (seclusion of women) and caste.[25] The main reason given for the need to train medical *women* in India was that cultural practices of *purdah* prevented Indian women from going to see male doctors. Indeed, cross-cultural studies in many parts of the world suggest that women prefer to be attended by women doctors during childbirth due to cultural notions of modesty, regardless of whether or not women are secluded for religious purposes such as in *purdah*.[26] The emphasis placed on *purdah* as a *cultural* practice in the colonial discourse may have served to legitimize the dominance of male obstetricians in Europe and the United States, where *purdah* is not prevalent. In colonial discourse not only was *purdah* represented as problematic insofar as it barred women from medical care, but the practice of *purdah* in and of itself was viewed as dangerous to women's health because it kept women away from sunlight and fresh air, and it was blamed for excessive female morbidity and mortality. In an official memorandum on maternity and child welfare relief, the director of public health for Madras Presidency (a British colonial province that included most of the contemporary state of Tamil Nadu and portions of the three states that border Tamil Nadu) in 1923 articulated all these anxieties about the effects of *purdah* on maternal health. In a discussion on maternal mortality he wrote:

> Amongst purdah women conditions are even worse, *tuberculosis* being particularly common. Under this system, the women are prevented from availing themselves of skilled medical advice in the absence of properly qualified medical women, and are also prohibited from taking advantage of the maternity hospitals. Even among the better educated classes the woman in travail is shut up in a dark dirty room where neither light nor fresh air can gain admittance, and she is usually surrounded by a crowd of female relations all prepared to resist to the utmost the introduction of any new-fangled notions of sanitation and hygiene. It is not surprising that the mother, weak and unhealthy to start with, very often succumbs in giving birth to a puny child.[27]

Indeed, *purdah* was an important Orientalist trope in constructing the colonized "other" society as repressive toward women, thereby legitimizing colonial authority.

Since in India *purdah* was primarily practiced by upper-caste Muslims and Hindus, the unstated implication was that the Dufferin Fund was intended to serve upper-caste women so as to make allopathic maternity care respectable and, ultimately, hegemonic. In fact, when female-supervised maternity wards in large hospitals did begin to open up, those women who tended to come at first were Hindu women from the lower castes and classes as well as some less-affluent European and Anglo-Indians.[28]

In order to lure high-caste Hindus and Muslims, therefore, hospitals began to establish separate wards for these communities. For example, in 1890 the Victoria Hospital for Caste and Gosha Women was established in Madras. Today the official name of this hospital is the Kasthurba Gandhi Hospital, though it is still colloquially referred to as Gosha Hospital. *Gosha* refers to the practice of veiling among Muslim women. Much of the ethnographic material in this book refers to this hospital. In 1904 a report put out by the Victoria Hospital for Caste and Gosha Women stated:

> We have much pleasure in noting the increasing popularity of the hospital. No pressure or inducement is now needed; patients come of their own free will, asking admission into the hospital. In fact during certain seasons of the year, it becomes necessary, from want of accommodation, to refuse admission to patients and they are advised to go to other hospitals. The influx of *mofussil*[29] patients is high as usual. . . . It is very satisfactory to find that

> there is a steady increase in the maternity every year. We are also pleased to state that several of the better class come into the hospital for their confinements. We have had no less than 33 Brahmin and respectable Hindu cases. There is no doubt that the new delivery ward, the gift of Lady Bashyam Iyengar,[30] will prove a special attraction as the accommodation and sanitary conditions are far superior to those of the old delivery ward.[31]

Lal points out the contradiction which this created in British policy. Colonial discourse represented *purdah* as a sign of India's barbarism and something to be reformed, yet the Dufferin Fund was structured to accommodate the practice.[32] By the same token, in the interest of attracting an elite clientele, hospitals supported by the Dufferin Fund were structured along caste lines at the same time that caste was rhetorically touted by the colonial regime as inimical to civilized society. Maternity hospitals were established in other colonies at the same time with the same intent of luring elite women, for example the Victoria Jubilee Hospital which opened in Jamaica in 1894. Victoria Jubilee, however, was staffed with *male* physicians, following the model established in maternity hospitals in Britain.[33]

Despite some reports that more high-caste women were using these maternity wards established under the Dufferin Fund, attendance remained low up through World War I. Within India, the Madras Presidency was known to be making greater strides in the provision of Western medical care for women than governments in most other provinces of the colony. Nevertheless, David Arnold reports that even by 1913, less than one-fifth of all registered births in the city of Madras took place in hospitals, and in rural areas of the Madras Presidency maternity hospitals were scarce.[34]

Despite the official rhetoric which emphasized *purdah* as the reason for the need to employ female medical practitioners in India, Lal makes the important point that there was also an imperialistic logic to this demand, which has often been ignored by historians. Lal argues that the rhetoric of *purdah* was used as justification for the establishment of the Dufferin Fund, but the fund initially provided employment and educational opportunities almost exclusively to women from Great Britain. Women interested in breaking into the medical establishment in Great Britain at the time faced fierce competition from male medical professionals. The "need" for women medical professionals in India, therefore, provided an alternative for British women who could not successfully compete with their male counterparts at home.[35] As Arnold writes, "Western medicine in India was a colonial science and not simply an extension or transference of Western science to a colonial outpost."[36] In reality, Lal and others suggest, most Indian women were prevented from accessing male medical practitioners primarily due to cost and patriarchal structures which rendered women's health care secondary to men's.[37] Furthermore, Meredith Borthwick's study of high-caste Bengali *bhadramahilas* suggests that even high-caste women were in fact willing to see male doctors, and that male doctors even entered *zenanas* to provide their services to women.[38]

Due to the colonial context, race was central to how the Dufferin Fund was executed. Initially, women doctors working in India all originated from and were trained in the West and then sent to India. Women began entering medical colleges in India in 1875 at Madras Medical College, but still these were mostly British and American or Anglo-Indian women. The Indian women who did enter the medical profession at the time came primarily from Christian communities. Hindu and Muslim women, particularly from the upper castes, tended to stay out of the women's medical professions just as they had stayed away from maternity wards as patients. The reason given for the lack of representation from these communities was that work associated with childbirth was culturally considered "polluting."[39] But racist attitudes in the recruiting policies of medical colleges must also be held responsible for this imbalance that existed up until the 1930s.[40]

One of the ways that women of European descent attempted to hold onto their privileged positions in nursing and midwifery was by arguing that better quality of care could be guaranteed only by providing training (and stipends for training) in the English language, as opposed to vernacular languages. In Madras Presidency this issue was, however, hotly debated in the 1930s, and the Madras government began to establish stipends and training programs in vernacular languages with the intent of spreading allopathic care to a wider population.[41]

By 1939 the Madras government explicitly stated that preference for candidates in midwifery would be given to "natives of the Province." Key restrictions for such candidates, however, were applied. First, candidates had to be between the ages of eighteen and thirty-five. And, in addition to the preference given to candidates who had received higher education, unmarried candidates were also preferred. Candidates who were pregnant or nursing would not be considered. And a student who married during the course of training would be considered to have resigned her training and would be penalized.[42] The combination of family and professional work was clearly viewed as inimical for women in the colonies, as it was for women in Britain. But such restrictions for candidates may have been particularly problematic in the Indian context, where marriage and maternity were expected at a younger age for most Indian women than for European women. Such restrictions may therefore have favored single European women seeking work in the colonies.

Proponents of the Dufferin Fund felt that part of their mission was to rid childbirth and medical care at birth of what they perceived to be a dominant cultural association of childbirth with "pollution," and therefore with untouchability in India. The profession of obstetrics thus had to be presented as both sanitary and noble. The success of the Dufferin Fund relied in many ways on the vilification of the *dai* as unsanitary and on the representation of home birth as inherently dangerous. Over time, however, it became eminently clear that due to the economic condition of colonial India it was not realistic to expect that all birthing women could be served by medical professionals in the short term. It was felt that intermediary measures had to be taken to improve the practices of the *dais*. It was to this end that the Victoria Memorial Scholarship Fund was established in 1903.

VICTORIA MEMORIAL SCHOLARSHIP FUND

Although individual civil surgeons and missionaries had provided training to *dais* as early as the 1860s,[43] the Victoria Memorial Scholarship Fund (hereafter called the Victoria Fund) represented the first systematic effort to train *dais* throughout India. Like the Dufferin Fund, the Victoria Fund was run by a voluntary organization consisting primarily of the wives of colonial administrators and headed by Lady Dufferin. Although it had government support, it was not a government program.

In 1918 a major report on the Victoria Fund, entitled *Improvement of the Condition of Childbirth in India,* reviewed the goals of the fund and assessed the extent to which these goals had been achieved. Civil surgeons, inspectors general of civil hospitals, and medical officers from several provinces, as well as "medical women" and "qualified midwives" all contributed papers to the report. Almost all contributors were men and women of British descent. An analysis of this report reveals the extent to which this project was conceived of as part of the civilizing process and was riddled with the contradictions regarding the question of whether this process would occur voluntarily or by force. These contradictions were played out in the representation of the *dai,* who was simultaneously depicted as a victim of "custom" and caste and as a criminal agent acting with free will. The question, therefore, was whether the *dai* could be enlightened and reformed, or whether she represented a threat to civility and should therefore be forbidden from engaging in her work assisting births.

The report states that the primary objective of the Victoria Fund was "to train midwives in the female wards of hospitals and female training schools in such a manner as will enable them to carry on their hereditary calling in harmony with the religious feelings of the people, and gradually to improve their traditional methods in light of modern sanitation and medical knowledge."[44] The emphasis on the *gradual* pace at which this transformation should take place was further underscored by Colonel C. Mactaggart, the inspector general of civil hospitals in the United Provinces, who wrote:

> I am strongly of the opinion that in all sanitary and medical matters in this country progress can only be made by carrying the people with us, and not by driving them. Progress in such matters can only be very slow and gradual and it can only be made as the result of a general advance in education and a gradual increase of the confidence of the people in the methods of Western medicine. No greater mistake can be made than to attempt to do too much and to endeavor to advance our methods by compulsion.[45]

The notion that the best way to achieve desired changes is through education so that the public comes to desire change of its own will reflects what Foucault has noted as a change from juridical power to discursive power that has been a hallmark of the discourse of civil society.[46] This attitude also reflects a general change in colonial policy in India following the Mutiny of 1857, after which the colonial government felt that it had moved too quickly to establish British-style institutions and morality under the leadership of Lord William Bentinck, and that it was too removed from the social lives of Indians to understand them and therefore to rule effectively.

Indian society was primarily conceived of in religious terms as "Hindu" society, and although there was a move to understand that society, there was also a retrenchment from becoming involved in or directly transforming "Hindu" institutions. Hence the reference above to the importance of training *dais* in such a way that their work is "in harmony with the religious feelings of the people." The post-Mutiny policy was to move into the inner spaces of Indian society in order to gradually transform and reform those spaces, to "carry the people with us" toward progress. Nevertheless, Christian missionary activity in India during this time continued to actively seek out converts in part through the provision of biomedical maternal and child health care.[47]

The private sphere of women, and in particular of mothers, became a great new frontier for colonists during this period of High Empire following the Mutiny. The "dark," "inner recesses" of women's space had to be penetrated in order to change the Indian public's attitudes about medicine and "sanitation." The representation of these spaces as "dark" in and of itself equated them with bad sanitation, and in the context of childbirth, the darkness and stuffiness of the space in which women delivered was repeatedly cited as a cause for disease. But by penetrating this space and bringing to it knowledge of Western medicine and sanitation, not only the private space but the entire nation could become en*lightened.* In short, embedded in the discourse on childbirth was the notion that the hope for the progress of the nation lay in the minds and bodies of India's women, who were homogeneously referred to as "the Indian woman." As the Scottish doctor Dagmar Florence Curjel, working with the Women's Medical Service in India, wrote in the Victoria Fund report:

> [T]he real solution to the problem lies in educating the Indian woman in the case of her own health, and that of her offspring, and in the elements of domestic hygiene, by every possible means. It seems to me that the question is truly one of *home* rule—for the woman is the heart of the Indian home, and it is *she* who will be the decisive factor in improving the conditions of childbirth in India.[48]

In the passage above, "home rule" refers to the growing nationalist movements for independence and in particular to the Indian Congress party's Home Rule campaigns, which were instigated by Balgangadhar Tilak and Annie Besant in 1916. Partha Chatterjee has argued that for Bengali nationalists during this time, Indian women—and the clothes draped around their bodies—became powerful symbols of superior Indian spirituality which was protected within the confines of the home and could thus resist internal colonization.[49] In colonial medical discourse, however, Indian women's desire and ability to improve the conditions of childbirth were construed as a prerequisite for political autonomy. As Scottish Dr. G. J. Campbell from Rainy Hospital in Madras wrote:

> Much requires to be done in the way of improving conditions of childbirth by securing legislation to raise the marriage age for girls in the country to

> 15 or 16. . . . This want of readiness for social reforms should be taken into consideration when claims for home rule are made. As I have said before, if some political genius of Indian birth would devise a scheme whereby in each section of the community the attainment of self-government could be made to depend on its ability to do this and other elementary acts of justice to its own weaker members, a useful stimulus to progress would be given. Then when every section of the community had achieved internal reform India would be ready to take her place with honour, as an equal, in the council of nations.[50]

It is important to note that although Indian mothers were constructed as being ignorant, they were also viewed as innocent victims of Indian "custom" who were eminently malleable. Like children, they could be reformed if given the right direction. It was the younger women in particular who were viewed as more inclined to accept and adopt Western notions of "progress," whereas their mothers-in-law were often viewed as conservative elements which had to be overcome or bypassed. Kathleen Patch, an English nurse working in the Winchester Mission in Mandalay, wrote:

> It has been said that the Burmese woman is one of the most charming of women, the best bargain-driver in the world, but the very worst mother. Just as we do not expect much in the way of self-help from young children so we cannot at present look for self-help from the native mothers. We have to help them to help themselves, and the gradual introduction of European methods can be best effected by giving the native midwives a first-class training and sparing no effort to inspire them with high ideals for their very important vocation.[51]

This infantalization of Indians was a central part of the psychological force of colonialism, as Ashis Nandy has argued.[52]

In the above passage the point is that "native" women are bad mothers because they are ignorant, not because they are immoral. This distinction between morality and knowledge was repeatedly used in judging "the Indian woman." As one woman doctor wrote, "The Indian woman is usually a *good* mother to her children, but her lack of knowledge often leads her to show her affection in ways inimical to the baby's well-being."[53] The colonial construction of "the Indian woman" as moral differed from constructions of womanhood in some other colonial contexts, such as in Jamaica, where high rates of infant mortality were attributed to the illegitimacy of the children and thus the immorality of the mothers.[54] Colonial notions of "the Indian woman" as moral were based on colonial and nationalist perceptions of upper-class, upper-caste propriety. In other colonial contexts where Indian women made up an important part of the indentured labor force on plantations and mines, such as in Fiji and Malaya, "the Indian mother" was in fact treated with greater disdain than her other colonized counterparts.[55]

In late-colonial India, in order to teach the moral but ignorant Indian woman how to become a "good mother," colonialists began to run classes in "mothercraft" and to disseminate information about "mothercraft" through public lectures, pamphlets, magic lantern shows, exhibitions, and baby shows. "Mothercraft" classes went beyond lectures on feeding and rearing children to include such things as the "art of housewifery," cooking, and needlework.[56] Beginning in the early 1920s, National Health and Baby Week celebrations were carefully organized to take place in districts throughout India simultaneously. As part of these shows, babies were entered into competitions for "most healthy" baby. A report of a 1928 celebration in Madras Presidency shows that all babies entered in these competitions were given such things as free baths, biscuits, and sweets. Winning babies were treated to prizes in the form of silk jackets, silver cups, soap, Horlicks malted milk, and toys, and their mothers sometimes received new saris. And "poor feedings" were distributed to all who attended.[57] Many of these "mothercraft" programs were modeled on similar projects being carried out in England and the United States.[58] A key goal of the "mothercraft" programs in the West and in the colonies was to get women to view their babies as "citizens" and therefore to care about their well-being not only on a personal level but for the sake of the future of the nation.[59] In the colonial context this was of course rife with irony: for India to become eligible for nation status, "the Indian mother" had to view her baby as a citizen even before the mother or baby was in fact granted citizens' rights.

Some colonists also argued that messages about such things as hygiene and "mothercraft" could only be imparted to Indian women through Indian men, who, because they were more often given English educations, were viewed as more accepting of Western "scientific" knowledge. As Dr. K. O. Vaughan, stationed in Srinagar, wrote, "In England women can and do manage their own affairs and those of other people too, intelligently, efficiently, and well. Without them where would be our educational system, our hospitals, our orphanages and a thousand other activities essential to the welfare of a great nation. Out here not only are the women not educated, but they have no power to reform things."[60]

Although the "Indian mother" in this report is generally constructed as ignorant but malleable and potentially reformable, the construction of the *dai* which emerges in this report is much more ambiguous. On the one hand, *dais* are represented as ignorant products of the "traditional" society within which they must live and work. On the other hand, they are depicted as self-serving criminal agents who are rigid in their opinions and are thus obstructing progress. Most of the *dais* at the time were at least forty years old, and their age was viewed as a marker of their conservatism. Some distinctions were made between rural and urban *dais*. Urban *dais,* it was felt, were more malleable, whereas rural *dais* were rigid in their ways and a force to be reckoned with.[61] But generally the report refers to *dais* as a homogenous category—sometimes calling them a "caste," an "institution," a "class," or a "race." Whichever label was used, they were always viewed as the lower rung of the social order, without access to education. Their low status itself was thought to preclude the possibility of their adopting Western knowledge and practices.

The *dai* was always depicted as dirty. In introducing two *dais* to the reader, Dr. Vaughan writes, "Their clothes filthy, their hands begrimed with dirt, their heads alive with vermin, they explain that they are midwives, that the patient has been in labour for three days and they cannot get the child out. They are rubbing their hands on the floor previous to making another effort."[62]

In fact, *dais* were constructed as being *inherently* dirty due to their low caste position. Thus, while most colonial reformers claimed that caste was an obstacle to building a civil society, they employed their view of the logic of caste to condemn the practice of the *dais*. In addition to being dirty, the *dais* were often referred to as "evil" and construed as being "meddlesome," echoing the condemnation of midwives in Europe and America by the church as well as the state and the medical profession.

In 1923, the director of public health for Madras Presidency even suggested that it was safer to deliver with *no* assistance at all than to be attended on by a *dai*. As he wrote:

> Excluding the few fortunate women who are delivered without any assistance or intervention, there still remains some 10 lakhs [one lakh is 100,000] of labor cases which are managed by barber midwives or *dhais [sic]*. Their ignorance of hygiene, or even of cleanliness, is stupendous, as may be recognized when it is stated that the duties of physician, midwife, and scavenger are all performed by them. Their methods, the instruments used by them, and the medicaments given to both mother and child are

> so revolting that no language sufficiently strong can be used to condemn them. It cannot therefore be a matter of great surprise that maternal deaths amount to the colossal figure of 25,000 annually.[63]

The introduction to the Victoria Fund report acknowledges that the *dai*-training schemes had not been wholly successful and attributes the lack of success to the active resistance of the *dais:*

> Many of the women were forty, fifty, sixty, or even seventy years of age: some were deaf, some were blind: none had any previous education or had ever exercised their mental faculties: they were very prejudiced and jealous of their reputation and in addition honestly convinced that no one could teach them anything as regards normal labour. They believed that doctors were required in abnormal cases, but they also believed that they themselves were the proper judges as to when a doctor should be called in. This was and is the general opinion of their patients and it is the attitude of the people of India at the present day. They are only very slowly beginning to realise that the great mass of the abnormal cases are due to neglect and ignorance in the treatment of normal labour.[64]

In the end, this report reflects extreme ambivalence about the value of working with hereditary *dais* through the Victoria Fund. Nevertheless, throughout the report there is a sense that despite the innumerable obstacles faced in training hereditary *dais* and in reforming "the Indian woman," the continuation of the work of the Victoria Fund remained essential to the stated goals of reducing infant and maternal mortality in India. The *dai*-training programs were viewed as necessary stopgap measures, while the long-term goals lay in the development of a cadre of professionally trained women doctors, nurses, and even midwives who would oversee deliveries in hospitals.

The director of public health for the Madras Presidency in 1923, quoted above, was less willing to concede that short-term government support of hereditary *dais* should be continued. He sought to prevent *dais* from practicing in the presidency and proposed to do so through the passage of a government act modeled after the Midwives Act of 1902 in England, which required all midwives to be licensed and penalized all midwives practicing without licenses. Through such an act, he felt that all *dais* would be replaced by certified midwives who would not be drawn from the pool of hereditary *dais*.[65]

In 1926 the government of Madras Presidency passed the Madras Nurses and Midwives Act requiring certification and registration of all nurses, midwives, health visitors, auxiliary nurse midwives, and *dais*.[66] Under this act, anyone working without a certificate of registration could be fined, as could anyone issuing false certificates or anyone falsely using such titles as "registered nurse" or "registered *dai.*" Applicants who wished to be put on the register had to pass standardized exams and had to provide testimonials of both their professional competency from medical personnel and their "good moral character" from persons of "good social standing." The council deciding who could and could not be on the register included representatives from all the above categories of practitioners except *dais.* Obviously, the administrative difficulty of officially training all *dais* and penalizing all those *dais* practicing without certification was insurmountable. Additionally, it would be interesting to know, although impossible to ascertain, how councils voted on the "moral" qualifications of *dais* given the construction of *dais* as inherently immoral. Clearly this legislation was more symbolic than pragmatic. Many *dais* then, just as today, of course continued to practice without any government training or licensing. Nevertheless, this act did represent the government's ongoing efforts to publicly condemn the traditional practices of the *dais* while simultaneously demonstrating a commitment to officially recognize and sanction the work of those *dais* who went through *dai*-training programs.

Throughout the Victoria Fund report, and in the numerous other government reports on maternal and child health at the time, the high rates of infant and maternal mortality are attributed to the general ignorance of the Indian population and specifically to the evils of the untrained *dai* in her (mis)management of birth. The report does not consider how maternal health during *pregnancy* results in high rates of infant and maternal mortality as well as miscarriages and stillbirths. A 1928 study of maternal mortality in India reported that 31 percent of "abnormal" obstetric cases and 54 percent of maternal deaths were caused by "diseases of pregnancy," whereas in Britain only 7 percent of "abnormal" obstetric cases and 35 percent of maternal deaths were caused by "diseases of pregnancy."[67] Poor maternal health during pregnancy is, of course, directly related to poverty and thus to broader structures of political economy.

The Victoria Fund report does not, however, consider how the political-economic structures under colonialism might have negatively impacted women's health. For example, colonial systems of labor and wage structures rendered women increasingly economically dependent on men, thereby diminishing their ability to take advantage of whatever medical services might be available.[68] Furthermore, colonialism was directly implicated in the spread of deadly epidemics of smallpox, cholera, and the plague, and was responsible for famines which devastated communities throughout the subcontinent. In the face of these man-made disasters, it was the health of women and children which suffered the most.

In sum, when we consider these two funds together—the Dufferin Fund and the Victoria Fund—it is clear that the status of health of Indian women and children served as the "grounds" for a discourse on childbirth in colonial India. Many goals were sought and achieved through this discourse, including the establishment of a network of allopathic institutions for maternal and child health (including hospitals and medical colleges); securing employment for European and Anglo-Indian women; providing the rationale for colonial administrators to move into the private sphere of Indian domestic life; and legitimizing the "civilizing" rule of the British. This is not to imply that individuals involved in these projects were not sincerely dedicated to the improvement of women's health; nor do I mean to deny that some Indian women benefited from the new forms of allopathic maternal health care available. But it is important to point out which other, unstated colonial interests were served through these projects.

These funds were structured by colonial interests and limitations as well as by local issues of caste and gender, which resulted in a very different scenario of the professionalization of obstetrics in India than in the United States and Europe. The first critical difference is that due to the intersection of imperialist and local interests, women dominated the profession of obstetrics in India from the beginning. Even in urban centers of India where childbirth has become heavily biomedicalized, it has not been accompanied by the domination of male doctors, as is the case historically in the West. Second, despite ongoing efforts to slander the *dais,* their central role in overseeing deliveries in India was viewed as inevitable in the short term by the colonial administration, and continues to be viewed this way today. Although ever since the Victoria Fund, many have decried the failures of the *dai*-training programs, these programs continue to be supported (to some degree) by national and state governments in India today. Unlike the situation in the United States and many parts of Europe, the biomedical establishment's control over childbirth in India can by no means be viewed as hegemonic.

Due to the combination of these two factors—the predominance of female obstetricians and the continued widespread practice of local midwives—the critiques which women have about the status of childbirth in India today differ significantly from the antihegemonic feminist critiques of the condition of childbirth in the West. The fact that women have dominated the field of obstetrics in India does not preclude the possibility that their practices are as saturated by patriarchal values as those of their male counterparts, since such values are to some extent inherent in biomedical obstetric training throughout the world. But the absence of male dominance in obstetrics in India does have important repercussions on the nature of the critiques of the professionalization of obstetrics in India. There is no significant "natural," "female-centered" home-birth movement in India today, even among the urban middle and upper classes. Rather, based on ethnographic material presented in the remaining chapters, I will argue that the contemporary criticisms waged by the lower-class women whom I met in Tamil Nadu are less concerned with issues of male domination in the hospitals and with the birthing woman's individual experience of birth, and more concerned with collectively experienced forms of class, caste, and gender discrimination which often prevented these women from getting the allopathic care they wanted.

CHAPTER 2

Maternal and Child Health Services in the Postcolonial Era

Having described the colonial context in which the professionalization of obstetrics emerged in tandem with a resigned acceptance of midwifery, I now move quickly through time to the policies and programs of the twentieth century which have informed the structure of public MCH services throughout much of the postcolonial era. In this descriptive chapter I hope to provide a general sketch first of the official structures of health care in India and in Tamil Nadu and then of the actual landscape of MCH care in Kaanathur-Reddikuppam and Nochikuppam. This chapter is intended to provide a basic framework through which to understand the more ethnographically and theoretically engaged chapters which follow. (See Appendix II for an outline of the *official* structures of rural and urban MCH institutions and practitioners in Tamil Nadu for 1995 that are described in this chapter.)

THE OFFICIAL STRUCTURE: THE BHORE COMMITTEE REPORT

A four-volume report by the colonial government's Health Survey and Development Committee was published in 1946, known as the "Bhore Committee Report" (Government of India 1946) after the chair of the committee, Sir Joseph Bhore. This committee drew heavily on the recommendations of the Indian National Congress's National Planning Committee, which was established under Jawaharlal Nehru's guidance. The Bhore Committee Report attempted to analyze the state of health care in India and to make recommendations for the improvement of health care services in India overall.[1] Drawn up on the eve of India's independence in 1947, the Bhore Committee Report became the template for the structure of health care services in India in the postcolonial era, as reflected in the postcolonial government of India's Five-Year Plans. The actual implementation of the institutional structures recommended in the report were initiated ten years following its submission. Many of the basic elements of this structure remain in place today.

The Bhore Committee Report called for the establishment of a socialist system of health care, emphasizing public health services and preventative medicine for the rural poor. Madras Presidency had been the first presidency to pass a Public Health Act in 1939, which put the responsibility for the provision of public health services, including maternal and child health, in the hands of the state. With the Bhore Committee Report, public health became the responsibility of the national government, although the implementation remained in the hands of the individual states. The model envisioned in the Bhore Committee Report was a three-tiered referral system, with primary health care services emphasizing preventative care available in primary health centers (PHCs) at the village level,[2] secondary curative services available at the district level, and tertiary services available in the urban centers, often attached to medical teaching and research institutions. Rural women seeking allopathic services during childbirth were encouraged and expected to use this three-tiered system according to their needs.

Following the Victoria Fund's approach, the Bhore Committee Report also posited that the hereditary *dais* would inevitably remain central to the care of Indian women during childbirth, at least in the short term. The report, therefore, supported efforts to provide basic training to the hereditary *dais* rather than trying to replace them with a new cadre of midwives. Government support of such *dai*-training programs continued in independent India, and these programs were included in the government of India's Five-Year Plans.

In addition to Madras Presidency's early move to take responsibility for public health services in general, the Madras Presidency's Department of Public Health also took an active role in overseeing the training and deployment of auxiliary health workers specializing in MCH care, known officially as "health visitors." In 1938 the Department of Public Health took over these responsibilities from preexisting voluntary organizations such as the India Red Cross Society. Based on a model borrowed from Britain, health visitors were women who were to be trained in such subjects as elementary physiology, home nursing and first aid, household management and dietetics, maternity and child hygiene, and character training and mental hygiene.[3] The Bhore Committee Report envisioned that, after completing their training, these health visitors would be appointed to medical institutions serving women and conduct outreach work in the communities surrounding these institutions to provide basic health services and educate others on the merits of these topics.

It was, however, an ongoing struggle to make the establishment of such a cadre of auxiliary health workers a basic structure of the postcolonial public health service sector. Ever since the implementation of the three-tiered primary-health-based structure, state governments have faced great difficulties in convincing urban-trained doctors to take up employment in rural hospitals. This made it politically difficult to establish a cadre of auxiliary medical staff attached to primary health centers who could serve as community health workers, since some felt that the presence of such auxiliary health workers would be an impediment to sincere efforts to staff the PHCs with more-qualified doctors. There were also concerns that these auxiliary workers would begin to work independently of the doctors' supervision, and that the rural poor would thus be served by under-qualified "quacks."[4]

By the mid-1970s, however, the multipurpose-health-worker (MPHW) schemes, modeled after the Soviet system, gained widespread acceptance and were implemented in many Indian states. These schemes called for both a male and female MPHW to be attached to each PHC. The male MPHWs were responsible for several vertical public programs, such as the leprosy, tuberculosis, and malaria programs, in addition to family planning. The role of female MPHWs has, however, been more limited in scope. Female MPHWs' primary task has been to educate women, collect census-type data, and provide services in the areas of family planning and maternal-child health care more generally. As I discuss in Chapter Five, the family-planning interests and services have largely overshadowed all other aspects of MCH care in India since its independence.

MCH CARE STRUCTURE IN TAMIL NADU IN 1995

Rural Tamil Nadu: The Official Structure for Public MCH Care for Childbirth

This combination of the three-tiered public hospital structure, MPHWs, and trained (and untrained) hereditary *dais* formed the basis of the official rural public health service structure for MCH care in Tamil Nadu during my research in 1995. It must be underscored that the *official* structure does not always represent the actual structure of MCH care services in any given area at any given time. What follows in this section is an account of the *official* structure provided by the Tamil Nadu Department of Public Health.

In 1995 the population of Tamil Nadu was approximately 58 million.[5] There were twenty-three districts. The city of Madras made up one district and the remaining districts comprised both urban and rural components. Each district had approximately fifteen to twenty "development blocks," each serving a population of approximately one million.[6] Within each development block, there was one PHC for every 30,000 people. In 1995 there were 1,416 PHCs in Tamil Nadu. Each PHC was to have at least five beds. The majority of the PHC services were outpatient, so few beds were deemed necessary. These PHCs were supposed to be staffed with two doctors (one female and one male), some paramedics, a pharmacist, and health support staff. Each PHC was to have one "sector health nurse" (previously called a "lady health visitor") supervising six "village health nurses," or VHNs (previously called "auxiliary nurse midwives" [ANMs]), the rural equivalent of urban female MPHWs. VHNs were responsible for MCH care, while male multipurpose health workers attached to the PHC were responsible for overseeing such things as public health, control of epidemics and specific diseases, and public emergencies. Each PHC was to have approximately six "health subcenters" (HSC) under its domain, which were overseen by the VHNs. In 1995 there were 8,681 HSCs in Tamil Nadu. In the plains areas where transportation was relatively easy, there was to be one HSC for every 5,000 of population. In areas with hilly terrain where transportation was more difficult, there was to be one HSC for every 2,000 to 3,000 of population. The VHNs attached to these HSCs were trained to provide essential obstetric care, including prenatal care, assistance with deliveries, postnatal care, family planning, and basic first aid for mothers and children. They were trained to detect emergency obstetric cases and refer those to the subdistrict-level hospitals, known as "*taluk* hospitals." These VHNs were trained to conduct deliveries in a subcenter building, if such a building existed, or in patients' homes. Only about 50 percent of all the HSCs actually had a building; the other 50 percent simply referred people to those services provided by the VHNs in homes.

In addition to the VHNs, the Department of Public Health also acknowledged that many home deliveries were conducted by local midwives, officially called "traditional birth attendants." According to the Department of Public Health, there were approximately 40,000 TBAs in Tamil Nadu in 1995, and 90 percent had received some form of training from doctors in tertiary-care hospitals. The Department of Public Health strove to create linkages between the VHNs and the TBAs such that the TBAs would contact the VHNs if they detected any obstetric problems. The Department of Public Health also recognized, but did not deal administratively with, a category of people that it referred to as "nontraditional birth attendants," which included members of the family who oversaw deliveries but who were not hereditary midwives.

For secondary health care, women and children were to be referred first to the *taluk* hospitals, of which there were approximately 200 in Tamil Nadu in 1995. After the *taluk* hospitals, patients would be referred to the "district quarter hospitals." There were twenty-three district quarter hospitals in Tamil Nadu in 1995, one for each district in the state. Finally, for tertiary care, women and children could be referred to the large "government hospitals" attached to research institutions in major urban centers.

Kaanathur-Reddikuppam: Options for MCH Care for Childbirth in a Semirural Village

As I discuss in the Introduction, Kaanathur-Reddikuppam was undergoing rapid transformation as it was becoming increasingly connected to the metropolis of Madras. This had greatly influenced the structure of MCH services in the area such that in 1995 approximately one-half of all deliveries were conducted in homes and the other half in hospitals. There was, however, much variation in the nature of both home and hospital deliveries. This section will briefly describe the range of MCH services in this particular area, with the intention of providing a framework for understanding how people made decisions regarding which kind of services to seek for health needs related to childbirth.

My first introduction to Kaanathur-Reddikuppam was through Muttamma, who was working as a "lay first-aider" for the Voluntary Health Services (VHS) in Kaanathur and who also did some work for the Lion's Club clinic in Muttukaadu. Muttamma was attached to the VHS "mini-health-center" (MHC), which was located on the main road in the middle of the small cluster of shops which made up the center of Kaanathur. The presence of this VHS mini-health-center, which was established in 1983, meant that the MCH services in this area already diverged from the official structure delineated above. Furthermore, although there was a government health subcenter building in the nearby town of Muttukaadu, south of Kaanathur-Reddikuppam, the post of VHN for the center was vacant during the time of my research. The building had not been used for deliveries for some time because it was damaged, and according to the block supervisor at the Kelambakkam PHC, the government had not provided the necessary funding to repair it. The VHN who was to fill that post was undergoing training in Madras during 1995. By the time I returned to Tamil Nadu in May of 1997 the VHN was working in the subcenter, though some complained that since she lived in the center of Madras her visits to the subcenter were somewhat sporadic and she was not available for off-hours emergency needs.

VHS was founded in 1966 by Dr. K. S. Sanjivi, a physician who strove to improve the health conditions of the rural poor.[7] Sanjivi felt that completely free health care created passivity among people and made them feel that they were not getting quality care. Therefore, in establishing VHS he proposed providing health services along similar lines as those provided by the government but required that families pay a minimal fee for these services. During the time that I was conducting research the annual fee was Rs. 50 per family for use of the rural facilities. A one-visit consultation fee to see a private doctor would cost at least this much.

Sanjivi's goal was to supplement rather than compete with preexisting government services. VHS's funding came from a combination of government, business, and individual sources. Just as the government health services were provided through a structure of HSCs and PHCs, VHS care was to be provided primarily through a network of mini-health-centers. And like the HSCs and PHCs, these mini-health-centers were to focus on preventative care. VHS had established mini-health-centers in two development blocks near Madras, including the Thirupoorur development block within which Kaanathur-Reddikuppam was located. The Thirupoorur block was one of twenty-seven development blocks within the Chennai-MGR District in 1995.

The headquarters of VHS lay on the southern edge of Madras. At the headquarter hospital, doctors provided curative services for emergency cases. In addition, this hospital was engaged in research and trained medical officers (doctors), multipurpose health workers (male and female), and lay first-aiders. The lay first-aiders, like Muttamma, were all women and were chosen from among the women living in the communities where the mini-health-centers were located. The lay first-aider was a part-time worker who was expected to conduct home visits in order to collect information about the health status—including information about pregnant and postpartum women, deliveries, and family-planning methods used—of members of the community. They reported this information to the MPHW in the mini-health-center. In addition, lay first-aiders could provide basic first aid care to people at home. Each mini-health-center was staffed by a male and female MPHW. The training for MPHWs was one year for male MPHWs and eighteen months for female MPHWs. The extra six months for female MPHWs was to provide training in MCH care. The VHS doctors working in the rural areas generally worked for VHS only on a part-time basis, making occasional visits to the various mini-health-centers to check up on the centers' status.

The mini-health-center in Kaanathur-Redikuppam consisted of a small cement-block room with a desk which was cluttered with vials of different sorts of medicines and packets of pills. And there were two metal fold-up chairs—one for the MPHW and one for the patient. Attached to the room was a tiny waiting area which was open to the outside road, though partially protected by a fence made of rough sticks and thatch. There was also a rubbish pile, haphazardly dumped to the side of this waiting area, which contained, among other things, medicine wrappers and bottles and used syringes that attracted a swarm of flies. I found myself spending quite a bit of time in this dingy waiting room since the open hours for this mini-health-center were fairly inconsistent. But the male or female MPHW in charge did usually show up, and many people from the area did come to seek his or her advice and get treatment for all sorts of ailments.

In Kaanathur-Reddikuppam, Muttamma's own son was the male MPHW during the time of my research. The female MPHW who was attached to this center when I began my research left VHS halfway through the year and established her own private practice seeing deliveries in her own home in a town about forty-five minutes away by bus from Kaanathur-Redikuppam. She was replaced by another female MPHW who also had to travel by bus to come to the center, which meant that she was not available for emergency care during off hours.

The female MPHWs were trained to conduct deliveries in homes if it became absolutely necessary that they do so. But their mandate, while working for VHS, was to educate women about prenatal care, deliveries, and postnatal care, and refer them to a hospital for deliveries. The headquarters of VHS only opened up its own obstetrics ward in 1994; the MPHWs were just beginning to refer women to that hospital for deliveries. Although the VHS female MPHW was an important source of information regarding MCH care in the vicinity, and she provided some pre- and postnatal care, she rarely in fact conducted deliveries herself.

Like the female MPHW who left to start her own practice conducting deliveries in another town, Shahida had been trained as a MPHW at VHS. After working for VHS and other voluntary health organizations in other regions of Tamil Nadu, she and her husband had come to Kaanathur-Reddikuppam in 1994 to establish their own clinic, and she was privately conducting home deliveries in the area. She and her husband were living in a room attached to the home of Murugesan (the *panchayat* president described in the Introduction), which was on the southern end of the main street of Kaanathur-Reddikuppam. They had set up their clinic in that house. Although Shahida would see prenatal and postpartum patients in the clinic if they came to visit her, she conducted all her deliveries in the homes of the laboring women.

Shahida's arrival had created a certain amount of resentment on the part of Chellamma, a fifty-five-year-old *maruttuvacci* who had been conducting home deliveries in the area for over twenty-five years. Chellamma's home was on a small path just off the main road near the minihealth-center. Like most hereditary *maruttuvaccis,* Chellamma had learned how to conduct deliveries through observation and apprenticeship at home rather than through any formal *dai*-training program. Karpagam, who lived in a thatched house off the open road leading from Kaanathur to Reddikuppam, *had* undergone a *dai*-training course at the Kelambakkam PHC in 1990 and also conducted home deliveries on occasion. This was not a hereditary profession for her. She was, however, quite critical of the training she had received since it was very time consuming and did not adequately compensate her for loss of pay due to missed work. She was also bitter that her clients did not pay her adequately and so she found herself seeing fewer and fewer home deliveries over the years. I have met some hereditary midwives in Tamil Nadu who complained that after they had gone through the *dai*-training programs their clients were *more* hesitant to pay them than they had been prior to the training, since these clients believed that the midwives were now receiving regular payment from the government.

For both Chellamma and Karpagam, the delivery work was very much part-time. Chellamma had worked most of her life as an agricultural laborer, and Karpagam was working as a laborer on construction sites.[8] Neither of these women provided prenatal care. They came only at the time of the delivery. Chellamma would also come for postpartum visits to bathe the baby and prepare postpartum medicines, but Karpagam did not provide these services.

There was one pharmacy in Kaanathur-Reddikuppam, which was located on the main road in the middle of all the shops. This pharmacy was run by a man whom most people referred to as a "doctor." He had MPHW training and had also taken a three-year course in Siddha medicine. When people asked this pharmacist what he recommended in terms of prenatal and postpartum care for mothers, he tried to encourage them to take Siddha medicines.[9] But he complained that people no longer had the patience required for Siddha medicines to really take effect, and they were increasingly demanding allopathic medicines, especially injections, for immediate results. It was because of this attitude, he said, that he was increasingly being summoned to accompany Chellamma to deliveries to give vitamin B_{12} injections to speed up labor. The pharmacist also occasionally gave mothers and newborns immunization shots. The pharmacist's shop was a private enterprise, so patients paid a fee for the medicines and services he provided.

In addition to the care provided by the VHS workers, Shahida, Chellama, Karpagam, and the pharmacist, women in the area could also get some government-provided prenatal and postpartum care at the local *balwadis* (day-care centers), which were run by the government's Integrated Child Development Services (ICDS). ICDS had become a national program throughout India, but it was modeled on a scheme initiated in Tamil Nadu during M. G. Ramachandran's term as chief minister in the 1980s. In Tamil Nadu, this program was often called by its original name, the Chief Minister's Noon Meals Scheme. This program had helped to establish *balwadis* in low-income communities throughout the state. The *balwadis* served as free day-care centers for children ages two to five and provided them with free lunches that were supposed to include rice, dal, soya flour, vegetables, and occasionally eggs. In addition, at these *balwadis,* packets of dried nutritious food (in Tamil referred to as *cattu uṇavu māvu*) were distributed to pregnant and lactating mothers and to children ages six months to two years. This *cattu uṇavu māvu* contained a mixture of wheat, ragi, soya, fried gram, and jaggery. In rural areas, such as Kaanathur-Reddikuppam, these *balwadis* also served as sites where VHNs from the PHC would come on a monthly basis to provide pre- and postnatal care, including immunizations, to pregnant women and postpartum mothers and their children. The ICDS in Reddikuppam was established in 1987, also during M. G. Ramachandran's term as chief minister. The ICDS in Kaanathur was established in 1994.

In addition to the above-mentioned MCH services for women within Kaanathur-Reddikuppam itself, services were also provided by various hospitals outside of Kaanathur-Reddikuppam. The PHC which serviced Kaanathur-Reddikuppam was located in the town of Kelambakkam. Very few women from this area chose to go to the Kelambakkam PHC just for their deliveries. This was partly due to the distance. As the crow flies, Kelambakkam was quite close. But the route there from Kaanathur-Reddikuppam was indirect and arduous. People would first take a bus going south to Kovalam and then get an auto-rickshaw or van to take them on a long dirt road riddled with potholes through the paddy fields back up to Kelambakkam, which lay on the east side of the canal. The trip by this route took about forty-five minutes. Most felt that travel to Madras was much more convenient even though it took a bit longer. Furthermore, they felt that the quality of care in the larger "government hospitals" in Madras was superior to that of the PHC. The "government hospitals" had emergency care for such things as cesareans, whereas the PHC did not. Those who did go to Kelambakkam for their deliveries only did so if they were planning to undergo sterilization following their delivery. Because the PHC in Kelambakkam was the central PHC for the entire Thirupoorur development block, there were more beds there than in most PHCs.

The other main option for women seeking care for deliveries in public hospitals was to go to the Kasthurba Gandhi Hospital in Madras. This large "government hospital" was usually referred to as "Gosha Hospital" because of its previous name as the Victoria Hospital for Caste and Gosha Women during the colonial era. The direct journey to Kasthurba Gandhi Hospital from Kaanathur-Reddikuppam by auto-rickshaw or van was approximately 20 km. and took about one hour. Many could not afford the expense of such private transportation (Rs. 150), however, and instead had to take two buses (costing a total of less than Rs. 10) to travel to Kasthurba Gandhi Hospital, thereby making the trip one-and-a-half-hours long. Some women from Kaanathur-Reddikuppam who were planning to deliver at Kasthurba Gandhi Hospital would go to the hospital in advance of their labor and, if there was room, stay in the prenatal ward until their labor began. Those who had female relatives (usually on their side of the family rather than their husband's) living in Madras would go and stay with them prior to their due date so that they could reach the hospital immediately once labor pains began.

Even though the main road connecting Kaanathur-Reddikuppam to Madras had made Madras's hospitals much more accessible and had led to the establishment of private hospitals along the main road, transportation still remained a factor in some women's decisions to remain home for their deliveries. This was particularly the case if a woman went into labor in the middle of the night, when no buses were available and an auto-rickshaw may very well not have been available either. None of the public hospitals had ambulance service to pick women up from their homes to transport them to the hospital. Those hospitals which did have ambulances only used them to transfer patients from their hospital to another hospital. Indeed, several of the women I met from Kaanathur-Reddikuppam who had had home deliveries said that they were planning on delivering in the hospital but they went into labor at night or very quickly, and there was no way to reach a hospital in time.

Cost was another important factor in women's decisions regarding where to go and whom to call for their deliveries. It might seem that when choosing between a government-subsidized hospital and a home delivery, cost would not be an issue, as the former would be free and the latter a negligible amount. In fact, this was not at all the case. I was told that the cost of bribes paid in public hospitals could be over Rs. 500 for a normal delivery. The problem of bribery, or forced tipping, within public maternity hospitals was pervasive and was cause for constant complaints among lower-class women in Tamil Nadu who availed themselves of the services in these hospitals. For the most part these bribes were demanded by the *ayahs*, watchmen, and ward boys in the large "government hospitals." Women living in Madras or other urban areas might go to a smaller public hospital in order to avoid these costs. In the large "government hospitals," like Kasthurba Gandhi Hospital, bribes were required for a woman to enter the hospital; for her family members to enter the hospital each time they visited; for the routine enema and shave in preparation for the birth; for the actual birth of the baby (usually Rs. 5 for a girl and Rs. 10 for a boy); for shifting the mother and baby from the delivery ward to the postnatal ward; for assistance going to the bathroom; and on and on. The individual bribes were minimal but they could add up considerably over the course of a woman's stay in the hospital. A more difficult delivery meant that a woman would require more help from the staff and that she might have to prolong her stay in the hospital—both factors adding to the total cost of bribes paid.

Home deliveries in Kaanathur-Reddikuppam cost as little as Rs. 50–100 if attended by one of the local midwives, Chellamma or Karpagam. (When Chellamma attended a delivery she would also provide postpartum bathing services, whereas Karpagam would not.) Both Chellamma and Karpagam typically would charge Rs. 50 if the baby was a girl and Rs. 100 if a boy was born. The families of those women whose home deliveries were attended by Shahida paid up to Rs. 700.

For women who were extremely destitute, therefore, there was no option but to remain at home and call Chellamma or Karpagam. Those a bit better off usually chose between the relatively equal costs of the public hospital and Shahida. And those who were more wealthy sometimes opted to go to a private hospital in Madras or in the town of Kovalam, where charges were significantly higher. I did not meet anybody (throughout my research in Tamil Nadu) who had health insurance to cover these costs. Since most of these poor people worked in the informal sector, there was no access to health insurance. Even in the formal sector, health insurance was extremely rare. Some large private hospitals, such as Apollo Hospital in Madras, were selling insurance policies to patients, but even these were not widely used.

People were often reluctant to say that cost was a factor in their decisions about where to deliver and who would oversee the delivery. Most people said that when they are dealing with the lives of both mother and baby, cost should never be an obstacle to care. Yet people were quick to point to the stinginess of others when it came to decisions based on cost, and they often noted that the cost of maternal health care was a problem for the community as a whole. What is interesting is that the cost of maternal health care for a woman during her delivery was talked about in the same context as the ritual expenses during pregnancy and the postpartum period, as discussed in Chapter Three. Thus, although many were critical of the corrupt system of bribery in the hospital and some were critical of what they considered to be Shahida's overly high fees, still they would talk about these costs as part of the overall burden of having girl-children. The ritual costs and health care costs were usually the responsibility of the woman's own natal kin. In short, the implicit critique seemed at times to be waged more against a patriarchal social system than against the medical establishment or the government.

Urban Tamil Nadu: The Official Structure of Public MCH Care for Childbirth

A long-standing criticism of the allopathic health care system in India, as in many parts of the world, is that it favors the urban sector over the rural sector, since urban-educated doctors and nurses have been unwilling to relocate to rural areas and the major research hospitals are clustered in urban areas. This has certainly been the case in the area of MCH services. It is because of the government's sense that it is economically impossible to provide allopathic MCH services to the entire rural sector that the government has been engaged in *dai*-training programs ever since the establishment of the Victoria Fund. Indeed, in Tamil Nadu, the largest government maternity hospitals are all in urban areas. In the capital city of Madras in 1995 there were five major government hospitals which had tertiary maternal and child health care facilities: the Kasthurba Gandhi Hospital; the Egmore Hospital for Women and Children; the Rajah Sri Ramaswami Mudaliar (RSRM) Hospital; the Kilpauk Medical College Hospital; and the Royapettah Hospital. Many women from all over Madras, other parts of Tamil Nadu, and even other states traveled to these hospitals for their deliveries.

In the early 1980s, however, there was a growing sense that the basic MCH care needs of the urban poor were not being met. The government of India established the Working Group on Reorganization of Family Welfare and Primary Health Care Services in the Urban Areas, colloquially known as the "Krishnan Committee," to assess the adequacy of health and family welfare services in urban areas of India. The Krishnan Committee's final report in 1984 argued that although the urban areas were sufficient in highly specialized curative medical institutions, they were lacking in basic primary health care for the poor, since there was no equivalent of the PHC in the urban areas. This was of particular concern since the urban populations, and particularly the urban poor populations across India, were growing rapidly due in part to migration from the rural areas. The Tamil Nadu census of 1991 showed 34 percent of the Tamil Nadu population living in urban areas; 35 percent of these urban residents were reported as living in the "slums."[10]

In 1985 the government of India initiated an "urban revamping scheme," which sought to establish urban health posts with attached outreach workers to remedy the situation reported by the Krishnan Committee. In the state of Tamil Nadu the government's urban revamping scheme was further supplemented and upgraded by the World Bank–aided India Population Project-V (IPP-V), which was established in Tamil Nadu in 1988.[11] The World Bank funding was to continue from 1988 through 1995. The governments of India and Tamil Nadu also provided financial support for this project. After the World Bank funding ran out, the national and state governments took over full responsibility.[12] The initial phase of the IPP-V project was carried out in Madras city and its suburbs. The project was later extended to other urban areas throughout the state.

Like the structure of the rural PHCs, under the IPP-V scheme there was to be one health post for every 30,000 of population. With the increase in urban populations since IPP-V was started, however, some health posts were covering populations of 35,000 to 40,000 in 1995. The health posts all provided outpatient MCH care, and some health posts also functioned as "maternity centers" where deliveries were conducted. Each health post was to have one "lady medical officer," supported by a "lady health visitor" and multipurpose health workers who were responsible for outreach work relating to MCH care in the surrounding areas. Each MPHW was responsible for a population of at least 5,000, out of which approximately 1,000 to 1,200 were "eligible couples" for MCH and family-planning services.[13] In large cities like Madras each MPHW was assigned to certain families that she was expected to visit once a month. An MPHW may have visited forty families in one day so that she could visit the same houses every month. The communities which were served by IPP-V were also supposed to choose female "link leaders" from the community who would serve as liaisons between the MPHWs and the families in the communities. Like the VHS MPHWs, the IPP-V MPHWs provided pre- and postnatal education and care as well as family-planning education and supplies. They were not expected to conduct deliveries in homes. Rather, they were mandated to make sure that women went to hospitals for their deliveries. Unlike the government's approach in the rural areas, which accepted the inevitability of home deliveries, one of the IPP-V goals was to have 98 percent of all urban deliveries in the state conducted in hospitals by the year 2000.[14] According to the IPP-V director for Madras Corporation, from 1975–1976 40 percent of all deliveries in Madras were conducted in homes, and 60 percent were institutionalized. By 1995, 99.9 percent of all deliveries were in hospitals. Thus, Madras met the IPP-V target before its 2000 deadline.[15]

In addition to the health posts and the outreach work of the MPHWs, the IPP-V program included an information, education, and communication (IEC) component which promoted educational programs relating to MCH care which were disseminated to the general public by television, radio, and posters, and brought directly to poor urban communities in the form of live theatrical and music performances as well as video programs.

In 1995 there were 120 IPP-V health posts in the city of Madras. Under the IPP-V scheme, Madras had been divided into fifteen zones. There was a "zonal center," or "zonal office," attached to one of the health posts in each zone, and eight or nine health posts were under the administrative jurisdiction of each zonal office. The health posts attached to the zonal offices had "operation theaters" and were therefore equipped to conduct cesareans, sterilizations, and abortions, whereas the other health posts were not.

Nochikuppam: Options for MCH Care in a Low-Income Madras Neighborhood

In this section I briefly describe the health care services relating to childbirth which were available to women from the neighborhood of Nochikuppam in Madras. My intent here is simply to make a sketch of the available services. In the remaining chapters I analyze various women's opinions and uses of the different services.

In Nochikuppam there were primarily two hospitals to which women could and did go for their deliveries: the large government Kasthurba Gandhi Hospital (Gosha Hospital) and the hospital at the IPP-V Santhome Zonal Health Post. Situated in the Triplicane neighborhood of Madras, the Kasthurba Gandhi Hospital was a short bus or autorickshaw ride away from Nochikuppam. The Santhome hospital, located between the Santhome church and Mylapore District in the southern part of Madras, was only a fifteen-minute walk from Nochikuppam.

The large Kasthurba Gandhi Hospital catered to women throughout Madras and even from other parts of Tamil Nadu, including Kaanathur-Reddikuppam. In 1993 there were on average 950 deliveries every month and sometimes as many as fifty deliveries in one day in Kasthurba Gandhi Hospital.[16] Some women from Nochikuppam went to Kasthurba Gandhi

Hospital only at the time of their delivery and went to the IPP-V hospitals for all their pre- and postnatal care. Due to the bureaucratic structure of the IPP-V zoning, Nochikuppam came under the jurisdiction of the IPP-V Rotary Nagar hospital rather than the Santhome Zonal Health Post, even though the Rotary Nagar hospital was much farther away. Therefore, women from Nochikuppam were often required to travel to the Rotary Nagar hospital for their pre- and postnatal care, although they could get some of these services and such things as iron supplements directly from the Rotary Nagar health post MPHWs who visited Nochikuppam.

The Rotary Nagar hospital was not a zonal health post, and, therefore, it had not been upgraded with operation facilities. The Santhome hospital, on the other hand, was a zonal post and had an operation theater. Women from Nochikuppam, therefore, did not generally go to the Rotary Nagar hospital for their deliveries since they could be admitted at the Santhome hospital at the time of delivery. Because the Santhome hospital had recently been converted into a zonal post, middle-class women from the surrounding areas, in addition to its predominantly lower-class clientele, were increasingly using the Santhome hospital. According to the zonal officer in charge of the Santhome Zonal Health Post, the average income of the patients using this hospital was Rs. 500–1,000 (approximately US $14–28) per month.[17] There were approximately sixty to seventy deliveries conducted each month at the Santhome health post in 1994.[18]

Although the majority of women from Nochikuppam had their deliveries in either Kasthurba Gandhi Hospital or the Santhome hospital, a few went to one of the other major government hospitals providing MCH care. Some went to the Kalyani Employees State Insurance (ESI) Hospital, a low-cost, private hospital option for working women employed in the formal sector. And those few women who could afford more costly private maternity hospitals (known as "nursing homes") went to those.

Nochikuppam also had a government-subsidized *balwadi* as part of the ICDS scheme, which provided the same pre- and postnatal services for women and children as did the *balwadis* in Kaanathur-Reddikuppam. An MPHW from the IPP-V Rotary Nagar hospital was employed to come to the *balwadi* once a week to conduct pre- and postnatal checkups and to provide immunizations, vitamin supplements, and other medicines for mothers and children.

The two WWF health workers who lived in Nochikuppam and the

WWF health supervisors who visited the neighborhood on a regular basis provided another important source of MCH education, service, and support to the women of Nochikuppam. They were in fact much more actively involved in the community than the MPHWs from the IPP-V Rotary Nagar hospital or the staff in charge of the ICDS scheme. The older WWF health worker, Kasthuri, became a "key informant" for me in Nochikuppam and facilitated my introductions with many of the women in the community. Several women in the community complimented Kasthuri by saying, "She is like a 'doctor' to all of us." The younger WWF health worker, Komala, also had a strong rapport with women in the neighborhood.

The WWF was founded by Mrs. Jaya Arunachalam.[19] Its headquarters are located in Mylapore, Madras, but the organization has grown rapidly, and in 1995 it had fifteen branches throughout South India and was beginning to establish partnerships with other women's NGOs in North India as well. In addition to its original project of providing low-interest loans to women working in the informal sector, WWF had also started its Health and Family Welfare Project in 1981 on the premise that large family size was making it difficult for women in the informal sector to pull themselves out of poverty. In 1995 the health program's name changed from the Health and Family Welfare Project to the Reproductive Health Project, reflecting a broader national and international trend away from a dominant emphasis on family planning toward a more inclusive emphasis on women's health throughout the life cycle. The bulk of the funding for WWF was generated from this bank program, but outside support was also provided by the governments of India and the Netherlands, the ILO and UNFPA, and a number of international nonprofit organizations such as the Ford Foundation and Appropriate Technology International.

The WWF Reproductive Health Project was essentially a community-outreach project. In Madras, between 1990 and 1996 the WWF had health projects in 232 low-income neighborhoods, covering approximately 93,000 families. One or two women living in those neighborhoods were chosen to work as WWF health workers, and these health workers were supervised and advised by WWF health supervisors who lived in other low-income neighborhoods and many of whom had been health workers themselves. To become a WWF health worker, women went through a fifteen-day training program in Gandhigram, outside of Madurai in central Tamil Nadu. This classroom training was followed by field training which included home visits as well as visits to various hospitals in the area. The health workers were expected to collect information about women's reproductive health status and needs and to provide education and minimal MCH and family-planning services, such as supplying iron tablets and vitamin supplements to pregnant women and distributing condoms and oral contraceptives. WWF health workers were not equipped to give immunizations. One of the most important roles of the health workers was to educate women about the governmental MCH and family-planning services available to them and to facilitate women's access to those services. Like the IPP-V MPHWs, the WWF health workers, who also worked primarily in urban and semiurban areas, were not expected to conduct home deliveries but rather were given a mandate to encourage women to go to hospitals for deliveries. In emergency situations, however, WWF health workers, including the health workers in Nochikuppam, have been summoned to assist at home deliveries, as demonstrated by the story of Mumtaz's delivery in the Prologue.

Like the presence of VHS in Kaanathur-Reddikuppam, the presence of the WWF in Nochikuppam meant that the structure of MCH care services diverged from the official structure. This of course means that these two communities may have been somewhat different from other semirural and urban communities in Tamil Nadu which did not have active NGO presences involved in MCH projects. Yet the NGO sector in Tamil Nadu (and India in general) is very extensive and has long played an important role in the provision of various social services. "Women's development" projects of various kinds have been a major component of the NGO sector. The government of Tamil Nadu encourages the NGO sector to play an active role in the provision of MCH care. Therefore, although the presence of these NGOs at my main field sites sets these communities apart, they could not be said to be anomalies in the Tamil Nadu social landscape. This does not, however, suggest that these communities are representative of all urban and semirural communities in Tamil Nadu.

Finally, another important source of MCH care for the women of Nochikuppam was Nagamma, a fifty-five-year-old *maruttuvacci* from the Chinna Pattinavar caste who lived in the neighborhood. She began to work as a *maruttuvacci* after her fourth child (of six) was born. She took up this work in order to supplement her income, since her husband went off to Andhra Pradesh at that time, leaving her and the four children. Her sister's mother-in-law *(cinna māmiyār)* was at that time conducting deliveries in the neighborhood and had assisted at the delivery of

Nagamma's third child. After her husband went to Andhra Pradesh, Nagamma began to learn how to conduct deliveries from her *cinna māmiyār,* and when her *cinna māmiyār* died, Nagamma began to conduct home deliveries in the area on her own. She had not been through any formal *dai*-training program. This kind of apprenticeship at the side of one's in-laws was typical of the training of *maruttuvaccis* I met throughout Tamil Nadu; usually they were trained by their mothers-in-law. Like Nagamma, most *maruttuvaccis* whom I met said they were motivated to take up this work out of economic necessity. A few, however, told me they became *maruttuvaccis* in order to help other women in their time of need.

With the steady trend toward hospitalized deliveries, however, Nagamma had not conducted home deliveries for several years by the time I met her. In fact, since the early 1990s, on those rare occasions when a woman in Nochikuppam delivered her baby at home, it was Komala who was hastily summoned to assist. Nevertheless, Nagamma's expertise in providing postpartum oil baths and medicines to mother and child was widely sought in the neighborhood, and she was often consulted about how to make *kaṣāyams* (herbal medicines), during pregnancy and at the end of pregnancy to induce labor. She was also known to be an important authority regarding pregnancy and postpartum rituals to worship the local goddess Desamma and to ward off the evil eye.

Thus far I have discussed the socio-economic backgrounds of the communities studied, the historical context which gave rise to the professionalization of obstetrics in India and now the structure of MCH care services available to women in the communities in Tamil Nadu where I conducted research in 1995. The following chapters (three through six) now turn to more in-depth ethnographic analysis of the impact of modernity on poor women's experiences during childbirth, focusing on the women's own accounts and interpretations. The next chapter examines pregnancy rituals in Tamil Nadu and how changes in the economy are affecting cultural constructions of pregnancy and the status of women more generally.

CHAPTER 3

Bangles of *Neem*, Bangles of Gold

Pregnant Women as Auspicious Burdens

JOURNEY TO THE CEREMONIAL HALL

It was seven o'clock in the evening when I stepped into Mohan's yellow and black auto-rickshaw near our apartment. Mohan jumped into the driver's seat and yanked the lever several times to start the engine. The engine sputtered and then calmed and we were off down the bumpy road leading out of Kalakshetra Colony, across the Adyar Bridge, and into the heart and traffic of Madras. We were on our way to Nochikuppam. Mohan was one of the auto-rickshaw drivers I had gotten to know traveling to and from my far-flung research sites. He was among the only ones who always used their meters and never asked for more than the meter fare. He was also keenly interested, perhaps perplexed, about what exactly I was doing.

Mohan made a sweeping U-turn and pulled the auto-rickshaw up to the archway leading into the Ellaiamman temple compound on the edge of Nochikuppam. As he dropped me off he asked, "What's special this evening?" I explained, "Tonight there will be a *cīmantam.* I've been wanting to see one for such a long time and finally I will see it." He nodded his head from side to side approvingly, saying "Oh yes, that is a *very* important thing," and sped off down the road.

Cīmantam is a ritual celebrated in Tamil Nadu during a woman's first pregnancy in preparation for her first delivery *(talai piracavam).*[1] It is a rite of passage into motherhood. This ritual was widely practiced in all the regions of Tamil Nadu where I conducted research. It was practiced by Hindus, Muslims, and Christians alike, with slight variations among these groups. In all cases the ritual was performed in or near the pregnant woman's in-laws' house, but the bulk of the expenses was borne by her own natal kin. It was customary for the pregnant woman to return to her own mother's house following the *cīmantam* ritual and to remain with her mother for her first delivery.

According to most of the people I met, the primary function of the *cīmantam* ritual is to satisfy the pregnant woman's *ācai* and to bless her to ensure an easy delivery and the birth of a healthy baby. In this context the term *"ācai"* is understood as "desire, cravings, passion" or, as Susan Wadley notes, "compulsion."[2] In this ritual the pregnant woman is revered for the auspiciousness of her fertility.[3] Within a framework of Hindu cosmology, she is worshipped as the Hindu goddess Sakti. Wadley defines *sakti* as "the female generative force of the universe,"[4] and this force is directly tied to women's reproductive capacities.

Many of the older women and men I met explained that these rituals had become increasingly elaborate and expensive within their lifetimes and that the form and meaning of the rituals had changed radically. Despite these transformations there was a growing sense of a moral prerogative to perform this ritual in the name of tradition *(paṛakkam),* "as it has been since time immemorial" *(anta kālattilē ceñca paḍi).*

The *cīmantam* ritual had increasingly become a context in which gifts of not only food but also gold, silk, and modern consumer items (such as kitchen appliances) flowed from the pregnant woman's own parents to her husband's family. The parallels between this trend and the historical trend of increases in dowry practices throughout India are obvious and are discussed later. Both trends indicate that in Tamil Nadu, as in the villages in Uttar Pradesh studied by Jeffery et al. in the 1980s, marriage alliances involve not only the exchange of women as labor (in the sense of both production and reproduction), but also increasingly the exchange of women as commodities.

The changes in the practice and meanings of *cīmantams* were tied to a growing consumer orientation in Tamil Nadu and in India more generally. In particular, the rising trend of conspicuous consumption has been occurring in tandem with a shift away from an emphasis on Nehruvian socialism toward an embrace of policies of economic liberalization and privatization. The seeds of this change were sown in the 1980s by Indira Gandhi's government and officially came to fruition in 1991 under the leadership of Rajiv Gandhi. This policy was continued by Prime Minister P. V. Narasimha Rao after the assassination of Rajiv Gandhi in May 1991. The official economic policies of privatization, or "structural adjustments," were implemented in 1991 as a condition for India's acceptance of a large loan from the IMF. India was at that time in the midst of a financial and political crisis. In exchange for the loan, the Indian government agreed to deregulate and liberalize all markets and to increase competition in all spheres of the economy. The government promised to make efforts to pull back from regulating the economy and agreed to pursue laissez-faire economic policies. The government undertook policies to liberalize the import market with the assumption that this would enhance exports as well. Overall government expenditure declined following the liberalization policies. Many critics argue that social programs were severely compromised by this decline and that liberalization has benefited the more privileged classes within India at the expense of the poor.[5]

Scholars of India have emphasized how consumption has become central to middle-class identity and practice in the wake of liberalization, as India soon became flooded with new import commodities, such as cars and electronics, that had previously been restricted from import. And they have underscored the importance of modern forms of media in constructing desires for new technological inventions.[6] And Christopher Fuller has pointed out that an increase in disposable incomes among the middle class in Tamil Nadu since the 1980s has led many to spend more lavishly on rituals as a form of conspicuous consumption.[7] Whereas these studies have emphasized the ways in which modern consumption patterns are transforming *middle*-class identity and practice, my study of changes in *cīmantam* practices among the poor underscores the effects that middle-class consumption has had on the lower classes as they struggle to gain and/or maintain prestige by emulating middle-class practices.

My study of *cīmantam* reveals a convergence of the desires for new consumer technologies and for the display of wealth through ritual. Thus, contrary to the common assumption that modernity is fundamentally antiritual and that the modernizing project replaces religion with science, in Tamil Nadu modern forms of capitalist consumption have brought with them an *increase* in the practice of this ritual. As Arjun Appadurai writes:

> The modernization theorists of the past three decades . . . largely accepted the view of the modern world as a space of shrinking religiosity (and greater scientism). . . . There are many strands in this view . . . but there is something fundamentally wrong with it. . . . There is vast evidence in new

> religiosities of every sort that religion is not only not dead but that it may be more consequential than ever in today's highly mobile interconnected global politics.[8]

Within the context of childbirth, there is the assumption that as birth becomes increasingly biomedicalized, women will put their faith exclusively in the powers of medicine to ensure the well-being of mother and child and come to rely less and less on religious faith and ritual. This certainly has been the trend in the United States. In Tamil Nadu in the late 1990s, however, the biomedicalization of birth and the intensification of some birth-related rituals, such as *cīmantams,* were occurring simultaneously.

The *cīmantam* ceremonies practiced in Tamil Nadu in 1995 were fraught with a fundamental tension. On the one hand, the ritual reflected and reconstituted a deep reverence for the auspiciousness of women as reproducers, as articulated through the concept of *sakti.* Yet, on the other hand, the economic dimension of the ritual in an increasingly consumer-oriented society placed greater strains on the family of the pregnant woman, thereby rendering her a financial burden to her natal family. Thus, women who were pregnant for the first time among lower-class communities in Tamil Nadu were often viewed as auspicious burdens. Auspiciousness is a multivalent concept in India. The Hindu goddess Laksmi is viewed by many as the ultimate symbol and purveyor of auspiciousness. But she is not worshipped in the hope that she will grant fertility as much as she is worshipped in the hope that she will bestow wealth upon the devotee. The fact that in 1995 the pregnant woman had increasingly become a conduit for wealth flowing to her husband's family also tended to heighten her auspiciousness in the public eye. Therefore, I am not describing a shift from an a-material cultural construction of pregnant women to an a-cultural economic construction of pregnant women, but rather a processual shift in the construction of pregnant women that has symbolic and materialist connotations which may be viewed as contradictory.

My analysis of the *cīmantam* ritual underscores the point made by some Marxist theorists that reproduction must be understood as production, thereby collapsing the notion that reproduction is part of the private domain while production is part of the public domain.[9] Engels's book *The Origin of the Family, Private Property and the State,* published shortly after Marx's death, hinted that a materialist theory must understand reproduction as the production of human beings, and thus as the production of one of the material essentials of life.[10] Claude Meillassoux argues that a complete materialist theory must explore the issue of reproduction more fully than Marx and Engels did. He wrote, "The reproduction of human beings is, in terms of economics, production of labour power in all its forms. But in spite of this foreview of Engels, little attention was given by historical materialism to this problem. Instead of granting to the production of this essential good the importance which could be expected from a theory of labour, it gives only partial attention to it."[11]

Although Mary O'Brien acknowledges the importance of viewing reproduction as the production of labor power, she argues that those theorists who view the product of reproduction—the child—as labor, or "use value," alone miss the fact that this product must also be understood to have the "value of the human being as human being, as objective species continuity." As she says, "Feminism insists that 'value' is not an exclusively economic category, but an ethical, affective, and genetic one."[12] An analysis of *cīmantam* rituals in this light shows that the value of what is (re)produced is indeed both economic and affective. The concern over satisfying a woman's desire, or *ācai,* was motivated by both affective and materialist concerns.

Within India as a whole there is a great deal of variation in the nature and degree to which pregnancy is ritually marked. One question is whether this variation reflects broad socio-cultural differences between North and South India and differences in women's status in these two regions. Studies have suggested that in general women have higher social status in South India than in North India. Differences in women's status in North and South India are inferred by such things as sex ratios;[13] "human development" factors, such as maternal mortality rates and female literacy; and cultural constructions of womanhood, as reflected through religious practice and ideology.[14]

A brief comparison of my study to studies addressing the cultural construction of and social practices surrounding pregnancy in different parts of North India by and large does reinforce this theory, if the ritual marking of pregnancy is viewed as a celebration of women's auspiciousness as reproducers and thereby grants them status. There are, however, important exceptions, and as I have noted, the marking of pregnancy by *cīmantam* rituals in Tamil Nadu has resulted in a contradictory status for women.

Jeffery et al. show that in both the predominantly low- and middle-caste Hindu and Muslim villages in rural Uttar Pradesh which they studied in the early 1980s, women remained in their in-laws' houses throughout their pregnancy and confinement. In these villages there were no rituals to celebrate pregnancy, and pregnancy itself was viewed as a shameful matter *(sharm ki bat).*[15] When Ruth and Stanley Freed conducted research in the Hindu village of Shanti Nagar, also in Uttar Pradesh, from 1958 to 1959, they found that there were no prenatal ceremonies performed. Yet their research suggested that two decades prior to their study some prenatal ceremonies had been performed by Brahmins. They speculate that the move away from performing these rituals related to the influence of the anti-Brahminical Arya Samaj movement in that region and the shift from having the first delivery in the woman's parents' house to having it in her in-laws' house.[16] Helen Gideon's work in a Sikh community in the Punjab in the 1950s showed that although women did return to their parents' houses for their deliveries there was no ritual marking of pregnancy.[17]

Tulsi Patel's recent study in a rural Rajasthani Hindu village provides a different picture. As in Tamil Nadu, the common practice in this village is for the pregnant woman to return to her parents' house for her first confinement. Patel shows that a ritual feast is provided for a woman during her first pregnancy, to fulfill her cravings as well as those of the fetus. In this case, unlike in Tamil Nadu, it is the mother-in-law who is seen as responsible for the gifting of clothing and food. Here great emphasis is placed on the notion that one gains *puniya,* or religious merit, through giving gifts.[18] Patel's study mitigates against the overarching generalizations about the construction of pregnancy in North versus South India and forces us to consider *which* social and cultural factors make a difference. A more thorough and specific investigation that compares pregnancy among different classes and castes throughout India would be required to draw out these factors and make conclusions.

My analysis of these *cīmantam* rituals in Tamil Nadu is based on extensive discussions with women about their own *cīmantams*—the reasons for performing them (or not performing them) and how they were performed. I also met with a Brahmin Sanskrit scholar and a Brahmin priest as well as with a Muslim Imam to get some sense of how some members of religious orthodoxies interpret these rituals. Most significant, I was able to attend five very different *cīmantam* rituals over the course of my year: one of a Hindu family from Nochikuppam; one of a Muslim family in Bapu Mastan Dargha; one of a rural lower-class Christian family near Dindigul; one of a lower-middle-class rural Hindu Nadar family near Adiramapattinam; and, finally, one of an affluent urban

Brahmin family in Mylapore, Madras. In this chapter I use the *cīmantam* of Anjali from Nochikuppam to guide the reader through the event and present a baseline against which I will point out differences among other *cīmantams.* After analyzing Anjali's *cīmantam,* I will discuss the recent historical changes in these rituals and situate the significance of these rituals and the exchanges which they entail in the context of women's reproductive life cycles more generally.

ANJALI'S *CĪMANTAM*

When Mohan, the auto-rickshaw driver, dropped me off by the archway leading into Nochikuppam, it was Anjali's *cīmantam* which I was going to see with such great anticipation. After Mohan drove away, I stood for a while by the archway. It was getting dark but there was a soft glow from the neon lights at the top of the arch which spelled out Ellaiamman's name in Tamil. Kasthuri and Komala emerged through the archway. Both were dressed in their finery: Kasthuri in her polyester sari and Komala wearing a brilliantly colored Kanchipuram silk sari and gold *jimikki* earrings. Both had fresh strands of jasmine buds dangling from their hair. Finally Annette (my research assistant) arrived and we were all ready to head off into Mylapore, where the *cīmantam* was to be held.

Mylapore is one of the oldest sections of Madras. It is known for its famous Kapeleswarar temple with its massive temple tank overgrown with a cover of green lily pads and algae. Mylapore is also a center for Brahmin families and for institutions of Sanskrit studies. Partly due to the Brahmin influence, Mylapore is filled with *cattirams,* or ceremonial halls which are rented out for weddings and other ritual functions. After passing by the road leading down to the Santhome IPP-V hospital, we made our way through the narrow winding streets of Mylapore. We walked by a Bhadra Kali temple from which we could hear the nasal trumpeting of *nātasvarams* signaling that a festive occasion was underway there.[19] This sound inspired us to pick up our pace so as not to miss the beginning of Anjali's *cīmantam.*

After walking for about twenty minutes, we finally came to the hall where the *cīmantam* was to be held. Tamil cinema music was blaring from crackly loudspeakers perched precariously outside the hall. Inside, the hall was filled with foldout metal chairs facing a stage. The walls were the same bright turquoise color which is painted on the walls inside many homes in Tamil Nadu. The large room was already quite full. Most of the people in the room were women and children, and the few men who were there stood clustered by the doorway. We were told to sit up in the front row by the stage, since Kasthuri was a close relation of Anjali's.

It was June 29th. The hottest of hot seasons had just passed but traces of it still hovered in the humid night air. *Cīmantams* are usually celebrated in what many Tamils refer to as the "ninth month" of pregnancy, shortly before the expected day of the birth. This "ninth month," however, is the equivalent of what in America we consider to be the eighth month, since in Tamil Nadu women are often said to be pregnant for ten months before the birth of the baby. There is an ancient Tamil calendar based on lunar cycles.[20] Some of the lower-class women I met knew only of the Tamil calendar. Others knew both the Tamil and the solar Gregorian, or cosmopolitan, calendars. They thought in terms of the Tamil calendar for ritual events and issues of auspiciousness (such as pregnancy and birth) but thought in terms of the cosmopolitan calendar in order to operate in the public spheres of the state and the marketplace.

Kasthuri gave the following explanation for why pregnancy is calculated to last ten months:

> After a baby is born people say that the baby is one month old as soon as the Tamil month changes. So if a baby is born at the very end of the Tamil month, people will say the baby is one month old when the month changes, even if it was only born two days prior to the change in month. Similarly with pregnancy, if a woman conceives at the end of the Tamil month, she is said to be one month pregnant when the month changes even if she is thought to have conceived only two days prior to the change.[21]

Although the *cīmantam* was most commonly celebrated in the "ninth month," some people had a series of ceremonies which were often all considered *cīmantams* beginning in the "fifth," "seventh," or "ninth" month of pregnancy. The choice of these particular months reflects the fact that in Tamil Nadu odd numbers are thought to be auspicious. The importance of odd numbers often dictates the timing of events and the quantity of things used in rituals. Poopathi from Reddikuppam had three such ritual celebrations during her pregnancy. She explained that those who have *vacati* will do it three times. *Vacati* is usually used to mean "wealth, means, or amenities," but Poopathi told me that she did not mean wealth in this case, since her family was poor and each of the ceremonies was very modest. In her case *vacati* meant a certain kind of familial caring—when a family takes special interest, each member wanting to do their part. For the fifth-month celebration, Poopathi's mother brought all the goods (including five varieties of rice) to her mother-in-law's house. For the seventh-month celebration, her maternal aunt *(citti)* did all the preparation and brought seven varieties of rice. And for the ninth-month ceremony, her maternal uncle *(māman)* brought everything, including nine varieties of rice. Sometimes if a celebration is done in the fifth or seventh month, it may not be done again in the ninth month.

There were some months in which these ceremonies were relatively rare. The Tamil month of Āḍi (July 15–August 15) is considered to be a highly inauspicious month for marriages. People often say that the reason for this is that if a woman conceives in the month of Āḍi her baby will be born in the Tamil month of Cittirai (April 15–May 15). Cittirai is the hottest month of the year, and it is thought to be a very difficult time for a mother and baby to endure birth and the postpartum period.[22] Although the extreme heat is the most common explanation, it is also possible that the rationale is tied to the agricultural cycle; since Āḍi is also the time for sowing seeds, there is no time for elaborate wedding preparations.[23] This theory is further supported by the fact that Mārkaṛi, which is considered to be the second most inauspicious month for weddings, coincides with the harvest time.[24] Whatever the explanation, I found that the maternity ward in the Santhome hospital was indeed virtually empty during the month of Cittirai. There are sometimes restrictions placed on intercourse during the Tamil month of Āḍi in order to prevent births in Cittirai. In some instances women will actually return to their parents' house during Āḍi as a preventative against pregnancy. Due to these restrictions it is relatively rare to perform *cīmantams* during Paṅkuṉi (March 15–April 15), the Tamil month which precedes Cittirai. Anjali's *cīmantam* was taking place in the Tamil month of Āni (June 15–July 15), and she was expecting her baby to be born in Āḍi.

Just as we had taken our places in the front row of the *cattiram,* Anjali's husband's two sisters came to distribute a rose, a piece of turmeric root *(mañcaḷ),*[25] and caramel candies to each of us as a token of welcoming. They gave us these gifts because Anjali's husband's family was hosting the event, as the husband's family typically does. Anjali's husband, Sekar, came from a very large Periya Pattinavar family and lived in Nochikuppam. Sekar's immediate family was very well-off as compared to many other families in Nochikuppam. Sekar himself finished his diploma in engineering and had a job in a private company earning approximately Rs. 3,500 (US $97) per month. It was because they were economically better-off than most that they were able to afford to rent the *cattiram* and hold the *cīmantam* there rather than in their home, as most people did. Kasthuri told me that the hall alone cost approximately Rs. 2,000 to rent. And then there were the added expenses of lights and cinema music and the catered meal following the ceremony, all of which were covered by the husband's family. This particular *cīmantam* therefore was not a typical one for the residents of Nochikuppam. But it was the one that the women of Nochikuppam wanted me to see first. And it was a significant one since it represented a kind of ideal against which other residents were always comparing themselves and each other in an ongoing competition of ritual display.

On the floor below the far right edge of the stage, and right in front of where we were seated, there were nineteen two-foot-high "ever-silver" (stainless steel) vessels and several bulging woven palm and plastic bags. Anjali's mother, a middle-aged woman with a thin, taut face and thin, taut arms, came over to untie the bags and remove the lids of the vessels. Soon this area in front of us became the focus of great activity and the topic of much conversation. Kasthuri and another woman assisted Anjali's mother. Each of these vessels was filled with a specialty food which had been carefully prepared by Anjali's mother and other female relatives on her mother's side. If the mother and other female relatives have to travel a long distance to come to the *cīmantam,* they may have to hire a minibus—a significant addition to the overall expense. Anjali's mother first uncovered the vessels containing five varieties *(tiṉucu)* of rice associated with Tamil ritual: tamarind rice *(puḷi cātam),* curd rice *(tayir cātam),* coconut rice *(tēṅkai cātam),* lemon/lime rice *(elumiccam cātam),* and, finally, *sambhar* rice *(cāmpār cātam).*[26] These rice varieties were specialty items; plain white rice is the staple food of South Indians, eaten by many at least twice a day. Members of extremely poor families I met explained that they rarely could afford to make all five rice varieties for the *cīmantam* but made at least one or three.

Next, Anjali's mother uncovered the vessels containing sweets and savories. The sweets included *badusha,* Mysore *pāku, poriviḷaṅkā uruṇḍai, cōmās, jeelebi, kāppu arici, atiracam,* sweet *ponkal, laddus,* and *rava laddus.* And there were two savories: *muṟukku* and *aval.* I had been told earlier that those who can afford it should always have 101 pieces of each of these food items.[27] It seemed to me that this family had certainly fulfilled this expectation. The fruits were next to be unpacked. Nine varieties in all: mangoes, plums, pineapples, grapes, guavas, *ca-*

pōḍḍās,[28] sweet limes *(cāttukuḍi),* two varieties of grapes, and bunches of sweet yellow plantains. All of the fruits were placed together on one huge "ever-silver" platter.

It was not long before two young girls dressed in their silk *pāvāḍai* came scampering over to peer wide-eyed into these giant containers full of all their favorite foods.[29] They used every tactic to try to convince the women to sneak some sweets to them. They began with their own artificially sweetened, high-pitched voices, like those of spoiled children portrayed in Tamil movies. When this tactic failed they resorted to whining and finally whimpering until one woman came after them with her hand held up in the air saying, "*Cē, cē, pō, pō, aḍippēn!*" ("Go, go, I'll hit you!") and shooing them off while discretely slipping some pieces of *muṟukku* into their tiny palms. The children secretly popped them into their mouths and ran off to join some of the other children who were romping around on the stage. This was clearly an evening for the children to celebrate. The girls dressed in their traditional finery and the boys duded up in Western wear[30]—blue jeans and vests—were all racing around the women, playing tag and practicing the latest Rajini Kant movie dance steps with incredible hip-jutting precision.

The children were not the only ones taking a keen interest in what was being unpacked. A group of five elderly men, accompanied by Anjali's father, all dressed in traditional white *vesdhi* with *tuṇḍu,*[31] now came to take their places on mats set on the floor just below the stage and beside the area where all the food and other ceremonial items were being prepared. These were the only men to play a role in this ceremony. Even Anjali's husband would be virtually absent, his main role being to greet the guests at the entrance of the hall. These men were each referred to as *periya manuṣaṉ* (big man) or *talaivar* (headman). These *periya manuṣaṉ* acted as unofficial *panchayat* members for their communities. They were not elected officials but rather well-regarded elders who were called upon to settle disputes within the community or between the community and other institutions (particularly the police).[32] They watched, criticized, and directed as the women arranged the goods and conducted the rituals of the ceremony. These *periya manuṣaṉ* were thought to have knowledge about how the ceremony should proceed, including such details as the number and order of items to be given to the pregnant woman.

The women then began to take a piece of each of the fruits, one of each of the sweets and savories, and small clumps of each of the rice varieties, and set them onto a separate platter. This was the platter which would satisfy Anjali's *ācai.* It is extremely important to satisfy a pregnant woman's *ācai* in order to ensure a problem-free delivery and the well-being of mother and child. In Tamil Nadu, being pregnant is thought to increase a woman's *ācai.* Here, *ācai* is not understood as sexuality in the sense of libido, as it is often assumed to be.[33] Rather, *ācai* during pregnancy is understood as connected to a combination of food cravings, an increase in "heat," the demands of the fetus *(cūl),* and a desire to return to the maternal home to be cared for. Often people point to connections among these aspects of *ācai.* For example, they say that a pregnant woman's food cravings during pregnancy (which some health workers say reflect basic nutritional needs) are not satisfied by her husband's family, so she longs to return to her own parents' home. Or, people attribute the food cravings to the demands of the fetus, which may in fact conflict with the desires of the pregnant woman. Vaidya Radhika and A. V. Balasubramanian explain that according to Ayurveda, a pregnant woman is understood to be *dowhrudini,* that is, one who possesses two *hrudayams,* the "seat of the mind." In this case, one *hrudayam* belongs to the mother while the second belongs to the fetus, and their desires may be in conflict. As they write:

> According to our *Aacharyaas* the foetus grows up to a period of four months and in the fifth month the "*chetna*" or the life gets associated with the foetus and this causes the longings of the mother. These longings and desires are to be satisfied. Not doing so may cause abnormalities of the foetus like dwarfism. These desires are not always beneficial, and may prove harmful to the foetus (even when fulfilled). In such cases one should use one's "*yukhti*" or power of reasoning, so as to fulfill her desire and at the same time render it harmless.[34]

The notion that pregnancy increases women's heat is tied to a construction of the body as fluctuating between states of "hot" and "cold" and health as a balance between these two states. In humoral theories of Siddha and Ayurveda, this heat is associated with the humor *pittam* (or *pitta*). (These notions of hot and cold and humoral theories are discussed in more detail in Chapters Five and Six.) According to Siddha and Ayurvedic theories, women in general are thought to have more *pittam* than men, and many health problems unique to women are attributed to an excess of *pittam.* During pregnancy, a woman's *pittam* is thought to increase substantially. Siddhars who detect the status of health through the pulse say that they can determine whether or not a woman is pregnant by feeling a twofold increase in the rate of *pittam* in her pulse.[35]

Certain physical problems during pregnancy are often attributed to the fact that the woman's *ācai* is not satisfied; she feels something is lacking or deficient *(kuṟai)*. These physical signs serve as a clarion call to the woman's natal kin that a *cīmantam* must be performed to fulfill her desires and restore her health. Several women in Nochikuppam told me that the swelling of a woman's legs and arms in the later stages of pregnancy would be interpreted this way, and a *cīmantam* would soon be performed. In these cases, in addition to the *cīmantam,* the woman would seek medical advice, since many of the women I met were aware of the fact that the swelling of the limbs was a possible indication of a serious medical condition, namely preeclampsia. *Cīmantams* were done not only in response to some perceived problem, but more commonly as a routine preventative to such problems. For example, a Muslim *mantiravāti*[36] in Bilal Nagar told me that if a pregnant woman does not get what she wants to eat, the baby will get pus on its mouth. Therefore, he explained, it is important to perform the *cīmantam* in order to prevent such a misfortune.

This intense *ācai* was viewed as normal during pregnancy. A pregnant woman does not have control over the *ācai.* In this sense, Wadley's notion of compulsion is very appropriate. It is a kind of compulsive desire, particularly when the *ācai* is said to derive from the fetus. If something goes wrong, it is attributed to the unfulfilled *ācai,* and the pregnant woman is not personally blamed; rather, the blame lies with the social group for not completely satisfying her *ācai* during her pregnancy. Thus, the *cīmantam* was a way of ensuring that the social group fulfilled its obligation of satisfying the woman. This differs from the premodern European situation described by Jacques Gélis, in which if a baby was born with a deformity the blame was usually placed on the mother's excessive sexual cravings and imaginings during pregnancy.[37]

The platter of food items arranged to satisfy Anjali's *ācai* was placed on a mat below center stage, right next to the group of *periya manuṣaṉ.* The trays and vessels containing the remaining food were also lined up just below center stage. This was called the "showing" *(kāḍḍu)* of the *varicai* (line of items). The food items were shown to Anjali once she was seated onstage. And, equally significant, they were shown to the *periya manuṣaṉ* and to all the guests.

As I discuss below, many older people suggested that this emphasis on showing the *varicai* in *cīmantam* was a relatively recent phenomenon tied to the fact that the *cīmantam* was increasingly a public event concerned with exchanging goods, particularly gifts flowing from the mother's house. Accordingly, these items were seen and scrutinized as a calculated exchange. But the emphasis on showing and seeing these things was also tied to key elements of Hindu worship through *puja.* Just as the flame of camphor is "shown" so that all worshippers can partake of its light, these food items were shown so that all could have a sense of *ācai* being satisfied. Just as worshippers are blessed through seeing and being seen by god in *darsan,* this food would be blessed when Anjali set her gaze upon it.

Now that Anjali's gustatory *ācai* had been attended to, there remained another central desire to fulfill: the desire of beauty *(aṛaku),* the desire to be beautiful. And so, on yet another plate, these women assembled a silk sari, a blouse, a comb, a piece of ribbon, lavender-scented Pond's powder, *kuṅkumam,*[38] sandalwood, and a bar of soap with a soap box. Last but not least, they placed one gold ring. This plate was also set on the mat below center stage.

Another plate was brought out onto which the women placed seven dozen glass bangles *(kaṇṇāḍi vaḷayal),* one bangle made of *neem* (margosa) twigs[39] twisted and braided together, and one gold bangle. Along with these bangles, the women put flowers and sandalwood paste. And finally, on the last plate, they placed neat piles of green, heart-shaped betel leaves *(vettilai)* and chunks of areca nut *(pākku),* along with more flowers and several glass bangles. This plate is known as a *tāmpūlam.*[40] Having arranged the items on these last two plates, they were now ready to begin the ceremony.

It was 8:30 P.M. when Anjali emerged from a back room and climbed the steps of the stage to take her place on a thin and low-lying bench *(maṇai)* covered with a white cloth. There was no fanfare accompanying her entrance—neither music nor silence. As was customary in many communities, Anjali was dressed in the same sari she had worn for her wedding, a dark rose-colored Kanchipuram silk sari. Her sparkling wedding jewelry was prominently displayed and her golden hair ornament *(cuḍḍi)* shone brightly on her forehead. The sari and ornaments were so copious that I could barely tell that she was nearing the end of her pregnancy. Light from the tall brass oil lamps *(nallaviḷakku)* flickered on her face. The expression on Anjali's face was a strange combination of solemnity and distraction. Her eyes darted from place to place without ever landing, as though she were uncomfortable with being the center of attention. There were about 300 people in the room by that time.

An elaborate flower ornament, known as a *jaḍai,* covered the back of her head and extended down the length of her long braid. The *jaḍai* was also worn for weddings and frequently for girls' puberty rituals *(vayatu aḍaital).* Because of the importance of this *jaḍai,* some people referred to the *cīmantam* ceremony as *pū muḍittal* or *pūccuḍḍal* (tying the flowers). Even if a *cīmantam* was done in a very simple manner due to economic constraints, the *jaḍai* was thought to be imperative, partially due to the fact that keeping a professionally made photograph of these rituals had become increasingly common. These photos were very standardized and usually included frontal, side, and back shots of the girl or woman. The side and back shots were taken specifically to highlight the *jaḍai.* Several times, when I asked women to describe how they had performed their *cīmantam,* they replied, "They put the *jaḍai* and took the photo. And that is all." At Anjali's *cīmantam* there was a professional photographer snapping away and an anthropologist (myself) with video camera in hand. The *cīmantam* ritual had indeed increasingly become a spectator event for those who could afford it, and for others, a few photographs could create the illusion that a spectacle had taken place.[41]

Once Anjali was seated on the *maṇai,* her sister-in-law placed a bounteous garland of flowers around her neck. A thin, shy smile spread momentarily across Anjali's face. The sweet fragrance of all the jasmine in the garland and the *jaḍai* wafted through the hall. All the closest women relatives from her family and her husband's family were now gathering around her, preparing to place bangles on her arms and to give and receive her blessings. Anjali seemed more relaxed now that she was surrounded by her closest kin.

The central activity of the *cīmantam* ritual was the placing of numerous bangles on the arms of the pregnant woman. For this reason many used the term "*vaḷaikāppu*" rather than "*cīmantam*" to refer to the ritual as a whole. Some used both terms interchangeably. *Vaḷaiyal* means "bangle," and *kāppu,* which is derived from the verb *kā* (to protect), refers to a protective band usually worn around the wrist and sometimes worn as an anklet. These bands are often made out of metals like iron and copper but they may also be made out of turmeric-soaked threads, and are felt to protect the general health and well-being of the wearer. Placing the various bangles on Anjali's arms was thus a way of protecting her and her baby from any misfortune during her first delivery.

For orthodox Brahmins, however, *cīmantam* and *vaḷaikāppu* were considered distinct rituals—the former scriptural and the latter not. According to orthodox Brahminical practice, the ritual I am describing was *vaḷaikāppu* or *pūccuḍḍal* and was *not cīmantam.* For Brahmins there was a separate rite called *cīmantam* involving worship of the sacrificial fire *(homam)* and officiated by Brahmin priests. The distinctions between Brahminical and non-Brahminical practice of these pregnancy rituals are important but are not the topic of this chapter.

Anjali's mother-in-law *(māmiyār)* took the twisted *neem* bangle from one of the plates and slid it over Anjali's right wrist. In this community the mother-in-law puts on this first and highly significant bangle. I was often told that the *neem* bangle contains *sakti.* The woman wearing this bangle thus gains and becomes *sakti.* As Muttamma in Reddikuppam once explained to me, "The reason we put the *neem* bangle first is that Sakti is our *mutal teyvam* (first goddess); this *neem* bangle is *sakti* so we put that first to give *sakti* to the woman."[42]

Next Anjali's mother came forth and, taking the gold bangle from the tray, she placed it on her daughter's right arm. Gold jewelry in Tamil Nadu was usually made of 22 karats and was exorbitantly expensive. Residents of Madras often commented that within the last decade gold shops had begun to spring up everywhere. Gold jewelry, they said, was increasingly felt to be central to the construction of womanhood in Tamil Nadu.[43] A woman without gold jewelry was not only a woman without beauty or wealth, but she was a woman who was not cared for by her parents; she was like an orphan. Therefore, despite the economic hardship entailed in purchasing gold, Anjali's family had to provide her with the gold gift for this public event. Now *neem*-twig bangle (placed by the mother-in-law) and golden bangle (placed by the mother) sat side by side, symbolizing Anjali's status as an auspicious burden.

Like Anjali's mother-in-law and mother, the other women who placed bangles in this ceremony were all *cumaṅkalis,* that is, women who were auspicious because they were themselves mothers as well as wives. To be considered a *cumaṅkali* for this ritual, the woman's first child had to be alive. These women came forward, one at a time. Anjali's sister-in-law, Vasanti, came first. She selected two glass bangles from the bangle tray and proceeded to place them on Anjali's right wrist. She had to delicately squeeze and pinch the fleshy place above Anjali's thumb before the bangles slid free onto her wrist. Vasanti then chose two more bangles and squeezed and pushed them onto Anjali's left wrist. The placing of bangles was done very cautiously, for the bangles had to be tight enough to be a proper fit, but if one bangle should break during this ceremony it was considered very inauspicious. Next, Vasanti tucked a small strand of jasmine into Anjali's hair. She then smeared sandalwood paste on Anjali's cheeks and forearms and on the backs of her hands and placed a dot of *kuṅkumam* on Anjali's forehead. This part of the ritual is called the *nalaṅku.* Next she sprinkled Anjali's head and body with rosewater, pouring it from a special silver canister *(pannīr cempu).*

On the floor near Anjali was a small metal water pot with a coconut perched on its opening. The pot had also been decorated, with thick lines of sandalwood paste with dabs of *kuṅkumam* centered on the paste so that the whole pot seemed to be covered in glowing eyes. This decorated pot with a coconut, known as a *kalacam,* is believed to embody god and is commonly found in Tamil Hindu worship, or *puja.* Vasanti now picked up the *kalacam,* circled it clockwise three times around Anjali's head, and then let it sway two times back and forth between herself and Anjali. Anjali then gave Vasanti two glass bangles and *vettilaipākku* (areca nut wrapped in a betel leaf) from the *tāmpūlam* plate.[44]

With the exception of the glass bangles, each of the ritual gestures and offerings made by Vasanti resembled the core practice of *puja* offerings to a Hindu deity. And the return gift of the betel nut paralleled the *prasadam,* or blessed leavings of a deity. Thus *cīmantam* was clearly a deification of the pregnant woman on the eve of her entry to motherhood. The fact that these *cīmantam* rituals were becoming increasingly public events meant that the pregnant woman had in some ways become increasingly deified. With no Brahmin priests officiating, the *cumaṅkali* relatives became ritual specialists guided in part by the opinions of the prominent elderly men *(periya manuṣaṉ)* of the community. As is the case with Hindu *puja,* the worshippers supplicate and seek to fulfill the deity's wishes in order to both gain the beneficent protection of the deity and forestall the dangerous outcome of the deity's unsatisfied wishes. In the case of the *cīmantam* the deity's wishes are understood as desire *(ācai)* emanating from both the woman and her soon-to-be-born baby. Should these desires go unfulfilled, the dangers could include death of the child, of the mother, or both. In short, in this case, the risks of unfulfilled wishes weigh heaviest on the goddess herself. The pregnant woman is regarded as the goddess Sakti but she is a very needy and vulnerable Sakti.

The concept of *sakti* is a key component of Hindu thought. In the 1980 edited volume *The Powers of Tamil Women,* Wadley and others suggest that the emphasis on the concept of *sakti* in Tamil culture is central to understanding the nature of women's power in Tamil society.[45] Wadley explains that the goddess Sakti "provides a motivating force for the inactive male: without the *sakti* of his goddess, no male god can act."[46] As the Tamil proverb goes: "Siva without Sakti is a corpse." S. B. Daniel elaborates further on this point:

> *Sakti,* to the villager, is a natural energy which is essential for all action from physical movement to thought processes. *Sakti* sustains hard labor and mental exertions and adds coercive force to prayers and curses. It is generally believed to reside in living creatures but because it is at base a form of energy, it is not limited to one medium. . . . *Sakti* is manifested primarily in females. Although males also possess a measure of *sakti,* it is believed that this is because they embody a small portion of the female principle. This *sakti* is the goddess within them.[47]

In *The Powers of Tamil Women,* both Wadley and Margaret Egnor (now Margaret Trawick) argue that in Tamil culture, not only are women innately powerful and "*sakti*-filled," due primarily to their reproductive abilities, but women also gain *sakti* throughout their lives through the control of their powers and particularly of their sexuality (here also referred to as *ācai*). This control comes both from without and from within. Wadley writes that "the dominant ideology states that the Tamil woman should be constrained and controlled by her male kin."[48] Furthermore, Wadley adds that women exert a great deal of self-control over their sexuality necessitated by their subordinate position in society in relationship to men.[49] As Egnor puts it, "If women have more *sakti* than men, this is (at least in part) because women stand in the position of servants with respect to men. This also helps explain why women, rather than trying to undo the sexual hierarchy, are often its staunchest supporters."[50] Egnor tries to preempt a feminist critique of this proposition when she says that although some might say that notions of *sakti* are created to mask the reality of women's subordination, in India action and idea are not separated from each other but are aspects of one reality.[51] The concept of *sakti* must indeed be seen as reflecting a real belief in female regenerative power and cannot be seen as simply a mystification and foil for male domination. But the women I met did *not* seek to perpetuate male domination in order to enhance their *sakti.* On the contrary, they articulated a deep critique of their subordination, particularly in the context of the multiple exchanges involved in puberty rituals, dowry, *cīmantam,* and postpartum gifts, as I discuss later. The problem is not that women do not critique the system, but rather that women often blame themselves and blame other women; it is a case of blaming the victim.

There is another way in which an analysis of *cīmantam* rituals provides an alternative view to that put forth by Wadley and Egnor. While Wadley and Egnor emphasize control and containment of women's *ācai,* *cīmantams* are performed for the express purpose of fulfilling and satisfying the pregnant woman's *ācai* rather that containing it, and in the *cīmantam* the *ācai* is satisfied primarily by other women. What Wadley and Egnor say about containment is not wrong, but things are different for pregnant women, and the concept of *ācai* is multivalent and cannot be understood only for its sexual connotation.

After Vasanti completed her worship of Anjali as *sakti,* each of the other *cumaṅkalis* followed Vasanti's example, copying her gestures and adding more and more bangles to Anjali's wrists. By the end, Anjali's forearms were filled with glittering glass bangles of all colors.[52] I was told by many people that if a woman has a home delivery, the bangles must be worn and should break on their own accord during the course of the stormy first delivery. If the delivery takes place in a hospital, however, the woman is required to remove all the bangles upon being admitted.

After all the bangles had been placed, Anjali's mother came forward and placed a gold ring on Anjali's finger, and her sister presented her with a new Kanchipuram silk sari. The tray with all the other beautification objects brought from her mother's house was then placed at Anjali's feet for her to see.

Two women then lit camphor on plates which were filled with vermilion-colored water known as *ālam.* They brought the flaming plates down from the stage and walked among the crowd. People reached out their hands, palms down, to capture the warmth of the flame in their fingertips which they then touched lightly and reverently to their eyelids. This gesture is *ārati,* and it marks the end of the *puja* ritual. *Vettilai-pākku* and fruits and flowers were then offered to the *periya manuṣaṉ.*

It was now nine o'clock. Anjali remained seated on the *maṇai* for a few more minutes, and the *periya manuṣaṉ* remained seated on the floor while the photographer took some posed shots of each. Finally, Anjali came down from the stage to where the *periya manuṣaṉ* were seated. The *periya manuṣaṉ* rose and Anjali genuflected to them. Then they all retired to the back room where all the guests were treated to a catered meal.

After the meal, Anjali accompanied her own parents back to their house where she would remain for the delivery of her child.[53] Her husband went with her to her parents' house. He would remain there for three days and then return to his own parents' house to stay. All the remaining food and vessels which had been brought from Anjali's mother's house were taken to Anjali's mother-in-law's house to be distributed and consumed there. The delicacies prepared to fulfill Anjali's *ācai* were brought back to Anjali's home, where she would consume them in the *puja* space in her house.

Following a *cīmantam* the pregnant woman typically went to stay with her own parents for her first delivery and for several months after the delivery. It was felt that she would be better cared for in her parents' house. She would be nourished with food and love and would be allowed to rest more than if she were to remain in her in-laws' house. It was, however, not so uncommon for her to remain in her in-laws' house for the delivery and postpartum period. In such cases she might go to her parents' house for a few days following the *cīmantam* in order to follow ritual prescriptions, then return to her in-laws' house.

There were several reasons why she might remain with her in-laws. Perhaps it was simply too far to travel to her parents' house. But, generally, lower-class women in Tamil Nadu did not marry into families very far away from their natal kin. Another reason for remaining with the in-laws was that, contrary to the common assumption, some women felt they would be better cared for in their in-laws' house. This was particularly true if their in-laws were wealthier than their parents. A third and very important reason for remaining in their in-laws' house was that their in-laws might live closer to big urban hospitals, and many women were choosing to have hospital rather than home deliveries. If the last two explanations were given for remaining with the in-laws, sometimes the pregnant woman's mother would come to the in-laws' house and remain as a guest in their house throughout the delivery and the postpartum period. This goes to show that despite the cliché of the mean mother-in-law and the beleaguered daughter-in-law, in reality these relationships are, of course, highly varied.

REINVENTION OF TRADITION

Generally when I asked young women why they performed the *cīmantam* ritual, they would reflect for a moment and then say, "I don't know; it is tradition *(paṛakkam),* that is all. It was done in those days *(anta kālatilē)* so we are also doing it today." Others would add that it was primarily done to satisfy the pregnant woman's *ācai.* Most felt that it was socially critical to uphold this tradition. Families which did not do so were said to be scorned. It was very bad for the family's prestige *(kowravam)* not to perform this ritual.

The moral position taken with respect to the need to perform a *cīmantam* varied in part according to economic status and a family's ability to cover the rising price tag of the ritual. Women whose families could not cover the costs would sometimes take the moral high ground, saying that such rituals are indicative of *mūḍanampikkai* (superstition) or that *cīmantams* are a waste of resources which should be put to more efficient and "modern" uses such as savings schemes and school supplies, not to mention daily meals. Most people, however, did perform some form of *cīmantam* despite their poverty, and they did so out of concern for both prestige and the well-being of the mother and child.

Another reason given for not performing a *cīmantam* was the conflicts arising from "love marriages" (especially across caste and religious communities). If the families of couples who had a "love marriage" did not accept the marriage, they would not conduct a *cīmantam.* The absence of this ritual was thus felt to be another scar—a symbol of illegitimacy. In some cases of "love marriage," however, the parents and family of the pregnant woman could not stand to have this occasion unmarked, and they would hold a small function in their home without any of the husband's relatives present. Others told me that feuds which arise due to "love marriages" may be resolved through the performance of *cīmantam,* because families that are unwilling to give blessings to the marriage itself find it emotionally and socially very difficult *not* to acknowledge the legitimacy of a newborn baby. Thus, the birth of the baby is cause for a reconciliation which is initiated at the time of the *cīmantam.*

Whereas younger women described *cīmantam* as a traditional practice, people from the older generations had a very different story to tell. Saraswati from Nochikuppam guessed that she must have been about eighty years old. She had moved from Cuddalore (near Pondicherry) to Madras following her marriage. The journey from Cuddalore to Madras in those days was long and tedious, involving a trip by boat to Hamilton Bridge and then a bumpy ride by horse-cart to Nochikuppam. Because of the distance, she did not return to her mother's house for her delivery. I asked her if they also did not perform *cīmantam* due to the difficulty in travel. She replied:

> Where was all that in those days? I had nothing. All these are new customs *[caḍaṅkukaḷ].* This custom *[cīmantam]* only began after the birth of my fourth child. It was only after the "evacuation" of Madras due to the bomb scare that this practice began. This was before independence. At the time of the bomb scare the white people [British] were here. So we all ran away. I went to my mother's house in Cuddalore. Everyone went to stay with relatives outside of Madras. After we returned, my husband's two brothers

were married. At that time we got independence. Then Nehru and Gandhi were here and it was at that time that these customs began. So for the wives of my brothers-in-law they did this *cīmantam.* But even then it was not like it is now. At that time they only made sweetened tamarind, puffed rice *(aval),* and unpolished rice *(paccarici).* We didn't put *laddus* like they do now. They didn't do any bangle ceremony. They only gave a very cheap sari and blouse that they bought from the side of the road for Rs. 1.25.

The evacuation of Madras occurred during World War II in response to the threat of Japanese invasion.[54] India gained independence in 1947, following the end of World War II. So Saraswati was suggesting that in Nochikuppam people only began to practice the *cīmantam* ritual at that time and that it had only recently become an elaborate ceremony.

As Eric Hobsbawm has said, "'Traditions' which appear or claim to be old are often quite recent in origin and sometimes invented."[55] The *cīmantam* ritual cannot be seen as a postcolonial invention since it does have roots in older Brahminical tradition and is mentioned in Sanskrit texts. But it is very likely that in the past this ceremony was performed only among the Brahmin community or at least among high-caste communities, whereas in 1995 it was widely practiced across caste and religious communities. Furthermore, the ceremony had taken on new form and meaning and did not reflect the same ritual that Brahmins referred to as *cīmantam.* Thus, it can be said to be a "reinvention." It is new wine in old bottles.

Many other people underscored Saraswati's point that the form and nature of the *cīmantam* rituals had changed dramatically in the past few decades. The most obvious change that people noted was that in the past, the ceremonies were relatively simple in terms of the number and quantity of food items brought from the pregnant woman's mother's house. And many noted an increase in the importance of sweets: *laddu,* Mysore *pākku, kēsari.* Another change that people noted was the increasing emphasis on showing *(kāḍḍu)* the various items which were brought, as was evident in Anjali's *cīmantam.* The number of people invited to these functions had also increased so that more people could *see* all the items being shown. This had led to the practice of renting out halls for the function. One woman explained to me: "Everything must be shown. Just like in the cinema." In fact, women frequently referred to the cinema in explaining various aspects of *cīmantam,* marriage, and other social practices. As Arjun Appadurai and Carol Breckenridge have claimed, "The commercial cinema provides a powerful emotional and aesthetic framework within which an Indian form of 'capitalist realism' . . . is learned. . . . Indian films contain models of celebrity and consumption that are pivotal to the new public culture."[56]

People also pointed out that in the past relatives brought things from the mother's house according to their wish *(viruppam).* But these days, members of the husband's household were increasingly making demands about what should be brought. And, whereas the emphasis used to be almost exclusively on the food offerings made by the woman's family, and on the glass bangles and flowers, these days her family was also often expected to give all the "ever-silver" vessels in which the food was kept, silk saris, and gold jewelry, as was the case in Anjali's *cīmantam.* In some cases, in addition to giving gold jewelry to the pregnant woman, the woman's family was also expected to present the husband with a gold ring. In many other *cīmantams* the husband's family also demanded the gift of consumer items such as food mixers and grinders, and even television sets and tape-recorders, all items usually associated with modern dowries.

I especially heard such demands for consumer items made in Bapu Mastan Dargha. Many of the Muslims in this area followed the practice of giving money *(paṇam vaccu kūppiḍṟatu)* during the *cīmantam.* In the past only small sums of money were given, often totaling about Rs. 50, and this money was discretely tucked into the hand of the pregnant woman during the ceremony or it was placed on a plate in front of her. In 1995 this continued to be the practice in some families, particularly very poor families. But people told me that increasingly the husband's family was demanding more money for the *paṇam vaccu kūppiḍṟatu.* And, rather than meet the demands of the husband's family by increasing the sum of money, many now preferred to give the amount in-kind by giving mixers and grinders. Their reason for doing so was that this way they felt assured that these items would be directly useful to their daughters as they worked in their in-laws' kitchens. Similar tactics were being used in the context of the dowry, as we see below.

Murugesan, the *panchayat* president of Kaannathur-Reddikuppam, summed up the changes in *cīmantam* practices: "In those days they gave according to their wish *(viruppam).* But after 1965 it has changed. Now it is all business *(viyāpāram)*—not just for the *cīmantam* but for life as a whole." So with a rise in consumption patterns a new kind of *ācai* is emphasized in the *cīmantam*—the desire for consumer goods. And the issue of prestige *(kowravam)* seems to be tied more to a display of wealth than to a need to uphold "tradition." Yet the concept of tradition was evoked to lend a moral grounding to this "business."

In my discussions with people about the changes in *cīmantam* practice, many different historical referents were evoked. Saraswati associated the changes in Madras, first, with the evacuation during World War II and the subsequent emergence of a postcolonial state and, second, with changes occurring "more recently." Murugesan tied the changes to the emergence of the road and buses connecting Kaanathur-Reddikuppam to the metropolis of Madras in the mid-1960s. Many others suggested that the changes had occurred in the past two decades and thus only affected the new generation of pregnant mothers. In particular, people associated the changes directly with the economic liberalization policies of the past decade. What sense can we make of these different historical references?

In considering the relationship between history and changes in *cīmantam,* it is useful to look at theories regarding the history of dowry in India. Two historical processes are evoked when describing the rise in dowry practice and dowry demands: the process of colonialism and the process of economic liberalization.

Bina Agarwal, Veena Oldenburg, and Madhu Kishwar each point out that under colonialism, new rules surrounding rights in land were established to facilitate taxation.[57] These rules had two important effects on women's power. One was that women were denied any rights in land, so that dowry in the form of moveable goods was the only form of property available to women.[58] The other was that because landowners were expected to pay taxes in cash rather than in-kind, dowry became one of the only ways a family could quickly access cash. Dowry thus shifted from being moveable property over which a woman had exclusive control to becoming property given by the bride's family to her husband's kin. The bride thereby lost control over the dowry and her in-laws gained access to a quick source of goods (such as gold) that could be sold for cash to pay the taxes.[59] It was during the colonial period under these rules of taxation that the practice of dowry became established as a pan-Indian institution. It has since been largely responsible for dismantling earlier systems of bride-price which existed in certain regions.[60] M. N. Srinivas argues that the shift from bride-price to modern dowry was largely due to the lower castes' emulation of the higher castes in the context of an increasingly monetized society with access to formal education and the organized sector which emerged during the colonial era.[61] This transition from bride-price to dowry is particularly noteworthy in South India, where in the precolonial period dowry was not so significant even among patrilineal communities, and it was nonexistent among some matrilineal and bilateral communities.[62] As Agarwal writes, "Reports from many parts of the subcontinent, including South India and Bangladesh, indicate that dowry demands from the groom's family have been increasing and acquiring a character similar to that in North India."[63] Having thus become established and entrenched throughout India, dowry demands and incidents of violence associated with dowry continued to spiral upward and have recently been exacerbated by an increase in conspicuous consumption accompanying economic liberalization policies within the past decade.

Although I do not have information regarding the effects of colonial policy on *cīmantam* practice, we may assume that if *cīmantam* was practiced during the colonial period, it may have also been viewed as a convenient means of accumulating wealth for the purposes of paying taxes and paying off debts. That of course would have to be proven by historians. What is clear from my research is that the connection between economic liberalization and increasing consumerism, which has led to a burgeoning of dowry demands, was also affecting the practice of *cīmantam* in the 1990s.

CĪMANTAM AND THE DISCOURSE OF COMMUNALISM

A few people whom I met speculated that the resurgence and reinvention of the practice of *cīmantam,* which is considered to be a historically Hindu ritual, and its spread to non-Hindu communities may be tied to the pan-Indian movement of Hindutva, or Hindu nationalism. When I met with the Imam of the Ismail Grounds mosque adjacent to Bapu Mastan Dargha, he very adamantly told me that in the Muslim tradition there are no *cīmantam* ceremonies. According to him, even the ceremony which many Tamil Muslims practice on the fortieth day following the birth of the baby is not part of Islamic religious practice. As he said (in English):

> We have no hard and fast rules that we have such functions from the purely religious point of view. It is all a social development. They are only recent developments. The bangle ceremony during pregnancy, the forty-day period after the birth . . . these are all social developments.
>
> As soon as the baby is born we whisper Allah's name three times into the baby's ears. That's all. Naming the baby can be done at this time or after seven or nine days. All these are mere customs and formalities. This is all social custom. There is no religion at all in this. Actually we must avoid all these things. It is against the Muslim religious principles. All this is unnecessary. It is all new Hindu influence. The only important thing is praying five times a day.

This Imam's shift from viewing these changes as generalized "social developments" to viewing them as part of "new Hindu influence" which goes "against Muslim principles," and thus as something to be "avoided," points to an undercurrent of rising communal friction in Tamil Nadu. At the time of my research in 1995 Tamil Nadu was one of the few Indian states which had been spared the violence of the Hindu-Muslim religious conflagrations of the postcolonial era. But even in 1995 tensions were rising and comments like this Imam's were increasingly creeping into public discourse. In the intervening years since I carried out this research, politically motivated communal violence has spread to parts of Tamil Nadu as well.

Despite the note of alarm in this Imam's comments about Hindu hegemony, the fact that most Muslims as well as most Christians in Tamil Nadu did practice some form of *cīmantam* in and of itself cannot be seen as a recent manifestation of a Hindu revivalist movement; religious communities in India have a long history of interconnected practices and ideologies which are not necessarily the result of a desire for religious hegemony. Furthermore, although, as I have mentioned, the *cīmantam* ritual is indeed patterned on Hindu *puja* practice and the pregnant woman herself is deified as the goddess Sakti, the orthodox Hindu Brahmin scholar and priest I met agreed with the Imam that the ritual of placing bangles is *not* a religious practice, even from a Hindu scriptural perspective. According to Brahminical practice the *cīmantam* ritual, which is very distinct from the *vaḷaikāppu,* or bangle ceremony, is considered part of the religious orthodoxy while the *vaḷaikāppu* is not. There are no Hindu priests officiating at the bangle ceremony, and there are no formal prayers, or *mantras,* to the gods.

In short, concerns about the relationship between Hindutva and the resurgence and moral necessity associated with *cīmantam* do not seem to be based on causal connections, but rather they reflect the subtle and powerful ways in which communal discourses are constructed. Despite the fact that the topic of *cīmantam* was seeping into communal discourses, most people argued that the economic changes and the concomitant trend toward increasing conspicuous consumption were responsible for the transformation of these *cīmantam* rituals.

THE BUSINESS OF REPRODUCTION

Jeffery et al. have noted, in rural Uttar Pradesh, "While the dowry is the peak of gift giving, the marriage establishes a long-standing pattern of *len-den* (taking-giving) mainly from the bride's family to her husband's family."[64] In Tamil Nadu in the late twentieth century, dowry was also the "peak" of gift giving tied to a series of exchanges. But whereas Jeffery et al. locate the beginning of these exchanges in Uttar Pradesh with marriage, in Tamil Nadu these exchanges began when a girl went through puberty, or "attained age" *(vayatu aḍaital)*. This may be attributed in part to the practice in Tamil Nadu of cross-cousin marriage and marriage between a woman and her maternal uncle.[65] During puberty rituals the maternal uncle as well as the girl's immediate family were expected to provide gifts and a feast for the community. The fact that the gift giving began with puberty also suggests that these exchanges were tied to women's reproductive capabilities rather than to marriage per se. The centrality of reproduction to the giving of gifts was underscored by the fact that in Tamil Nadu the gift giving ended following the birth of the first child. I refer to this period between puberty and the birth of the first child and its associated exchanges as the "reproductive continuum."

Throughout the reproductive continuum by far the bulk of the expenses were the responsibility of the girl/woman's own parents. This led to tremendous grief on the part of the parents, to elaborate strategies to minimize expenses, and to numerous accusations. An animated discussion in Kaanathur-Reddikuppam among Muttamma, Karpagam, Annette, and myself revealed many aspects of the problems which this community faced with respect to these exchanges. I will therefore quote the interview verbatim in order to discuss its key points. The discussion took place in Karpagam's thatched house. Karpagam was busily cooking her husband's lunch over a smoky fire while we spoke. This excerpt begins with a discussion about the problems of dowry demands which persist after the wedding has taken place.

Dowry Dealings

Annette: So, if you call your daughter, since she's educated, and tell her that this is wrong, won't she agree?

Muttamma and Karpagam: She will agree.

Annette: What about her in-laws?

Karpagam: Suppose we give our daughter to you. We have to do all that is expected of us. Only then will she be happy there. Supposing I don't do it; they will say "your mother is useless *[kati illātaval]*[66].

She has dropped her daughter here." The mother-in-law will ask my daughter: "Does your mother have enough resources *[vakku]* to buy a meter of cloth? She has left you here without anything."

Muttamma: That's the cruelty *[koḍumai]* of dowry.

CVH: What will happen if you don't give?

Karpagam: What!? . . . My girl will not be married.

Muttamma: Prestige *[kowravam]* will go down. It will be less. "Why did they give their daughter away like an orphan *[anāti peṇ]?*"

Karpagam: The mother-in-law's family will say to the daughter-in-law: "Even if your family has to beg to eat, can't they spend even ten rupees and get you married? They just sent you without anything. Despite the fact that they live in a condition of poverty *[kēvalam],* couldn't they at least give a little oil lamp *[kuttuviḷakku]?* They didn't spend even ten paise. They simply married you off without giving anything."

Muttamma: Even if the girl decides to go away and be in the mother's house, the pestering of one's own brothers and sisters-in-law is too much. That's why many commit suicide by hanging or by drinking medicine. This is what the dowry problem is.

Karpagam: Listen to Muttamma's story. When her daughter was married she didn't take many ornaments. Now her daughter is coming and asking for property *[cottu].* She is asking for a share of the property *[pākam].* The brothers are refusing to give her a share.

Earlier we used to give smaller things and less. Like only one copper pot, one big pot to use for ceremonial cooking *[aṇḍa],* one tiffin carrier, one hand dipper, one small vessel. . . . Just giving five or six countable things *[uruppaḍi],* marriages were conducted. But nowadays instead of five varieties of things we must give 200 varieties. Everything has to be given. Just the gifts alone have to go in a "lorry." The husband and wife should go in one "lorry." And a "cot," "bureau," "almirah," and cooking vessels will all go in another "lorry."

Muttamma: They are asking for "grinders," "mixers," "TVs," sewing machines. If there is no electricity in the boy's hut we still have to give these things so that when the electricity does come they can use them. If we are a little well-off we have to buy a "motorbike"!

Annette: A "motorbike"! Even if he doesn't know how to ride?

Karpagam: If he doesn't know how to ride, they'll give it as money. For those who have a girl it is very difficult.

Muttamma: If we have a girl, it is tears for us until the end.

Annette: Can't we stop this problem?

Karpagam: How can we stop this? Supposing in my house my mother does it for me but for my brother his wife is not able to. Then I myself will say to my mother: "You did so much for me. Why did you allow a woman without resources for my brother? Did they send even a *pūri*[67] roller *[pūrikkaḍḍai]?*" I myself will ask.

Annette: The asking should stop.

Karpagam: Why me alone? The whole world is like that now.

CVH: Was it not like this earlier?

Karpagam: No, it was not like this. Since the nation *[nādu]* is improving it's become like this.

What does Karpagam mean when she says "since the nation is improving"? This was a comment made in fact by many people in reference to visible changes in the display of wealth, particularly in major urban areas such as Madras. In particular, people pointed to the fact that since the liberalization policies of 1991 were implemented, there had been a dramatically visible change in the number and kinds of cars on the streets and in the use of cellular phones and a wide range of other electronic equipment, and a proliferation of shops selling gold. Such conspicuous consumption had become a marker of upper-middle- and upper-class identity. So "the nation" which Karpagam sees as improving refers primarily to the upper classes. For residents of Kaanathur-Reddikuppam and Nochikuppam, the need to maintain prestige in this new improved "nation" had led to a desperate struggle to obtain new consumer items as well as new wealth in the form of such things as gold. Exchanges in the context of the reproductive continuum were one means of obtaining such goods. The burden of this struggle fell on the family of the reproductive girl/woman. As Muttamma said so poignantly, "If we have a girl, it is tears for us until the end."

I was curious to know whether such demands were placed on families when the marriage took place between relatives, such as cross-cousin marriage. Karpagam gave me a surprising response:

> The relatives will ask the most. Everywhere it is the same. The relatives know as well. They know what we have. They will think, "Yes, our sister

> will give us 'weight.' She has quite a lot of money. If we ask our sister, she'll give." We'll think, "After all, we're giving to our brother. What's going to happen? He won't destroy it. So let's give a lot." Shouldn't we give more for our own brother than we would to others? If it is *acal* [outside the family], how do we know whether he is a good or bad man? So if it is *acal* we will only give a little now and afterward we'll give the remainder.

In her study of changing marriage practices among non-Brahmin Tamils, Karin Kapadia notes that this is in fact one reason for the shift away from kin marriage to nonkin marriage.[68] Obtaining the money for dowry expenses was a constant struggle. Many people took out loans to raise the money for dowry. But these loans were often taken from local moneylenders who charged exorbitant interest rates. Property in the form of land or a house was sometimes mortgaged in order to take out loans. The very poor in Kaanathur-Reddikuppam could not afford to save for the dowry so they had to borrow at the time of the marriage.

Many would give only a portion of the dowry initially and then give the remainder after they were convinced that the marriage would last. So the remainder of the dowry might be paid off in the context of pregnancy and postpartum ritual exchanges, including *cīmantams.* In these cases the new bride was often ceaselessly pestered by her in-laws. Nevertheless, this was considered by many to be a wise move because if the couple should separate the dowry money would not be returned. As Karpagam explained: "No, they won't give anything back if the couple separates. They will keep it and spread some lies about the girl. 'Your girl was immoral *[tappu];* she was wayward.' Even if we go to the court they'll prove that our girl did something wrong. Even if we go through this with a fight they will start planning for a second marriage for their son."

In addition to the need to take out loans and give dowry payments in installments, parents of the bride-to-be strategized carefully about how to give the dowry in such a way that they could be sure it would benefit their own daughter and provide her with some economic security rather than be squandered on something like her husband's drinking habits. This is similar to the point made above about Muslims in Bapu Mastan Dargha giving cooking gadgets rather than money for the *paṇam vaccu kūppiḍṟatu* in the *cīmantam* ceremony. When negotiations for a dowry were being made, the bridegroom's family would offer something as a contribution for the dowry. The bride's family was then expected to offer a contribution for at least double the amount offered by the bridegroom's family. It was in such negotiations that the bride's family was careful to solicit contributions which would benefit their daughter.

Karpagam and Muttamma explained that the bridegroom's family might borrow jewels from another person and display these as jewels to be given to the bride. Her family would then have to give her jewels for double the amount. But after the wedding, the bridegroom's family would return the borrowed jewels to the original owner. They would also demand that the bride hand over the jewels her parents provided, and those jewels might promptly be pawned off. To prevent such problems, the bride's family would demand that the bridegroom's family's contribution go into the bride's *tāli* (wedding necklace) since a wife was not supposed to remove her *tāli* as long as her husband was alive.

Muttamma and Karpagam felt that the degree to which a new bride was pestered and threatened about dowry related to the nature of the relationship between her husband and his own mother, sisters, and sisters-in-law (his brothers' wives). The following excerpt from the discussion points to how different kinds of relationships resulted in different degrees to which the wife was hassled about dowry:

Karpagam: If the husband's favoritism is toward the mother-in-law or sisters-in-law, then the girl is all alone. Even if she discusses the matter with him it's still no use. Sometimes the husband and wife will be on the same side and they will stand up against his mother. "Mother! Go away! We would like to live separately!" There are people like this. Here the husband and wife are undivided *[orukai]*[69] in their thoughts. So they will live separately from the mother-in-law's house. But some husbands are slaves *[aḍimai]* to their mothers or sisters and keep the wife away. Then she is all alone. Some are divided like this.

Annette: Are there more people like this [i.e., divided]?

Karpagam: There are various types in the world. There is nothing which says this is what should be or that is what should be. Supposing my son doesn't give food for me. . . . He lives separately with his wife. I'll say, "Look, you give me something. You are earning and living together. Why are you allowing her to take everything to her own mother's house? Don't you have a sister? Don't you have to get her married? You are giving everything you earn to her [your wife]. You give me four *aṇās*[70] or eight *aṇās* so that I can save it in a thrifty manner and get your sister married. Your father is old. Please

> give me some income son!" So, hearing this, you will also start giving to your mother.
>
> So why should I be there as a wife? As a wife that has to put the *tāli,* why should I stay there? I will think: "I am the wife, sleeping with him and giving him all the *cukam* [health/pleasure],[71] why can't we have what he earns? I am not wearing flowers, not even going for a 'cinema.' We are not even spending ten rupees. We are not even buying a biscuit for our child. What is the use of my man? Why? See, he gives his mother everything!" This becomes a problem.
>
> "When we stay with the sisters-in-law and mother-in-law all that my husband earns is getting wasted on their family. Somehow we should fight with the mother-in-law and get out from the family so we would get a lot of money, isn't it?"

Although the husband is often blamed for squandering the dowry on such frivolous things as liquor, it is interesting that Karpagam and Muttamma, as well as numerous other women, tended to exempt men from culpability when it came to the issue of the overall problem of dowry demands. As Muttamma said, "If you look at the dowry problem it is not caused by men at all. It is only by women. The mother-in-law and sister-in-law." Muttamma and Karpagam were keenly aware of how women themselves participated in the perpetuation of this form of patriarchy. Once again, contrary to Wadley's and Egnor's assertions that women feel they gain more *sakti* from their subordination, women in fact articulated a *critique* of the ways in which they become implicated in their own subordination.

The Reproductive Continuum

I have discussed dowry in-depth to show that, indeed, dowry did mark the "peak of gift giving" and was the gift that caused the greatest anxiety. But Karpagam and Muttamma's discussion also situated dowry within the context of the giving of a series of gifts in the reproductive continuum. This series of exchanges begins with puberty and ends with the return of a woman to her mother-in-law's house following her first delivery and the subsequent stay with her own parents. Although dowry is the most substantial payment in this continuum, it is only part of this longer process. The following excerpt from the same discussion makes this clear:

Muttamma: It has just been one month since my daughter attained age *[vayatu aḍaital]*. We have to have a big function for that. My daughter will wear new clothes, and jewelry. Just like a wedding, it is very expensive. We have to call everyone and make different types of rice and sweets and give a grand dinner. For my first daughter we did this on the third day itself, after pouring the water,[72] but for this daughter we are doing it later and it will not be so grand. For the first daughter it was very expensive. Money, *jimikki,* clothes, silk *pavadai, ḍāvaṇi,* silk sari . . . everything was given by her *māman.* All my brothers will have to bring things.

Annette: What will happen if we don't follow this custom?

Karpagam: No, we have to do it. My relatives have to know that my daughter has come of age. We have to tell ten villages.

Annette: Let them know on their own. Why do we have to tell?

Karpagam: No, it is a prestige *[kowravam]* issue. We should have respect from the town *[ūrkkowravam]*.

Annette: How ever much money is lost it's okay, but respect in a village shouldn't be lost. Is that it?

Karpagam: You are doing it for your daughter, isn't it? So I want to do it for mine.

Muttamma: When a girl is getting married the boy has expenses in his house but the girl has twice that amount of expense in her house. After a baby is born they ask: "Is it a girl or boy?" "Oh, girl, is it?" [in low, disappointed tone of voice]. If there are five girls: "Oh! The father will become poor!" The elders will talk like this. With four girls his prestige will go down. That's why when a child is born if it is a girl they feel a sense of weary dissatisfaction *[calippu]*. If they have four boys already and another boy is born they will not say: "It's another boy!" They will hide this fact and say it is only a girl. That's because they are afraid of *drishti* [the evil eye] if they say it is a boy. So they'll say, "Only a girl was born."

Karpagam: So many girls are born while they wait for a son. If all five are girls it becomes very difficult. All five will get sick. How much trouble we will take to look after all five. When they mature, he has to give so much for the puberty ceremony, and then again for marriage, and then for *cīmantam.* For *cīmantam* he has to give five rice dishes and provide gifts. He has to arrange for the radio in the village to provide songs. The people in the village will be called. Again food has to be prepared for all before the delivery. Again, after the delivery they have to make three types of sweets and for the baby they have to give one gold sovereign and silver anklets, and clothes for baby, and for the husband and wife. After delivery they have to give all that and send them. That is the last *cīr* [ritual gift]. Then it's all over.

Muttamma: Until the girl has her first child and we send her back to her mother-in-law's house we have difficulty.

Occasionally *cīmantams* were not performed, when the baby was born before the ritual took place either because the baby was born prematurely or because the woman had miscalculated her due date.[73] Miscalculated due dates were therefore a cause for much suspicion. I heard of several cases where the mother-in-law accused her daughter-in-law of intentionally miscalculating the due date for the express purpose of circumventing the *cīmantam.* The anger in such cases arose around the issue of gifts ungiven, and mothers-in-law felt their daughters-in-law were protecting their own parents. Most women denied such conscious strategizing. Indeed, often the miscalculations were related to the fact that the woman had little or no prenatal care at all during her pregnancy. One woman, however, admitted to me that she had in fact intentionally miscalculated the due date to save her parents from the expense of the *cīmantam.* Among most communities, missed *cīmantams* were not performed following the birth.[74] Thus, whereas the demands of dowry continued to haunt women following their marriage, unfulfilled *cīmantam* payments might be circumvented, usually unintentionally but sometimes purposefully, due to the biological basis of the ritual itself. When the ritual was circumvented, however, it meant that the delivery took place while the pregnant woman was still at her in-laws' house, and many women said that their in-laws were not likely to treat them as well as their parents to begin with, and even less so if *cīmantam* was not performed. Furthermore, the in-laws might put extra demands on the woman's parents for gifts following the baby's birth.

CONCLUSION

The notion of prestige *(kowravam)* was repeatedly evoked as people explained to me why it was imperative that they perform the *cīmantam* ritual. The grander the event, the greater the prestige bestowed upon the pregnant woman's family. And the more the family spent on gifts and food for her husband's kin, the more her pregnancy was viewed as auspicious. Furthermore, the more public the event, the more the pregnant woman was deified as the goddess Sakti, whose desires had to be fulfilled and whose blessings were sought.

However, the rise in economic demands on the woman's parents in the context of these ritual gifts during the reproductive continuum was often cited to me as the underlying cause of the preference for male children which, when taken to its most horrific extreme, has led to the practice of female infanticide in parts of Tamil Nadu and elsewhere in India. Although people I met often associated female infanticide with the ignorance of a past era *(anta kālatilē),* they simultaneously linked it to the rise in the expenses associated with the reproductive continuum, which they saw as related to the increase in consumer orientation that is one manifestation of modernity.

How did this contradictory construction of the pregnant woman as auspicious burden among lower-class communities in Tamil Nadu impact how these women experienced the biomedicalization of pregnancy and birth? The fact that women were revered for their reproductive capacities meant that their families felt they should do everything in their means to provide them with the best medical care. For most (though not all) people, the best medical care meant allopathic care, either because allopathic care was associated with modernity and prestige or because they were convinced that allopathic care was more effective, even if they were critical of how it was provided in public hospitals. Pregnant women's own demands for allopathic prenatal care and hospital deliveries were in fact sometimes associated with the intensification of women's *ācai.* Most of the women whom I met in Tamil Nadu did receive some basic allopathic prenatal care. For some this meant regular and repeated visits with a multipurpose health worker, a nurse, or a doctor. For others it meant one or two visits to get iron tablets and vitamin pills, and a tetanus shot administered during the fifth month of pregnancy. Women in urban centers like Madras tended to have more frequent prenatal visits than women in more rural areas like Kaanathur-Reddikuppam. Women planning to deliver in a public hospital made sure to have at least one prenatal visit in order to receive their prenatal registration card *(aḍḍai),* which they needed in order to be admitted to the hospital. These cards meant that women carried their own medical records of their pregnancy with them.

Despite the increasing problem of women using ultrasound and amniocentesis for sex-selection purposes in India, none of the women whom

I met had had amniocentesis, since it was only available in private practice and the cost was exorbitant. Some of the women I interviewed had had ultrasounds in the public hospitals for a fee of Rs. 10 when it was deemed medically helpful. Doctors working in public hospitals generally abided by the laws which forbade informing parents of the sex of the fetus, and none of the women I met reported getting an ultrasound privately. One doctor at an IPP-V hospital in Madras, however, did tell me that although she didn't inform mothers directly about the sex of the baby, if the baby was a boy she (the doctor) would simply say to the mother, "You should be very happy." The doctor told me that this was a way to get women to make arrangements for a sterilization operation following the delivery. This attitude is not altogether surprising since, as I discuss in Chapter Four, the emphasis on family planning often overrode other MCH interests.

The growing economic burden of *cīmantam* (and other ritual gifts associated with the reproductive continuum) was compounded by the fact that the pregnant woman's family in Tamil Nadu was also largely responsible for the medical expenses associated with childbirth. This was particularly true of the first delivery, since the pregnant woman almost always returned home for that delivery but not necessarily for consecutive deliveries. Sometimes families had to sacrifice the prestige of the *cīmantam* ceremony in favor of spending their slim resources on the expenses of allopathic care. Or they might sacrifice the prestige of the allopathic care in favor of the ritual prestige. More often, they felt they must compromise somewhat on both allopathic care and ritual costs in order to ensure that some of each of these needs was met.

CHAPTER 4

Invoking *Vali*

Painful Technologies of Birth

The first time I visited Nochikuppam, Kasthuri, one of the WWF health workers, summoned a group of pregnant and postpartum women from the neighborhood to gather in a dank room used primarily to house cows and chickens on the ground floor of her government-subsidized housing complex. We were well into a discussion about women's childbirth experiences when I asked whether women were given any medication to reduce the pain of birth in hospitals. "Oh, yes," they all agreed. "They give us injections and 'glucose drips' and then the pains come and the baby will be born right away." I was sure that my Tamil had failed me and that I had not asked the question properly, so I asked Annette to pose the same question. And again they responded with the same answer. When we asked a third time and underscored that we wanted to know about medicines to *decrease* rather than increase the pain, we were met with baffled looks. "The baby will only be born if the pains are strong," they explained. Nagamma (the elderly *maruttuvacci*) joined in, saying, "When you are grinding, it is only if you go on grinding and grinding that you will get a good paste. Like that, without pain how will you deliver a baby?"

Wherever I went in Tamil Nadu I encountered precisely the same response to my question—a misunderstanding followed by a sense that the premise of the question itself was incredible. In fact, I discovered that it was common for women to have their labor accelerated with oxytocin drugs called epidocin and sintocin when they gave birth in government hospitals. Like pitocin, used in the United States, these drugs are manufactured to simulate the effects of oxytocin, which is a naturally produced hormone. Epidocin helps to dilate the cervix, and sintocin works to amplify the contractions. What I found most surprising and disturbing was the fact that women themselves believed that this was the preferred way to deliver a baby. When I inquired with a doctor from the Santhome IPP-V corporation hospital in Madras whether women sometimes asked to have their labor accelerated, she replied (in English): "They don't ask; they insist! Given the choice, everyone wants to be induced." This remark was supported by my observations and discussions with women in maternity wards throughout Tamil Nadu. Women sometimes evaluated different hospitals based on how readily they would accelerate labor. And one nurse told me that she had even been compelled to give women placebos to satisfy these demands when it was medically dangerous to accelerate labor. The practice of medically accelerating labor was not confined to hospitals alone. Vitamin B_{12} injections as well as stronger oxytocin drugs were increasingly being administered for home births as well.

Why had the use of drugs to accelerate labor pains become so normalized in urban and some rural parts of Tamil Nadu? And why did the use of analgesics to reduce the pain of birth seem to be such a far-fetched concept to lower-class women? This chapter is an attempt to address these twin questions. The fact is that as birth becomes increasingly biomedicalized throughout the globe, modern medical technologies may be used in different ways and given different meanings in particular contexts. In Tamil Nadu, cultural notions about female power *(sakti)*, local constructions of the body, and traditional medical practices to accelerate labor pains combined with the political-economic situations of large government hospitals to make accelerating economically efficient and render the use of analgesics an unaffordable luxury. Taken together, these factors resulted in this particular use of technology during childbirth.

A high level of technological intervention in all realms of life has been considered a hallmark of modernity by both advocates and critics of the modernizing project ever since the eighteenth-century Enlightenment. The nature of technological innovation and intervention has been a key area of inquiry for some feminist scholars studying the biomedicalization of childbirth in Europe and the United States. Critiques of the biomedical models of birth in Europe and the United States have argued, first, that these models have become overly technologized and, second, that they bestow too much authority on the doctors and strip pregnant and parturient women of any real power. Birth has come to be viewed as something that is always potentially pathological; pregnant women thus are constructed as "patients" who must always be managed by the medical establishment. Critics assert that due to an economically driven imperative to always seek newer technologies, and a tendency to routinely use whatever technologies are available, not only is biomedicalized birth in America detrimental to women's authority but it also has negative repercussions for the health of mothers and infants; many medical interventions have iatrogenic consequences and are often responsible for precipitating the need for further interventions, such as cesarean sections. The biomedical model of birth that emerged in the context of the Industrial Revolution, like biomedical models of the body more generally, conceived of women's reproductive bodies as machines with standardized time limits for production. These machines then came to be judged as efficient or inefficient based on normative production schedules, and technology was brought in to improve "inefficient" bodies.[1]

Feminist scholars, of course, do not all agree that technological interventions in the context of birth are necessarily a means of controlling women. Catherine Reissman and Judith Leavitt, for example, focus on how women have both benefited and suffered from the medicalization of women's health. They look at women as engaged agents in the promotion of technologies used in reproduction. Reissman argues that by ignoring women's agency in the medicalization process, scholars only "perpetuate the kinds of assumptions about women that feminists have been trying to challenge."[2] Of particular interest for this chapter, they both discuss women's role in advocating for the use of analgesics during delivery beginning in the mid-nineteenth century, when the first analgesics, ether and chloroform, were used by doctors during births.[3] In the second decade of the twentieth century, the American National Twilight Sleep Association was formed as a middle- and upper-class feminist organization to demand the use of "twilight sleep," a combination of scopolamine and morphine that put women in a state of amnesia so that after the birth they were unaware of having experienced any pain. Doctors often felt pressured into administering these earlier forms of anesthesia to satisfy the demands of their patients, despite the risks attached. As the dangers of these drugs became increasingly apparent, women's organizations began to mobilize against these particular drugs, but the movement had established that women had a fundamental right to painless childbirth.[4] It wasn't until the middle of the twentieth century that the natural childbirth movement began to gain momentum and to question the value of painless birth. This movement, in its various forms, has viewed pain as a natural part of the process of birth that can be managed through such things as breathing techniques, birthing positions, and psychological orientations, rather than through pharmaceutical drugs. However, despite the fact that the ideals of natural childbirth are embraced by some women in the United States, the use of anesthesia, particularly epidurals which suppress the experience of pain without altering women's consciousness and without completely taking away their muscle control, are on the rise and are fast becoming routine. Pitocin, which increases the intensity of the pain as it induces contractions, is dreaded by most American women and rarely given to American women without being combined with anesthesia to mask the pain. The inverse is also true. That is, the heavy use of epidurals and other analgesics has also led to an increased use in pitocin, since these analgesics are known to slow down natural labor, thereby precipitating the need for pitocin or, possibly, cesareans.[5]

Of course, biomedicalized pregnancy and birth in the United States are not as uniform as critics often make them out to be. There is, for example, variation in how births are managed based on race, ethnicity, class, gender, and region. The same technological intervention may be interpreted, experienced, and acted upon in different ways within the United States.[6] There is dispute over how socio-economic status influences the process of medicalization. Some argue that women in higher socio-economic brackets will experience greater degrees of technological interventions while others argue the opposite.[7] With respect to pain medications, recent reports suggest that patients on Medicaid in the United States are sometimes not provided with epidurals (unless they pay for them themselves) due to the higher cost of administering epidural anesthesia as compared with other analgesics such as Demerol.[8] There is also a great deal of variation in the dominant models of birth throughout the so-called Western world. Brigitte Jordan's seminal comparative study showed variation in modern obstetrics in three different Western nations: the United States, Sweden, and Holland.[9]

Yet, as discussed in the Introduction, Jordan has recently expressed grave concerns about the export of a monolithic Western model of biomedical birth to the Third World.[10] Although such statements serve important political strategies, they tend to detract from understanding the crucial historical and cultural distinctiveness of the biomedicalization of birth globally. While Robbie Davis-Floyd points to an increase in the use of analgesics during labor (particularly epidurals) among American women, the women in Tamil Nadu whom I met were hardly aware of anesthesia as an option and were wary of the concept when I presented it to them. And whereas women in the United States tend to dread the prospect of having their labor induced with pitocin, women in Tamil Nadu were demanding to be induced. Neither the American nor the Tamil Nadu scenario is "normal." Each may be equally "exotic" from the other's perspective. How, then, do we explain the particular nature of the biomedicalization of childbirth pain in Tamil Nadu? The answers lie in the nexus of cultural and political-economic contexts; in cultural understandings of gendered bodies as well as in unequally allocated funds for health care services.[11] In the remainder of this chapter, I attempt to unravel the many factors contributing to this situation.

In their book *Conceiving the New World Order,* Faye Ginsburg and Rayna Rapp argue that we must move beyond analyses which simply demonstrate how ideas and practices associated with modern reproduction reflect or support preexisting local social and cultural structures or combine to form new hybrids. Rather, they urge us to view reproduction itself as a critical site within which *new* cultural meanings can emerge. As they state, "Regardless of its popular associations with notions of continuity, reproduction also provides a terrain for imagining new cultural futures and transformations."[12] In this vein, this chapter also examines how notions of maternity, and of gender more broadly, are *refashioned* through the biomedicalization of birth in Tamil Nadu. Specifically, I argue that through the routinization of administering drugs to accelerate labor, a contradictory discourse on *sakti* has emerged, creating a debate as to whether modernity has increased or depleted women's power and transforming cultural conceptions of maternity.

VALI AND THE BODY

Vali is a Tamil word meaning "pain" or "ache" and is frequently used to describe all sorts of generic aches and pains in the body. Labor pains are called *piracava vali* (birth/delivery pains) or *iḍuppu vali* (hip/waist pains). *Piracava vali* and *iḍuppu vali* refer to both the sensory experience of pain and the function which the pain serves—the contractions. In Tamil, no distinction is made between these two aspects of *piracava vali.* From the perspective of most of the women I met, the two were inseparable. That is why my question about reducing the pain was so incomprehensible. It was as though I was asking whether they are given any medicines to stop the contractions.

My question was not merely confusing but somewhat ominous, for it conjured up the specter of prolonged labor and the very tangible associated dangers to both mother and baby. Many elderly women I met had lost their babies in childbirth and knew women who had died in childbirth when no emergency care was available. The tragedies of Murugesan's first wife and six out of his nine children are testimony to this. Despite the rising critique of the overuse of cesareans in urban hospitals in Tamil Nadu, most women I met expressed great relief that such emergency procedures were increasingly available to them in case of problems such as delayed labor.

The rates of maternal and infant mortality had come down significantly in the state of Tamil Nadu in the last two decades of the twentieth century and were generally much lower than the national rates. In 1970 the infant mortality rate (IMR) for India as a whole was 129 (per 1,000 live births); for Tamil Nadu, it was 125. By 1991 the national IMR was down to 80, while the Tamil Nadu IMR was 57; and by 1993 the IMR for Tamil Nadu was down to 56.[13] The neonatal mortality rate and the under-five-year mortality rate in Tamil Nadu (50.1 and 20.6, respectively) were considerably lower than the national rates (56.4 and 29.9), but neonatal mortality rates remained high in both cases. The perinatal mortality rate in Tamil Nadu (53.8) was noticeably higher than the national rate (47.2).[14] Most infant deaths in Tamil Nadu in the 1990s were due to low birth weight, and many were stillbirths. These statistics reflect the fact that in Tamil Nadu immunization programs had been relatively successful but more attention needed to be placed on improving maternal health, particularly during pregnancy, and improving care during delivery.[15] Discrepancies between rural and urban MCH care were also evident; in 1993 the rural IMR in Tamil Nadu was 65, while the urban IMR was 42.[16]

Maternal mortality rates (MMR) in Tamil Nadu had also been steadily declining. In 1982 the MMR for Tamil Nadu was just over 250/100,000 live births, and by 1991 it was down to 130/100,000.[17] The national MMR was reported to be 500/100,000 live births in 1995.[18] According to a 1990 UNICEF report, approximately 20 percent of *all* maternal mortalities worldwide occurred in India—the highest percentage in any one country.[19] Mari Bhat et al. have shown that maternal mortality rates are extremely difficult to determine in India given the absence of a reliable national vital registration system. While they agree with the assertions of Visaria's earlier work that the national MMR has been declining since the early part of the twentieth century, they also contend that overall maternal mortality rates for the country and for individual states may be inflated because deaths from other causes have been attributed to childbirth.[20] Other community-based studies, however, indicate that maternal mortality rates may be much higher than official reports suggest.[21]

Despite the fact that infant and maternal mortality rates in Tamil Nadu generally compare favorably to national rates, they are still high when compared with the rates in industrialized countries and even when compared with the neighboring country, Sri Lanka, or the neighboring state of Kerala. Among industrialized countries, Sweden has consistently had the best record with respect to mortality rates. For example, as early as 1979 the IMR in Sweden was 7.5/1,000 live births, while in the United States it was 13.8.[22] And in 1983 the MMR in Sweden was 1/100,000 live births, while for the United States it was 10/100,000.[23] The national data for Sri Lanka from 1991–1993 indicated an MMR of 40/100,000 live births and an IMR of 18.2/1,000 live births.[24] In 1988 the IMR in Kerala was reported to be 28, while that of Tamil Nadu was 74.[25] In Tamil Nadu one in every fifteen children died within the first year of life, and one in every twelve died before the age of five between 1988 and 1992.[26] Furthermore, recent studies have begun to point out that if we are truly to understand the nature of risk associated with pregnancy and childbirth in India, particularly among poor communities, we must look more closely at the issue of morbidity and not only consider rates of mortality.[27] In a study carried out in the South Arcot District of Tamil Nadu and in Pondicherry, Dr. D. K. Srinivasa et al. report that the "ratio of morbidity to mortality was higher than expected. For every maternal death there were 478 morbidities. There were 328 serious life-threatening morbidities per maternal death."[28]

The high risk associated with childbirth in the not-so-distant past, and continued risks in the present, meant that for many, childbirth and particularly prolonged labor continued to be associated with danger for both mother and child. This was not a problem of the medical establishment's pathologizing childbirth, as some critics of biomedicine suggest. Rather it reflected a very real close association between birth and death. Durga, a health worker with an unusual combination of biting wit and compassion, once spun a wonderful pun, saying, "Don't you see, 'Madam'? The word *"piracavam"* [delivery] itself contains both birth *[piṟa]* and death *[cāvu]*."[29]

VALI AND POWER

In addition to "pain" and "ache," the word *"vali"* means "strength, force," or "power." It was due in part to the combination of pain and danger which women must endure during childbirth that Tamil women were often constructed as valiant beings. They were thought to derive their strength from the patience and perseverance *(poṟumai)* required to withstand the strains of childbirth and the sacrifices of motherhood. As discussed in Chapter Three, *sakti* is located primarily in women's reproductive capacities, which must be assiduously controlled but which are also celebrated through *cīmantam* rituals. It was partly because of women's ability to suffer nobly the pains of birth that they were said to be *sakti.*

A key concept which arose in discussions about the relationship between suffering and *sakti* in the context of labor pains was that of *tapas.* Margaret Egnor explains *tapas* thus: "The power acquired through suffering and servitude is a special case of the Hindu theory of *tapas,* whereby through certain forms of self-denial (called *tapas*) the individual accumulates a certain internal heat (also called *tapas*). The longer and more harsh the suffering, the greater the heat accumulated. This heat may be used, but unless it is spent in sacrifice, another form of self-denial, it is lost."[30]

In short, *tapas* is the bodily experience of internal heat from self-inflicted suffering as well as the power derived from that heat. This power can sometimes be visionary and bring the sufferer into contact with a divine world. Some women I met gained such visionary experiences through the pain of childbirth; a few connected these visionary experiences directly to oxytocin drugs. Kavita had just delivered her first baby four days before I met her and was very eager to tell me the following visionary experience.

• • •

Shortly after her marriage, Kavita had discovered that she had a myoma (a tumor consisting of muscle tissue) and had had a myomectomy. After the operation there was some risk that she might not be able to conceive and in fact she did not conceive for some time. This caused a great deal of tension between her and her husband's families. Her in-laws were suggesting a divorce and her own parents felt that if her in-laws were going to cause her so much grief she should come back to live with them, even though Kavita and her husband were living on their own.

Kavita's parents came and took her back with them to their house, whereupon her husband put out a legal notice saying that she should stay with him, so she returned to his house.

Her in-laws all speculated that these problems had arisen due to the fact that the mediator who was helping to arrange the marriage had mistakenly gotten their horoscopes mixed up with those of another couple, for it was later discovered that Kavita and her husband both had the same birth star, which astrologically speaking is not auspicious for marriage. Since they could not change their birth stars they turned to numerology. According to numerology their wedding date added up to eight, which is considered an inauspicious number, so her husband removed her old tāli *and replaced it with a new one and thus they were remarried on a different date. Furthermore, Kavita explained, according to numerology the number totaled by one's birth date should correspond to the numerological total of one's name. If these correspond it is said to be good for one's health. So during all the family problems both she and her husband changed their names to correspond numerologically with their birth dates. It was soon after these adjustments were made and they were remarried, she explained, that she was finally able to conceive.*

While she was in labor on the delivery table she saw an image of a powerful woman who was crying. The woman was crying to tell people to reduce the number of children they have in order to prevent so much suffering. Along with this crying woman, there was an image of a globe which was closed on the bottom and in the process of closing on the top. The crying woman showed her that the globe was divided into horizontal layers. The bottom, closed portion of the globe represented the first generation, when women were having sixteen to seventeen children. These women had to suffer through hardships equal to 100 *years. The next layer up represented the second generation, in which women were having five to ten children and suffering fifty years. The next layer up represented the present time, in which women were having two to five children and suffering twenty-five years. The next layer up represented the best period, in the future, when women would have only one child and suffer ten years. And, finally, at the vertex of the globe which was closing as the crying woman spoke, sat god. With no children, god will be there to help us, she explained. And when we reach the point where the globe closes we will know that all is one.*

With each dose of oxytocin Kavita received the pains intensified, and each time this happened the crying woman elaborated on a different layer of this globe. As her contractions accelerated the globe closed faster and faster. And the crying woman urged her to write down what she was saying so that she could research it afterward. So during her labor Kavita insisted on having a pencil and paper, and she scribbled down the image of the globe which she showed to me. While she showed it to me she said, "That crying woman said that I should research this after the baby was born and look, you have now come to research it with me!"

• • •

This was an extraordinary vision driven as much by her own familial demands as by the demands of the nation's pervasive family-planning propaganda. Familial conflicts and national propaganda here coalesced in the message that women's reproductive capacities are ultimately a source of suffering for women. The vision, however, seems to make a mockery of both family and state by claiming that it is only with no children that a woman can join god and avoid suffering. Yet it was because of the suffering she endured during labor, which was augmented by shots of oxytocin, that she was able to have such a vision and to have this brush with god, which she had never experienced prior to giving birth. Due to cultural constructions of power, some women felt that because of their *sakti* they could withstand the added intensity of oxytocin-induced labor. More important, some felt that the additional intensity of induced labor, and the *tapas* one accrued through it, added to their *sakti*.

The pain of birth also contributed to the construction of women as *pāvam*. Although *pāvam* can refer to an act of sin, in this case it connotes a kind of pity or sympathy. While this, too, can be viewed as a certain kind of power, like the power attributed to a martyr, it is a very circumscribed power which requires comfort and protection. It is interesting, therefore, that although both men and women mentioned notions of *sakti* in discussing the pain of birth, only men alluded to women as *pāvam* in this context.

To say that women in Tamil Nadu are often discursively constructed as valiant and powerful is not to say that they are always given the respect that such qualities might demand. In fact, these constructions can serve to perpetuate women's subordination. Women themselves were keenly aware of this. Nevertheless, they felt that their ability to withstand the pain of birth did warrant special respect. Muttamma in Reddikuppam laughed nervously when I told her that my husband had been present at my first delivery, and she was shocked to hear that this was even going on in some of the private hospitals in Madras. In Tamil Nadu men were not permitted to be present during either home births or public hospital births. Birth was considered so much the exclusive domain of women that husbands were sometimes not informed that their wives were in labor, and only came to know after the baby had been born. After her initial surprise, however, Muttamma reconsidered and said: "Yes, that would be a good thing here, too. Only then would men give us some respect when they see how strong we must be."

VALI AND DISCOURSES OF MODERNITY

Although women were categorically constructed as having inner strength due to their ability to withstand the pain of childbirth, there were also discourses about variation *among* women and across time in terms of both thresholds for tolerating pain and women's need for various drugs to alter the nature of labor pains. These were fundamentally discourses about modernity. I frequently heard women comment that "in those days," women's bodies were stronger and healthier. "In those days," women labored more in the fields right up until the day they delivered, whereas now women were not necessarily engaged in such labor-intensive work outdoors; even if they were involved in such work, now they stopped working during their pregnancy, believing that it was their prerogative to sit in front of the television and get fat and have each and every wish, or *ācai,* fulfilled. "In those days," women were healthier because they ate food that was not tainted by pesticides. One result of the degrading effects of modernity on women's bodies, so these arguments go, is that women's threshold for tolerating the pain of childbirth has diminished.

Similar discourses were constructed in Europe and the United States during the Victorian era, equating increased sensitivity to pain with the "civilized races" and indifference to pain with "primitives" and criminals.[31] At the turn of the twentieth century, upper-class American women used these theories to advocate for the use of anesthetics, such as "twilight sleep," during delivery. But, rather than using discourses of modernity to press for the use of analgesics to numb the pain, as American women did, the Tamil women I met explained that due to the effects of modernity, women increasingly wanted to be induced because they could no longer withstand the long, drawn-out pain of labor, and they were hoping to be induced in order to get the pain over with as quickly as possible.

Others said that it was not simply the tolerance of pain which had diminished, but women's *bodies* had changed such that they were no longer getting the strong contractions that they got in the past, and therefore it had become increasingly *necessary* to induce labor. Gertrude Fraser has noted a similar kind of discourse in an African American community in the American South about how modernity has transformed the bodies of mothers and infants, thereby requiring new forms of maternal and child medical care.[32] Although there is no denying that cultural practices can and do transform bodies, in these cases such explanations appear to help people make sense of practices which are often structured by political-economic constraints that they may not be able to control, as discussed below.

Those women who *were* aware of the use of analgesics to reduce labor pain often explained the use of such drugs in terms of class, saying that it was those middle- and upper-class women who led a more languid lifestyle who could no longer tolerate the pain of birth at *all* and now required anesthesia. They argued that this was the reason for the fact that analgesics were much more frequently used in private hospitals than in government hospitals. I conducted very cursory research in Apollo Hospital, one of the most prestigious private hospitals in Madras, and I also met with a doctor at the E. V. Kalyani Nursing Home, a private maternity hospital which has long been a favorite of the elites. Indeed, in these private hospitals anesthesia, including epidurals, was provided, and some women did avail themselves of these drugs. Further research should, however, be done to determine how frequently women attending private hospitals do in fact get epidurals, or other analgesics, and how they feel about using these drugs. Based on the few discussions I had with patients at Apollo Hospital, it seemed that not very many women opted for epidurals despite their availability. It is interesting to note that women who went to Apollo Hospital were encouraged to attend prenatal birthing classes at the hospital, and those who attended the classes emphasized the importance of using breathing techniques to manage the pain of birth. In some sense, it seems that attending these classes and using natural childbirth breathing techniques was itself viewed as a sign of the modern and of prestige, since such classes were not provided in public hospitals.

Although the discourse among the poor in Tamil Nadu regarding pain medications was tinged with a certain amount of jealousy toward the leisure class, it was fundamentally a *critique* of modernity. This was also, I would contend, a critique of a perception of "Westernized" modernity, since the upper-class, urban women often came to symbolize a kind of

"Westernized" modernity or at least were thought to be emulating such a modernity. This demonstrates how discourses of modernity are framed in reference to one another. As Kalpana Ram has written, "An internal tension that seems common to many postcolonial projects of modernization and subject formation" is that along with the "lack of faith in 'tradition' goes a fear of becoming over-modernized. Here the Western subject stands as a constant reminder of the hazards of an overly modernized population."[33] Furthermore, one of the problems with constructing oppositional categories of "modernity" versus "tradition" in the first place is, as Margaret Jolly notes, that in postcolonial locations "the organic and the traditional are unduly linked with the indigenous while the technocratic and the modern are intimately entangled with the foreign."[34] Yet, although these discourses among women in Tamil Nadu reflected a kind of class critique and a critique of "Western" modernity, their implication was that because of modernity women of *all* socioeconomic classes no longer had as much *sakti* as they once did. One negative political consequence of such discourses is that as they begin to circulate widely, they tend to foster an underestimation of the real dangers that overwork in modern times often poses to the health of both mother and child during pregnancy, delivery, and the postpartum period.[35]

How women mapped their constructions of "those days" versus "these days" onto historical chronologies varied. Further studies are required to determine patterns in these constructions. However, in general, women in both Madras and Kaanathur-Reddikuppam seemed to view this change as having occurred within one generation, so that the mothers of women who were having babies in 1995 had not routinely used drugs to induce deliveries when they were birthing in the 1970s. It would be useful to trace the changes in the use of inducing drugs from the perspective of the medical establishment and pharmaceutical companies in order to better understand women's own changing conceptions of their bodies.

KAṢĀYAMS

Another reason that women in Tamil Nadu so readily accepted medicines to induce labor is that there has been a widespread tradition of making herbal medicines at home which serve the same purpose. In Tamil the generic word for such herbal concoctions is "*kaṣāyam.*" It is interesting that there were numerous *kaṣāyams* which were made to induce labor but, as far as I could tell, there were no *kaṣāyams* to reduce the pain of labor.

Starting at the beginning of the last month of pregnancy, some women I met took a mild, diluted *kaṣāyam* every night just before going to sleep. Most people made this *kaṣāyam* by boiling ground dried ginger and jaggery in water and drinking the mixture while it was warm. Others made it out of individual ingredients—dried ginger, jaggery, cumin, anise, black coriander seeds—and took one such *kaṣāyam* each night. These mild *kaṣāyams* were said to enable the pregnant woman to pass urine easily and frequently and to help bring on labor pains gradually.[36]

More commonly, *kaṣāyams* were taken once the woman had the first inkling that her real labor pains had begun. Although the ingredients were generally the same, these were far less diluted and were expected to have immediate, dramatic results. The dried ginger was the most important ingredient, and at times it was made into a paste and consumed plain for extra potency. In addition to the ingredients already mentioned, some people included pepper, drumstick leaves, coconut milk, *ōmam, cittirattai,* or dried *cuṇḍakkay* in this *kaṣāyam.* The *kaṣāyams* were usually made by the pregnant woman's mother or mother-in-law (depending on whose house she was staying in), but they could also be made by a local *maruttuvacci.*

These stronger *kaṣāyams* were taken as a kind of litmus test to determine whether or not the pains which the woman was experiencing were genuine labor pains. If the pains increased in frequency and intensity soon after the woman consumed this *kaṣāyam,* then it was a sure bet that they were real labor pains, and the *kaṣāyam* was credited with speeding up the contractions. If, however, the pains subsided after the woman took the *kaṣāyam,* then the pains were said to have been caused by "heat" *(cūḍḍu vali),* and the *kaṣāyam* was thought to have been effective in diminishing the "heat pains." In general, when people complained of having "heat pains" they were referring to indigestion caused by gas. Ginger is a well-known antidote to gas. In addition to the *kaṣāyams,* some women took milk mixed with plain soda or with a sweet soda drink such as Limca as soon as they felt strong pains; this, too, was thought to determine the nature of the pains, since it was said to either increase labor pains or decrease "heat pains." Coffee was also given to increase labor pains, and in some cases castor oil was consumed to induce labor, but neither of these was used as a diagnostic in the same way that the *kaṣāyams* and soda-based drinks were.

Drinking *kaṣāyams* and other homemade concoctions to speed up labor was not perceived as a substitute for stronger allopathic medicines such as oxytocin drugs. Most women I met were given both, since weaker bodies now required stronger medicines. The *kaṣāyam* served to confirm that labor had begun in earnest, and the oxytocin drugs ensured that it would be over quickly. The widespread use of *kaṣāyams* and other homemade medicines to induce labor seems to have made the ground fertile for the acceptance of allopathic drugs to induce labor.

INSTITUTIONAL CONSTRAINTS

The heavy use of allopathic drugs to induce labor and the infrequent use of anesthesia in public maternity wards cannot be wholly attributed to cultural constructions of womanhood or the use of *kaṣāyams*. There were also very clear political-economic issues which constrained the practices within Tamil Nadu's maternity wards. These economic constraints were due not only to the relative poverty of India as a Third World nation, but also to structures of patriarchy and class within the nation-state and within the state of Tamil Nadu which influenced the distribution of monies for poor women's reproductive health services. The per-capita expenditure for health in India in 1988 was Rs. 57, compared to Rs. 142 for education and Rs. 153 for defense.[37] Per-capita expenditures for health in Tamil Nadu during the same time were slightly higher than for India as a whole. However, per-capita expenditures in family welfare, which encompasses maternal and child health care services, were lower in Tamil Nadu—at Rs. 5.23—than the all-India rate of Rs. 7.19 in the mid-80s.[38] Although these figures are outlays from the mid- to late eighties, they reflect the situation when I began conducting research in 1993.

The large government hospitals in urban centers and even many of the primary health centers in more rural areas were often severely overcrowded. In 1993 there were on average 950 deliveries every month and sometimes as many as fifty deliveries in one day in Madras's Kasthurba Gandhi Hospital.[39] The "normal" (i.e., vaginal) deliveries all took place in one room, so it was common to see four or five women in the final stages of labor at the same time in the same room. In the Chengalpattu Medical College Hospital, another major government hospital located in the smaller city of Chengalpattu, in 1995 there were on average twenty deliveries daily. About sixteen of these were "normal" and took place on four delivery tables in one room.[40] So there, too, women labored side by side in the final stages of delivery. In some of these government hospitals a thin curtain divided the delivery tables for minimal privacy; in others there were no such barriers. The prenatal and postnatal wards in these hospitals consisted of huge open halls in which rows upon rows of women lay right next to one another enduring the pain of early labor or recovering from delivery and breastfeeding their newborns. Often there were not enough cots in the pre- and postnatal wards for all the women, and some were required to lie on thin mats on the floor.

In this context, drugs to induce labor could be seen as a form of crowd control. Ann Oakley, Emily Martin, and others have pointed to the use of drugs to induce labors which, in Europe and the United States, are thought to be "inefficient" in relation to an abstract, scientifically derived "normal" length of labor. In the overcrowded hospitals in Tamil Nadu, however, the concern for efficiency did not seem so abstract, but may at times have arisen from a concrete need to keep women moving from the prenatal ward to the delivery ward to the postnatal ward and out in order to free up space for the steady influx of new women in labor.

Political-economic constraints also contributed to the fact that analgesics were not given to women in these hospitals. In some instances, if the medical staff were unable to sufficiently calm down a woman who was anxious due to the pain she was experiencing, they gave her Valium (diazepam, locally referred to as "Calmpose"). This tranquilizer was given to induce sleep and to relax the woman in labor. It can, however, slow down contractions, so doctors were reluctant to administer it unless it seemed necessary. The goal in administering Valium was to calm down an unruly woman rather than alleviating the pain for her own sake. Doctors working in maternity wards were not trained to administer analgesics other than local anesthesia used for such things as episiotomies.[41] For more powerful analgesics it was necessary to call in the help of a specially trained anesthesiologist. Most public maternity wards in Tamil Nadu, like those in many primary health centers or in small IPP-V corporation hospitals, did not have anesthesiologists in house. In the larger government hospitals which did have an anesthesiologist, that doctor was often so overextended that he could only attend to emergencies, such as cesareans. (Although the majority of the obstetricians working in hospitals in Tamil Nadu were women, the anesthesiologists were typically men.) The severe economic constraints on public maternity hospitals are, of course, not unique to Tamil Nadu or to India. In fact, the situation is far more extreme in some other places. In Jamaica, for example, 25 percent of all deliveries in the country take place in the Victoria Jubilee Hospital. In 1987 due to budgetary shortages 65 percent of the women delivering in that hospital were completely *unattended* by any kind of medical staff, whether they be doctors or nurse-midwives.[42] This is clearly a *global* issue for poor women everywhere. Another political-economic factor which requires further research concerns the role of the pharmaceutical companies marketing both analgesics and oxytocin drugs in India.

EXPRESSING *VALI*

The problem of overcrowding also influenced how the medical staff responded to women's expressions of pain. One of the most common complaints I heard about the large public hospitals was that the nurses and *ayahs* would scold women for yelling out in pain and at times they would go so far as to hit women for making too much noise. Giruja was nineteen when I met her with her mother-in-law at the Santhome IPP-V corporation hospital where she was coming for a prenatal checkup. She had a two-year-old boy who had been born in Kasthurba Gandhi Hospital (Gosha Hospital), and she recounted her experiences there:

Giruja: In Gosha nurses and *ayahs* will scold. Sometimes they will beat women.

CVH: Why?

Giruja: Some of the *ayahs* will yell at us.

Mother-in-law: They are not able to bear the pain. So they will scream. But the nurses and *ayahs* will use dirty words *[keḍḍa vārttai]*, saying, "When you were with your husband you didn't shout out in pain. When you were with your husband didn't you know this would happen? You are shouting now; didn't you know this would happen during the delivery?" They will make faces *[muñci kāḍḍuvāṅka]* and say these things.

CVH: Can't you tell them that you will shout when you feel the pain?

Giruja: No. We can't say anything. Whatever they say, we have to listen. We are in the delivery ward so we have to keep quiet.

CVH: Did they beat you?

Giruja: No. I was clever *[uṣār]*; I didn't shout. I saw so many patients nearby who were being scolded. So I knew that if I shouted I would get the same treatment.

CVH: Why do they say you shouldn't shout?

Giruja: If we shout and make noise they will say not to cry. But if we cry out and make a lot of loud noise and go beyond a limit they get fed up *[veṟumai uṇarvu tōṉṟutal]*. When there's too much noise in the room, four or five people making noise together, then they will scold and beat this way.

Giruja clearly linked the harsh punishment meted out to those women who loudly expressed their pain with the problem of overcrowding and the general need for order in delivery wards where four or five women might be laboring simultaneously.

The snide comments that the pains are the just deserts for women who had indulged in sexual pleasures with their husbands were repeated to me on numerous occasions throughout Tamil Nadu.[43] Some even said that if laboring women called out: "*Amma! Appa!*" (Mother! Father!) the nurses and *ayahs* would ask: "Did your father come and sleep with you?" These condescending comments served to create social distance between the medical staff and the patients and seemed to be derived in part from a general critical discourse on the reproductive practices of the poor.

Studies have shown that emotional support given during delivery helps to relax the birthing woman and consequently reduces the intensity of her pain.[44] Patel's ethnographic study of a Rajasthani village shows that a group of comforting and encouraging female relatives and neighbors surrounding the laboring woman helped to relieve her stress and reduce the intensity of her pain. She writes, "The people around provide mechanisms that effectively prevent the laboring woman from turning hysterical or even losing her calm."[45] Women who were laboring in most large government hospitals in Tamil Nadu, on the other hand, had no such familial or emotional support. No family members or friends were allowed to be present in the delivery ward. Once again, this was partially due to the problems of overcrowding. When four or five women are laboring side by side and the medical staff have to maneuver around and between them, additional people in the room could at times become obstacles. More space is therefore desperately needed to allow for family members to be present. But space was not the only concern. Many medical staff told me that they did not want to be bothered by nosy relations who acted as if they knew what was best for the birthing woman or by relations who got so worried about the birthing woman's health that they themselves needed reassuring. In short, the medical staff wanted to have full control and authority over what transpired in the delivery room, and there was concern that relatives might upset that authority. Often older women were present at home births. They did indeed have their own opinions on how a delivery should be managed and were used to debating such issues with a midwife.

Because women had to labor alone, they felt extremely alienated in the confines of these hospitals. Many women told me that their primary fear of a hospital delivery was the fact that they would have to be alone. In the smaller public maternity wards, such as the Santhome IPP-V corporation hospital, where the boundaries between the delivery ward and the public waiting area consisted of a curtain in the doorway, these rules were not so rigorously enforced. In the large government hospitals, on the other hand, the delivery wards were closed off by heavy doors which were assiduously guarded by strict hospital matrons. There is little doubt that the fear brought on from being alone in these hospitals served to exacerbate the experience of the pain. So although women were frightened into silence, some could not control themselves, and many said there was a greater tendency towards panic in the hospital than at home.

Doctors were rarely implicated in the accounts of medical staffs' intolerance for women's expressions of pain. It was the nurses and, even more commonly, the *ayahs* who were viewed as the perpetrators of these acts of violence. This was not due to the fact that there were no doctors around. For although it is true that deliveries in some smaller public hospitals were often conducted by the nurses and *ayahs,* this was not the case in the large government hospitals, where most of the problems of verbal and physical mistreatment were reported to occur. Rather, doctors were not implicated because the scolding by the *ayahs* and nurses stemmed from issues of professional hierarchy and were sociological in nature.

On the one hand, *ayahs* were taking advantage of the professional power accrued by their being a part of the institutional framework of the medical establishment. They were exerting what Eliot Friedson has called "professional dominance."[46] Since most of the *ayahs* came from a similar class and caste background as the patients, they may have been more inclined to resort to verbal and physical forms of control in order to establish social distance from the patients and thereby gain some authority. In his discussion of "professional authority," Friedson says that in those relatively rare instances in which a patient's social status is superior to that of the physician, "the physician must allow the patient to dominate treatment at the risk of losing them."[47] The situation of the use of "professional dominance" by the *ayahs* varied from this model in two important ways. The *ayahs* did not risk losing patients because the patients were coming primarily for the services of the physician, and also because the *ayahs* were working in public hospitals and most patients had no other options. The situation of the *ayahs* in public maternity wards was more akin to the role of the lowest-level staff in what Erving Goffman has called a "total institution." In his discussion of prison wardens, he writes, "Sharing the culture of the inmates' home world, they can serve as a natural communication channel between high staff and inmates. . . . But, on the same ground, they will have difficulty maintaining social distance from their charges . . . This may merely complicate the warden's role, further opening him to inmate derision and to inmate expectation that he will be decent, reasonable, and corruptible."[48] The *ayahs* responded to this precarious position by resorting to verbal and physical violence to assert their authority. And, far from being corruptible to the patients' benefit, the *ayahs*—viewed as the most corrupt members of the medical staff—extorted bribes from the patients for every small service provided.

It was not only their social proximity to the patients that led *ayahs* to act harshly. It was also the fact that these *ayahs* were at the bottom rung of the social hierarchy *within* the medical profession. They were under extreme pressure to make sure that everything within the hospital ran smoothly. Since they were the first to be blamed for problems or disruptions, they lived in constant fear of becoming scapegoats and being summarily dismissed from their jobs with no legal recourse.

Doctors, too, sometimes exerted their authority by verbally harassing and hitting women whom they considered to be "unruly." One doctor at a government hospital in Railway Colony in Madras explained to me that sometimes it was necessary to control women in these ways and that afterward the patients would thank the doctors for being so firm and would apologize for being "rude" and "uncooperative." Indeed, several women said much the same to me. They giggled with embarrassment as they recounted how loud they had been and said that they were grateful to the doctors for controlling them. Thus, doctors took on parental roles while patients were infantalized.[49]

The notion that women should stoically endure the pain of birth without making too much noise was not confined within the hospital walls. Many said that women delivering at home should refrain from shouting out too loudly because men in nearby houses might hear the screams and moans and that would be embarrassing or unseemly *(aciṅkam)*. Anthropologists have long been interested in cross-cultural studies of the expression and experience of pain during birth. In their cross-cultural study on this subject in 1950 using the Human Relations Area Files, Lawrence Freedman and Vera Ferguson concluded that contrary to earlier theories which stipulated that it was only "civilized" women who felt pain during birth, in fact pain during birth is universal.[50] But they acknowledged that in some cultures great value is placed on exhibiting restraint during birth and cultural psychological techniques have been developed which may in fact mollify the pain.[51] Carolyn Sargent also notes that Bariba women in Benin who often go through labor and deliver their babies all *alone* exhibit intense stoicism and self-discipline during birth with virtually no verbal expression of pain whatsoever. She argues that although behavioral responses should not be viewed as correlates of the severity of the sensation of pain, cultural techniques may indeed reduce the sensation of pain. In particular, she points to the need to overcome fear in order to reduce the sensation of pain.[52]

The women I met in Tamil Nadu tended to emphasize the need for restraint in their homes primarily due to a sense of embarrassment around men. They repeatedly used the word *aciṅkam* to explain this to me. *Aciṅkam* can mean "unseemly" or "gross" in a generic sense, but it usually has the connotation of something dirty. So here women seemed less concerned with controlling expressions of pain to prove their bravery and more concerned with being discreet about a dirty bodily process. This does not negate the fact that the experience of the pain of birth (whether it is expressed or not) is reflective and constitutive of women's *sakti.* One woman from Reddikuppam who had delivered one baby at home and one in a government hospital said she preferred the hospital because in the hospital she could make as much noise as she wanted since she was anonymous there, whereas at home she felt as though she had to control herself more so as not to offend any male neighbors. Whether in the hospital or at home, the motivation to control the expression of pain for the women I met usually seemed to be based primarily on social fears. In such situations, the silencing of discomfort is not likely to reduce the sensation of pain.

The fact that the woman from Reddikuppam felt free to express her pain in the hospital indicates that the forms of verbal and physical control described above were not completely pervasive throughout the government maternity wards. Several women praised the doctors, nurses, and *ayahs* in government hospitals for using soothing tones *(āṟutal col-*

vāṅka), telling them to pray to god and assuring them that they need not worry since the delivery would soon be over. One nurse working in a government hospital said to me: "We may tell them not to shout out too much in order to conserve their energy. But generally we let women cry out in pain. Labor pains are painful. What to do?"

Furthermore, threats to beat women who made too much noise did not in fact always materialize and were sometimes viewed more as maternal gestures of discipline which were intended to tease rather than torment. These were viewed as *maternal* gestures since obstetricians in public maternity wards were almost always women. Even when they were beaten, women sometimes experienced it as a form of caring. In her ethnographic study of love in Tamil culture, Trawick shows that harshness and cruelty *(kaḍumai and koḍumai)* are important modes through which love is expressed and experienced, particularly the love between parents and children. She reports that children often attest to the love an adult has for them by telling stories of being beaten by that adult. She points out that children are beaten to study out of love. And they are even beaten to eat when they are sick. Furthermore, she writes, "Acts embodying the cruelty of love could also and simultaneously be acts hiding its tenderness. Thus, physical affection for children was expressed not through caresses but roughly, in the form of painful pinches, slaps, and tweaks, which left marks or drew blood."[53] The threats and slaps of the medical staff seemed to be experienced sometimes as "professional dominance" and other times as expressions of maternal love. Patients often wavered in ambivalence, uncertain whether to respond with disdain or gratitude. Women tended to interpret the doctors' harshness as a form of caring and the *ayahs*' harshness as abuse, thereby legitimizing the structures of hierarchy within the medical establishment.

Due to the ambivalent responses women had to their treatment in these hospitals, and the fact that women's expressions of pain were controlled in the home as well as the hospital, it would be a gross misrepresentation to suggest that in Tamil Nadu hospital deliveries were repressive and home deliveries were liberating. Nevertheless, the economic constraints which led to problems of overcrowding in government hospitals, combined with the issue of professional dominance, created a situation in which women delivering in public hospitals were being more severely punished for expressing their pain than they would have been in their homes. The woman who told me that she preferred the hospital because of its anonymity was an exception. On the other hand, numerous women told me that one of the factors in their decision *not* to go to a government hospital for their delivery was their fear of being mistreated for expressing their pain.

INVOKING *VALI* AT HOME

In Kaanathur-Reddikuppam it used to be that if a woman remained at home for her delivery, the *maruttuvacci* and female relatives could splash hot water on the woman's hips and give her homemade *kaṣāyams* to try to speed up the labor. If the labor seemed to be protracted, they might pray to their *kula teyvam* (family goddess) or to Desamma[54] to protect the mother and child during the delivery. If the delivery still did not progress, they might summon a local woman known for becoming possessed by a goddess in order to communicate with the goddess and ascertain what the trouble was. In some instances, they might resort to ritualized acts of grinding or pounding paddy, as practiced in many parts of Tamil Nadu.[55] A trained *dai* in a village outside of Kanchipuram described this ritual to me:

> At the time that they begin to feel the labor pains and they are shaking and throbbing in pain *[tuḍikkiṟāṅka]* we will do the ceremony of pounding and kicking the pounding stone *[ammikkal]*.[56] We take a measuring vessel *[padi]* and fill it with paddy and put that in the middle of the room. Then we take the pounding stone and go around the paddy and kick the pounding stone as we go around. Next we take the pounding stone and make it stand up straight in the paddy. As we do this we say to the birthing woman, "Look, you will get the baby quickly today." We kick the stone over and over and pray to god. Many women come and do this. This is good luck for the women who do the ceremony. They will surely have a baby themselves if they do this ceremony for another woman. Sometimes the baby is born only because of this ceremony.

If, however, after a day or two passed and still the baby was not born, women might be transported to Kasthurba Gandhi Hospital in Madras for emergency care. But prior to the late 1960s, when the connecting road to Madras was built, the journey was arduous, and the mother or baby sometimes died en route.

In 1995 women from Kaanathur-Reddikuppam still employed many of these techniques to speed up labor during a home birth. In addition, however, they were increasingly having their labor induced with vitamin B_{12} injections administered by the local pharmacist or with oxytocin drugs administered as either injections or drips in conjunction with glucose by Shahida, the former MPHW who had a private practice overseeing deliveries in the area. As in the public hospitals, it was almost routine for Shahida to accelerate women's labor with oxytocin drugs. This fact not only gave Shahida an air of professionalism, but it also served to fulfill a demand that so many women had come to view as a fundamental right. Several women told me that the only reason they had decided to stay home for their deliveries was that with Shahida they now had access to oxytocin drugs *and* the emotional support of being at home, surrounded by their relatives.

The use of oxytocin injections for home deliveries is not unique to Tamil Nadu. Jeffery et al. reported that over one-third of the women delivering in the North Indian village of Dharmnagri in 1982–1983 received such injections from private male compounders.[57] Jordan's Yucatan study also showed that Mayan midwives were using B_{12} injections to induce labor at home.[58] And Carolyn Sargent and Grace Bascope's more recent study in the Yucatan revealed that midwives are increasingly administering oxytocin during home deliveries. There, too, oxytocin use is viewed as the only thing that gives the midwife specialized knowledge. And they note that local women and midwives share the notion that a speedy delivery is desirable to avoid the risks of prolonged labor.[59] Shahida was, however, not a midwife, but a multipurpose health worker with more generalized medical training akin to a nurse's. I never came across a *maruttuvacci* (trained or untrained) who was administering oxytocin herself in home deliveries. From most women's perspectives, this was the aspect of Shahida's services that distinguished her from the *maruttuvaccis*.

Although people who called Shahida for their deliveries expected to be surrounded by their relatives, Shahida in fact often insisted that most family members be kept out of the room during the delivery as part of her professional persona. Yet, unlike in the hospitals, family members were right on the other side of the often thinly thatched wall or a sari that Shahida set up as a curtain. Ultimately, she was on their turf and had to constantly negotiate between her role as a professional and her need to be accepted by the community. The following story of Kaveri's delivery exemplifies how Shahida was forced to accommodate the desires of a family during a long labor.

• • •

Kaveri was the eighth born of nine children in a Hindu family. She was married when she was about sixteen, and her first baby was born in

1995 when she was around seventeen, though she was not sure of her exact age. Her delivery took place in her mother-in-law's home.

Kaveri began to feel labor pains around three o'clock in the afternoon. So she walked down the road to inform Shahida, whom she referred to as "doctor." Kaveri's family had decided to call Shahida in part because they knew she had "English" medicines. Shahida told Kaveri to go back home, take a hot bath, and wait for some time. Kaveri's mother-in-law made a dried ginger kaṣāyam, *which she drank.*

When Kaveri's husband returned home from work at 8 P.M.*, he went to summon Shahida, who came back with him. Shahida hung saris around the door and windows of the one-room thatched house and insisted on total privacy to conduct the delivery. She immediately gave Kaveri an enema and a shot of oxytocin and asked her to walk around the room. Kaveri's contractions became extremely painful but she was not dilating significantly. Kaveri's mother and mother-in-law were waiting outside along with several other female relatives. Shahida kept administering more and more shots of oxytocin but still the baby was not born.*

The next morning just as the sun began to rise Kaveri's cousin, who had converted to Christianity, grew concerned. She began yelling at Shahida from across the saris, telling her that she was incompetent and that she should let others in to help. Shahida yelled back, telling the cousin not to disturb her and that no one should come in because they might bring in germs. The cousin poured some coconut oil into a cup, took it to the church next door, and asked the priest to bless it. She hurried back to Kaveri and implored her to drink it. Shahida protested, saying this was all superstitious (mūḍanampikkai). *And Kaveri herself refused, fearing that this cousin was practicing Christian magic* (mantiravātam). *But the cousin's resolve was firm and the other relatives waiting outside felt it was worth a try, so Shahida and Kaveri were forced to comply. The cousin began to enter the house with the cup of coconut oil, but Shahida snapped at her and told her to stay outside. Shahida said that Kaveri would be ashamed and get the evil eye* (drishti) *if anyone came in, and she pushed the cousin back out. The cousin handed the cup of coconut oil through the sari curtain and Kaveri drank it up.*

By 8 A.M.*, however, the baby had still not been born despite the numerous shots of oxytocin and the blessed coconut oil. Everyone was exasperated and all the relatives outside agreed to try to ask the goddess to prophesy what would happen. Kaveri's mother's younger sister was summoned since she was known to become possessed by the local* kula teyvam, *known as Tulukandamma. Tulukandamma "came on" Kaveri's aunt, and she began to dance just outside of the house. The aunt held a brass plate with burning camphor in the palm of her hand and circled her head around and around as she danced. Speaking through the aunt, Tulukandamma prophesized that the baby would be born within three hours. Then, in order to cool down the goddess, the aunt ate a handful of* neem *leaves and returned to her normal state.*

A baby boy was born one hour later. Kaveri was in the lithotomy position.[60] *Shahida insisted on this position for all the deliveries she saw. By the time the baby was born, Shahida had administered thirteen shots of oxytocin.*

• • •

This story provides a clear example of how people in Kaanathur-Reddikuppam employed multiple techniques to attempt to speed up labor. It is particularly interesting insofar as it demonstrates the tensions which sometimes arose between allopathic and non-allopathic approaches to managing birth. The most dramatic moment was when Shahida told the cousin to remain on the other side of the curtain so as not to inflict the evil eye. This marks a distinct shift from her previous admonitions to stay out so as to avoid the spread of germs. In the end, Shahida was able to maintain some level of professional dominance by keeping others out of the house, yet she had to use non-allopathic notions of the evil eye to legitimate this distance. Furthermore, she was forced to accept the cousin's demands that Kaveri consume the coconut oil. And ultimately, there was an unspoken assumption among Kaveri's relatives that the presence of Tulukandamma was to be credited for the successful birth of the baby, rather than Shahida's drugs and professional knowledge.

The credit given to Tulukandamma may have also served to establish an unspoken assertion of the supremacy of Hinduism within the community as a whole. This birth seemed to dramatize tensions among Hindu, Christian, and Muslim actors, as well as between biomedical and non-biomedical systems of knowledge. This was, however, never articulated to me as being a religious issue, either because the question of religious conflict is so highly contentious or, to the contrary, because it in fact plays a much less significant role in Tamil Nadu than it does in other parts of India.

The story of Kaveri's birth demonstrates that biomedicine has not attained the level of hegemony that it has in the United States, and its value is continuously debated. But it seems to be debated in partial and uneven ways. For example, many women I met embraced the authority of biomedical knowledge when it came to using drugs to induce labor (and in this case they actually shaped the nature of biomedicine). On the other hand, they also strongly valued non-biomedical notions of health and diet for mother and baby during the postpartum period and resisted attempts by biomedical practitioners to persuade them to give up their dietary practices, as we will see in Chapter Six.

Kalpana Ram's (1998) research on childbirth in the southern regions of Tamil Nadu suggests that women there were more evenly critical of biomedicalized birth than the women in my study. Ram argues that most women preferred to give birth at home with a midwife, partly because they wanted to avoid the condescending attitudes of the hospital staff. Women are also critical of the medical staff's impatience regarding pain, as reflected in rising rates of cesareans and episiotomies, which goes against the Tamil value of women enduring pain.[61] In short, the women in Ram's study in no way appeared to value biomedicalized birth, and their critique was primarily based on the fact that biomedicalized birth has denied them "religiously informed experiences of femininity."[62] My study suggests a messier and more uneven representation of biomedicalized birth on the part of lower-class women in Madras and Kaanathur-Reddikuppam. In my experience, the critiques of biomedical knowledge and practice did not spring only from a concern with cultural constructions of femininity. Furthermore, even when religious notions of femininity informed this discourse, they did so in very complicated ways, given women's common belief that biomedical technologies to induce labor either enhanced *sakti* or helped to revitalize it.

There are serious risks with using allopathic drugs to induce labor without immediate access to emergency care, as was the case in Kaanathur-Reddikuppam. These include uterine rupture and decreased oxygen supply to the baby.[63] Kitzinger explains that extremely powerful contractions, such as those induced by oxytocin drugs, "are likely to interfere with the blood flow through the uterus and so cause fetal distress."[64] If the cervix is not "ripe" and ready for labor and oxytocin is administered, the uterus may not respond to the hormones and it may then be necessary to proceed with a cesarean.[65] Furthermore, Kitzinger writes that if labor is induced, it is critical to monitor contractions using an electro-fetal monitor.[66] Such technology was never used in home deliveries in Tamil Nadu and was rarely available in public maternity wards. Davis-Floyd also points out that these drugs are strong antidiuretics and when given with IV fluids to fasting women, they "can result in water intoxication, which itself heightens the woman's risk of pulmonary edema in those rare cases of gastric aspiration."[67]

Shahida was not alone. Along with the growth of the private health sector in India generally,[68] there was a growing trend in Tamil Nadu for women with training as multipurpose health workers to establish private practices to oversee deliveries in rural and semirural areas. In fact, the Voluntary Health Services MPHW who was working at the VHS mini-health-center in Kaanathur when I began my research left that position to set up a private practice in her home in a rural area about one hour away. She, too, was using oxytocin drugs on a somewhat routine basis. Such in-home MPHW care during deliveries of course can provide a much-needed service. But with women's demands to be induced, stricter forms of monitoring must be established to ensure that these drugs are not abused.

Furthermore, there are costs associated with the trend toward privatization. Not all can afford to pay the fees for private in-home care. An increase in the reliance on the private sector can lead to a decrease in the availability and quality of government-subsidized health care. For the poorest families in Kaanathur-Reddikuppam the cost of a delivery in the government hospitals in Madras was already out of reach, given the combined cost of transportation and the endless bribes demanded by the hospital staff for virtually every service provided. People calculated that the cost of the bribes in the government hospitals for a normal delivery was on average 500 rupees, which was close to the cost of Shahida's services at approximately 600 rupees. The very poor, therefore, continued to use the services of the local midwives who charged 50 rupees or 100 rupees for a girl or boy, respectively, but who had received little or no biomedical training. The rise in the private sector could mean that less effort will be placed on redressing some of these preexisting problems within the public sector.

CONCLUSION

In addition to the potential health risks associated with the routinization of labor-inducing drugs, we need to consider the implications of induced labor on constructions of gender, specifically of maternity. What is at stake for women's cultural identity with the routinization of drugs to induce labor? If women were previously constructed as powerful because of the long, drawn-out pain they experience in childbirth, what happened to that power when that pain was short-lived and no longer naturally produced? The women I met were increasingly dependent on medical technologies to deliver their babies; what was the social and cultural significance of this?

Many critics of medicalization ground their arguments in the work of Ivan Illich, who argued that medicalization is a form of mystification which "expropriates the power of the individual to heal himself and to shape his or her environment."[69] For women in Tamil Nadu, however, the process of mystification was by no means complete, as the story of Kaveri demonstrates. In fact, women were actively engaged in reconstructing their lives and bodies in response to the availability of new drugs. But the process of reconstruction was limited by the class and gender position of these women and the political-economic realities which dictated the nature of their care both at home and in public maternity wards.

The critical question is not whether biomedicalization is controlling or liberating. It can of course be both. I certainly do not want to suggest that nonbiomedicalized births are "natural" and do not involve forms of control, as some romanticized depictions of "traditional" birth suggest.[70] What is interesting is that as women made sense of this form of biomedicalization, they drew radically different conclusions about the relationship between modernity and *sakti*. Using the *same* technology—in this case, oxytocin drugs—some women viewed modernity as increasing and some viewed it as decreasing this female regenerative power. Some women felt that the intensification of pain caused by these modern drugs *increased* their *sakti,* yet others argued that forces of modernity had *depleted* their *sakti,* making it necessary for them to use these drugs. What is significant here is not simply that local context influences the nature of biomedicalization, but that this specific process of biomedicalization has created the space for a new, contentious discourse on *sakti* and a disputed reconceptualization of maternity. The final question which remains is: How might this emergent discourse influence other arenas of social life outside of the realm of reproductive health? How might this process of biomedicalization transform constructions of maternity, and of gender more generally?

The following chapter examines how discourses and projects surrounding population control have also transformed the experience of maternity for lower-class women in Tamil Nadu.

CHAPTER 5

Moving Targets

The Routinization of IUD Insertions in Public Maternity Wards

Foucault has argued that in eighteenth-century Europe "'population,' with its numerical variables of space and chronology, longevity and health, [began] to emerge not only as a problem but as an object of surveillance, analysis, intervention, modification, etc." and that "the project of a technology of population" was therefore initiated.[1] It was during this period that a concern over the health of the "population" became central to the art of governance. And scientific expertise (both social and medical) was deemed essential to this project. David Horn has further suggested that in the nineteenth century the reproductive practices of men and women came to be viewed as a critical site of intervention for the construction of a healthy population.[2] In short, the notion of the reproductive population as a positivistic, quantifiable, and malleable object of governance can be viewed as a distinctive feature of modernity. But how a given population is constructed and the means for fashioning an alternative, ideal population have varied greatly across time and space since the eighteenth century. For example, Horn points out that at the same time that Mussolini was constructing a pronatalist policy in Italy in the early twentieth century, the first World Population Conference in Geneva in 1927 was being chaired by the American birth-control advocate Margaret Sanger.[3]

As discussed in Chapter One, in nineteenth century colonial India, as in other British colonies, pronatalist concerns that high rates of infant and maternal mortality were desecrating populations (particularly the labor class) led to the state's interest in improving maternal and child health care. Ever since independence, however, the drive to reduce population size through family-planning initiatives in India has been of paramount concern at the national and state levels. India was the first country to include family-planning programs in its postcolonial national planning. In this chapter, I examine the particular ways in which this modern preoccupation with controlling reproductive practices in order to construct an ideal population has impacted the experiences of lower-class women in Tamil Nadu during childbirth.

During my research in 1995, medical staff in many of Tamil Nadu's maternity wards were routinely inserting IUDs immediately following deliveries and abortions, often without informing women beforehand and sometimes explicitly against women's wishes. This practice was the manifestation of government policies which established "targets" to "motivate" women to "accept" family-planning methods. As a result, the form and experience of biomedicalized birth was very different in Tamil Nadu than in the West. I emphasize the practice of routine IUD insertions in part because this issue has received very little public attention and because women repeatedly voiced their concerns about it. I argue, however, that despite these concerns, local conceptualizations of the body which emphasized the uniqueness of each body in time and space at times precluded the possibility for collective resistance.

International and national family-planning pressures are, of course, not unique to India. Anthropologists working in other parts of the world have also explored the problematic issues which family-planning programs pose for women's reproductive choices and women's health in general.[4] My study, however, focuses specifically on the ways in which the policies of family planning directly impact women's experiences of and decisions regarding the birth event itself. In 1996 the government of India inaugurated a new policy and promised to put an end to its top-down numerical family planning targets. In 1997 I conducted follow-up research to assess the nature of this change. In this chapter, therefore, I also discuss the motivations, goals, and realities of this policy-in-transition in Tamil Nadu.

THE EMERGENCY

When scholars of India think of how family-planning policies have flouted human rights in India, they usually recall the excesses of Indira Gandhi's Emergency (June 1975–January 1977) and of the campaign of forced sterilization, particularly of men, undertaken by her son Sanjay Gandhi. The strategy behind that campaign was based on a system of family-planning targets which was initiated in the late 1960s. At that time the national family-planning program was incorporated within the MCH program, and government MCH workers were given and required to meet targets to motivate a particular number of men and women to "accept" different kinds of contraceptives. Every month, each health worker was expected to convince a particular number of men and women to undergo sterilization, accept contraceptive pills or condoms, or have an IUD inserted. If these goals, or targets, were met, the health worker could be rewarded with an increase in pay or a promotion. If they were not met, the health worker could be punished by a reduction in pay or by a demotion. Similar numerical targets were established for public hospitals and district and state governments, creating an elaborate system of competition among hospitals and governments for public funding, which could be gained or lost depending on target-achievement rates. The implementation of these policies was a response to increasing pressure by international lending organizations, including the World Bank and USAID, to step up population-control programs as a condition for economic development.[5]

Such policies are based on a neo-Malthusian view of economic development which argues that overpopulation is a cause for poverty rather than a result of poverty.[6] The assumption is that Third World countries, and particularly lower-class communities, are to blame for their "unfettered fertility,"[7] which leads to their poverty. Their fertility, therefore, must be controlled to ensure greater economic prosperity for the families of the poor, for their nations, and for the world as a whole, since the large poor populations in the Third World are considered a drain on the world's resources.

Such neo-Malthusian theories have been convincingly refuted on many levels by scholars and activists in India.[8] Some argue that overpopulation is a result of poverty rather than a cause. Others show that it is not necessarily the poorest of the poor who in fact have the largest families. And many also argue that it is the overconsumption of the First

World which puts the world's resources at risk and not the poor of the Third World. Despite these critiques, neo-Malthusian theories have had and continue to have many proponents who are setting economic development policy. Imrana Qadeer argues that neo-Malthusian theories create the illusion that governments and international organizations are trying to alleviate poverty without their having to actually make any fundamental changes to the global socio-economic order.[9] During the Emergency, family planning became a priority at the top-most level. Government and public officials, as well as public service employees of virtually every type, were directed to fulfill family-planning targets and were penalized for failing to do so. Not only health workers, but also railroad employees, public-school teachers, labor contractors, government ration shopkeepers, policemen, and others were given instructions to motivate a certain number of people to accept various forms of contraception and were penalized if they did not meet their quotas.[10] Many of them eventually resorted to coercive means in order to achieve those targets.[11] The ruling Congress-I party's loss of the elections to the Janata Dal party in 1977 has often been attributed to the coercive family-planning tactics used during the Emergency.[12]

Due to this political fallout, subsequent strategies have focused almost exclusively on women. During the Emergency there were more vasectomies than tubectomies performed. By 1994, 96 percent of all sterilizations in India were done on women.[13] A similar trend is reflected in Tamil Nadu as well. According to the Tamil Nadu Department of Demography, during the 1970s there were more vasectomies than tubectomies performed. But from the 1980s onward the emphasis shifted dramatically toward the sterilization of women. Department records show that for the fiscal year 1994–1995 in Tamil Nadu there were 280,938 tubectomies, 44,362 laproscopic sterilizations for women, and 580 vasectomies. Of these three sterilization methods, vasectomies are by far the simplest and quickest operations, requiring the least amount of recovery time.

Since the early 1980s the family-planning tactics have not been as draconian as they were during the Emergency; but the system of targets continued, though it was confined to the health sector. Targets were set for MPHWs, hospitals, zones, districts, and states. Punishments and rewards were meted out based on "target achievement rates." The state of Tamil Nadu provided monetary incentives for male and female sterilization and IUD insertions and for those who "motivated" these men and women to "accept" these methods. In 1995, men who accepted vasectomies were to be given Rs. 105, and those who "motivated" them were to receive Rs. 50. Similarly, women who agreed to undergo sterilization could receive Rs. 160, their "motivators," Rs. 50. A purely "self-motivated" woman could therefore receive Rs. 210. Rs. 11.50 was given to a woman who accepted an IUD. In 1995 the government claimed that these monies should not be viewed as incentives but rather as compensation for loss of work time. In reality these schemes were neither incentives to opt for family planning nor compensation for loss of work, because the amount of money extorted in bribes or tips within these hospitals was usually much greater than the amount of money given to the patients.

The people who could benefit somewhat from these schemes were the health workers who "motivated" women to accept various forms of family planning. Conflicts frequently arose between two health workers, particularly between governmental and nongovernmental health workers in the same locale, both of whom claimed that they were the real "motivators" of a particular woman. In some places, if a woman chose to go to a private clinic for sterilization the MPHW working in that woman's area tried to get a certificate of proof that she herself had motivated that woman. In other places the MPHW automatically received compensation for any woman within her jurisdiction who underwent sterilization.

In addition to the monetary incentives for the health workers to get "acceptors," these health workers continued to be haunted by the need to achieve targets for family-planning acceptors. If they did not achieve their targets, their pay was sometimes cut. This target system worked at all levels of the health structure. Each health post, hospital, and zone was also given a set of targets to achieve. These institutions were given monetary compensation for reaching targets, or their allocations of money were cut if they failed to reach their targets. For example, within the All-India Hospitals Postpartum Programme a "sterilization bed scheme" was implemented, wherein the government provided hospitals with a certain annual rupee-outlay-per-bed provided that the hospitals performed a certain number of tubectomies per bed each year.[14] The family-planning "performances" of various districts within the states were also noted and ranked by the state government, and prizes were given accordingly, and the central government distributed prizes to individual states based on their "performance." The government of Tamil Nadu had often received crores of rupees (one crore equals 10 million rupees) from the central government for winning first or second place.[15]

The system of targets was supplemented by an equally elaborate state propaganda machine under the rubric of an information, education, and communication (IEC) program, which in 1995 was funded and administered by the World Bank's IPP-V program. According to the State Family Welfare Bureau of Tamil Nadu, the IEC strategy "aims at creating more demands for various kinds of family welfare services and greater involvement of the community by providing additional and differential Information, Education and Communication inputs with reference to backwardness and resistance prevailing in various areas."[16] Using various forms of media, IEC propaganda attempts to convince women and men of the value of the "small family norm" (two children per family) to individuals, families, women, the state, and the nation. A health administrator put it very succinctly when he told me (in English), "We are insisting on sterilization after two children. We also encourage use of the IUD for three years' spacing. If they don't accept family planning we may have to brainwash them better." Although these words may sound extreme, I found this reformist sentiment to be quite widespread, particularly among MPHWs who were given the mandate to "motivate" women to accept these family-planning methods.

THE ALL-INDIA HOSPITALS POSTPARTUM PROGRAMME

In 1995 the state's tactics were not confined to propaganda and the establishment of targets alone; they also included pressure and coercion. But these tactics were no longer being practiced in an overt, public way as they were with the sterilization "camps" during the Emergency. They were now being carried out on delivery tables immediately following childbirth or abortions, within the confines of public maternity wards.

The All-India Hospitals Postpartum Programme was established in 1970 as a "maternity centered hospital approach to Family Welfare" in national, state, and district hospitals. The program was later extended to the subdistrict *(taluk)* hospitals as well. The program's mandate was "to motivate women within the reproductive age group (ages 15–44) or their husbands for adopting the Small Family Norm through education and motivation particularly during prenatal, natal, and postnatal periods."[17] This program was also intended to supplement other MCH programs, such as immunization and the distribution of iron pills, within the hospital. But its primary goal, as stated in *The Family Welfare Program in Tamil Nadu: Year Book 1989–90,* was to involve the entire hospital staff attending to obstetric and abortion cases in the family-planning campaign.

It was within this program that targets were set for the "acceptance" of various forms of family planning by postpartum and postabortion patients coming to these hospitals. According to the demographer for the Tamil Nadu Department of Family Welfare, in 1995 the goal was that 70 percent of all women leaving the hospital after delivery be covered by some family-planning method, namely sterilization or an IUD.[18] A maternity assistant working in one of the IPP-V health posts in Madurai explained to me that they try to encourage women to prolong their stay in the hospital after delivery so that there will be ample time to "motivate" them. As she said:

> After delivery women stay a minimum of three days. We try to keep them here for one week. Village people want to go home right away because they need to take care of their family. We get them to sign some paper stating that we are not responsible for complications like postpartum hemorrhage. So most will stay for one week. If they stay one week it is good because we can motivate them to get sterilized. Some are afraid of getting sterilized so they go back within three days.

For many years American women were forced to return home within one day of a normal delivery because their insurance policies covered only such short hospital stays. On September 26, 1996, a bill was passed in the United States ensuring forty-eight-hour hospital stays for mothers and newborns after normal delivery and up to four days after cesareans. This was viewed as a major victory for women. In India many women stay in the postpartum ward for three to five days after a normal delivery and up to a week following a cesarean, at relatively low cost. While this seemed very humane to me initially, repeated comments like those of the maternity assistant above made me realize that even this issue of hospital stay seemed to be driven as much by the family-planning agenda as by a concern for women's health and well-being.

Health administrators claimed that family-planning procedures were integrated into the postpartum ward as a convenience to women, who can get both of their needs met at one time. Although it is true that some women may indeed find this to be a convenience, others find it extremely inconvenient when the family-planning element is presented not as an option but as a government-mandated policy. Although the All-India Hospitals Postpartum Programme was initiated prior to the Emergency, I suggest that following the resistance against the Emergency's vasectomy "camps," this program provided the site within which covert and coercive family-planning practices could continue.

FAMILY PLANNING IN TAMIL NADU: A STATISTICAL SUCCESS

Tamil Nadu has undoubtedly been successful in regulating population growth vis-à-vis the nation as a whole. A comparison of total fertility rates (TFR) is indicative of the state's family-planning "success." According to one report, in 1995 the TFR for Tamil Nadu was 2.2, the national TFR was 3.6, and the TFR for the state of Uttar Pradesh was 5.1.[19] Furthermore, by 1995 the disparity between urban and rural TFRs was much less significant in Tamil Nadu than in the nation as a whole. Another report states that the national urban TFR was 2.7 and the national rural TFR 3.7, indicating 36 percent higher rates in rural areas.[20] In Tamil Nadu, on the other hand, the urban TFR was 2.4 and the rural TFR was 2.5.[21]

Tamil Nadu's "couple protection" record was so impressive in 1990 that the government of India set different contraceptive target goals for Tamil Nadu than for the nation as a whole.[22] What the nation was to achieve by the year 2000, Tamil Nadu was to achieve by 1991–1992.[23] It is important to note that many statistics for Tamil Nadu show well over 100 percent "achievement" of targets for IUD "acceptors," whereas the achievement of targets for other forms of contraception fall short of 100 percent. The statistics for the IPP-V Santhome hospital zone in Madras show that for 1994–1995 the achievement for the IUD target was 145.9 percent, whereas for sterilization it was 73.9 percent, for oral pill use it was 83.9 percent, and for condom use it was 68.9 percent.[24] A comparison with IUD target "achievements" in other states is also interesting. During 1986–1987, Tamil Nadu reached 197.7 percent of its IUD-acceptor target, and in 1987–1988 the state reached 171.4 percent of its target. For both years the state far exceeded the targets of all other states and union territories.[25] In 1988–1989, Tamil Nadu's IUD success rate dipped to 101.2 percent and was no longer the highest of all states, but the numerical targets for Tamil Nadu were more than double those of 1986–1987, whereas other states' targets were not increased so dramatically.[26] Given that a high percentage of deliveries in Tamil Nadu took place in hospitals (as compared with the national averages) and given the All-India Hospitals Postpartum Programme's emphasis on maternity wards as a site for implementing the family-planning program, it is no wonder that Tamil Nadu had had such high rates of success in its family-planning program. The fact that it had been particularly successful with respect to rates of IUD "acceptance" seems to be clearly linked with the practice of routine IUD insertion following delivery and abortion.

THE ROUTINIZATION OF IUD INSERTIONS

This historical background is necessary for understanding the situation for lower-income women in Tamil Nadu in 1995 who were delivering their babies in public maternity wards. By 1995 many women in Tamil Nadu were indeed accepting and choosing to use various forms of contraception, including IUDs. And many did so without major complications. The Tamil phrase used for family planning is *kuḍumpak-kaḍḍuppāḍu*. *Kudumpam* means "family," and *kaḍḍuppāḍu* means "self-control" and is also translated as "bounden duty; obligation; and indebtedness."[27] This phrase is understood as the duty of the family to curb reproduction for the sake of the family itself, the state, and the nation. Many women had internalized these moral prerogatives. And many others opted to use modern contraceptive methods for the sake of their own health and well-being. Policymakers and others have indeed argued that Tamil Nadu's "success" in reducing fertility rates is attributable to the "cooperative" nature of the family-planning campaign.[28]

Yet there were also many women who did not choose to use IUDs for a variety of reasons but who nevertheless received IUDs through routine insertions. Some of these women were in fact satisfied with this routine procedure, since they did not want to get pregnant again soon anyway and they did not experience any negative side effects from the IUDs. Other women, however, suffered socially, psychologically, and physically as a result of the routinization of IUD insertion following deliveries and abortions. Therefore, I agree with Swaminathan that the family-planning tactics in Tamil Nadu cannot be summarily described as "cooperative."[29] These negative experiences became factors in women's decisions regarding where to seek care for deliveries and abortions, sometimes dissuading women from using hospital services at all or forcing women with little economic means to seek care in private hospitals. The following accounts demonstrate the scope of the problem.

The Experiences of Women as Patients

The following conversation took place in Nochikuppam in 1995. The women participating were Kasthuri, a young mother named Selvi and a middle-aged woman named Thilakkam, both of whom also lived in Nochikuppam, myself, and Annette. (In Tamil Nadu an IUD is commonly referred to using the English terms "loop" or "copper T" in reference to its shape and make.)

Kasthuri: They don't tell us before putting in the "loop." They don't ask us. When we are a little unconscious they put it. As soon as the delivery is over they come and ask whether we will get operated. Suppose we say yes, they'll tell us to put the signature. If not they'll put the "loop" and send us. They will not ask us whether we want a "loop" or not.

CVH: What if we don't want the "loop"?

Kasthuri: No, we cannot say like that. They will not ask us. Even if we say we don't want it, they will start up again saying, "Why should we listen to you? This is the government law so if you want to get the operation you tell us and we'll remove it." The minute the baby is born they will insert the "loop." They put their hand to remove the placenta and they put the stitches [episiotomy]; at that time itself they put the "loop" and send us to the ward after fifteen minutes. If there are ten cases in the ward, for all ten they have to put it. Even if they forget for one or two they'll record it as if they have put the "loop."

CVH: Do you think it is good that without your permission they are inserting the "loop"?

Kasthuri: It is good. But for some people it becomes difficult *[kaṣḍam]*. For some people it does not agree *[ottuvarātu]*.

Selvi: I was having pains for eight months after my first delivery. I was bleeding a lot. When I went for checkups they told me nothing was wrong. Finally I went to a private hospital. They told me I had a "loop" and removed it for Rs. 30. For eight months I had a "loop" without knowing it. For those eight months I was using *nirodh* [condoms] which these health workers gave me.

Thilak: If she had gotten it removed in the government hospital she could have saved Rs. 30.

Kasthuri: Only for putting the "loop" you can go to the government hospital. It is very difficult to get them to remove it. You *can* get them to remove it but you should have proper reasons for removing it. There must be something wrong with it. They don't simply remove it. In the private hospital if you give Rs. 30 they will remove it. They are not bothered whether you have the next baby.

Thilak: There was a girl who delivered her first baby at Gosha Hospital. They put a "loop" but she didn't know that they had put a "loop." For two years she did not conceive so she thought she must have a "loop" and she went back to Gosha to have it removed. They told her there was no "loop." Two more years passed and still she did not conceive. Her husband and her mother-in-law started mistreating her, saying they would find another wife. Finally, she went to a private clinic. They took a "scan," found the "loop" and removed it. She conceived again right away.

Habiba was a thirty-two-year-old Muslim woman from Bapu Mastan Dargha. She had had a love marriage with a Hindu man when she was fifteen years old and since their families did not approve of the marriage, they were living on their own. When I met her in 1995 she had seven children ranging from ages sixteen to three months. All seven children had been born in Kasthurba Gandhi Hospital. She had not used any family-planning method until after her sixth child, when she had had an IUD inserted. After her seventh child she had undergone sterilization. I asked her to describe the events of her last delivery.

CVH: When did the pains come for the last baby?

Habiba: In the last, the tenth month of my pregnancy, on Thursday morning at 8 A.M., my water bag *[panikkuḍam]* burst. I took no notice. I changed my sari three times because of all the water. It had not happened like this for any other baby. There was a little pain. Suddenly my stomach became lighter and dropped down because the water had come out. At 12 midnight the pain increased. After 12 midnight I knew I had to go to the hospital definitely. So I poured hot water on my hips and went with my sister-in-law and my husband to the street to call an auto-rickshaw.

Annette: Why did you wait such a long time before going to the hospital?

Habiba: I had to make sure that the baby was going to be born. I do not like to go to the hospital unnecessarily.

It was 1:30 A.M. when we reached the hospital. The doctor said the baby would be born by 3 A.M. The doctor scolded me for being so late. They wanted to know why I had not come for help earlier. They cleaned and shaved me and gave me an enema and sent me to the labor ward. I had a friend who was working as a "sister" [nurse] there and she took me to a bed. I was not shouting. The doctors were attending on others who were in pain. No one was there with me because I was quiet. All at once I had a strong pain; I shouted and pushed down and the baby was born. Only then did the doctor come to attend on me.

When I had first come to the hospital I had told them that I only had three children—two sons and a daughter. I didn't want to tell them I already had six children because I was afraid they would beat and scold me. But when the baby was born, the nurses and doctors were surprised that I made no fuss and that I had managed the delivery myself. And they began to have a doubt, thinking that maybe I had more than three children.

I had also told them that I wanted to undergo sterilization following this delivery. But after the delivery they told me I was very anemic and because of that they would not be able to do the sterilization operation right away. So they wanted to insert a "loop." I told them that I did not want the "loop" because I was going to get sterilized. But they did not ask me for my opinion; they put the "loop."

Then my nurse friend came by and said, "How can you say that she should put the 'loop' when she has seven children?!" That way the doctors came to know that I had so many children. When they knew I had seven children they said I shouldn't use the "loop" but they decided to leave it in and said I could get it removed when I got operated.

CVH: What do you think about the fact that they are putting the "loop" in for everybody after childbirth?

Habiba: I think it is good. It will prevent pregnancies. But it is better if they consult the mother first. If she has five or six children it is good to have the "loop." But for those of us who want to be sterilized, they should not put the "loop."

Habiba was sterilized four days later. They removed the IUD before performing the operation. Some women, however, told me of instances where the hospital staff had failed to remove IUDs prior to performing the sterilization operations. The following story of Manjula, a Nochikuppam mother of two children, both of whom were born in Kasthurba Gandhi Hospital, gives evidence of forced IUD insertion *and* failure to remove the IUD prior to sterilization, which itself was forced upon her by her husband and the medical staff.

• • •

I didn't have any children for the first five years after my marriage. After my first child [a girl] was born I had a "loop" put in. It fell out but I didn't know that it had fallen out and soon I got pregnant again.

After my second baby was born, while I was in the hospital the doctors wanted me to get sterilized. I was on the delivery table and said, "No! I want a boy." They said, "What if the third is a girl?" So they put a "loop" without saying anything about it. Then my husband gave his consent and forced me to get sterilized on the third day. He said that it was too expensive to have more children, to dress and educate all of them. At the time of the operation they didn't take out the "loop." One year later, after my first period, I was having stomach pains and went to see Komala [WWF health worker]. Komala realized that I had a "loop" and she removed it herself.

• • •

This story underscores the fact that not only the medical staff but husbands, too (as well as other family members), sometimes take decisions about women's reproductive bodies into their own hands.

Janaki also complained to me about the fact that the doctors in Kasthurba Gandhi Government Hospital had inserted an IUD against her will. In her case this was following not a delivery but a miscarriage. She was married when she was sixteen years old and had four miscarriages before she finally gave birth to twins by cesarean. After the third and fourth miscarriages, the hospital staff had insisted on inserting an IUD. But she told them she didn't want the IUD because she hadn't even had a baby yet. They told her it was good to postpone the pregnancy so that her uterus would have time to recover and get stronger after the miscarriage. Still she refused, saying it would cause her abdominal pain. She said that they repeatedly beat her when she refused, and they went ahead and inserted the IUD each time. And each time she went to a private hospital and paid to get the IUD removed. So when she conceived again the fifth time she refused to go to back to Kasthurba Gandhi Hospital. Instead she went to the Santhome corporation hospital.

One day Kasthuri and I were sitting on the steps of her housing block when a young woman named Chandira came running up to us out of breath. She held a baby in her arms:

Chandira: This child is seven months old. She was born in Gosha Hospital. They have sent me home without a "loop" and now I am pregnant again!

Kasthuri: How long have your periods been overdue?

Chandira: It's been two months now. I had a cesarean. I thought they had put the "loop." Don't they put the "loop" for everyone? I thought they had put it and I was careless.

They will not abort the baby now. I went to Gosha. They said that if they do "MTP" [medical termination of pregnancy, i.e., abortion] the uterus will get perforated, or they may have to do a hysterectomy. I said that I would sign the papers. But they said I must sign a paper saying I don't want another child ever. So my husband and I hesitated and came away. We decided to see a private doctor even if it is expensive.

Chandira's story points to another situation, namely abortions in public hospitals, in which IUDs are often inserted against the will of women and in which women are often pressured into "accepting" sterilization. Although abortions are performed free of charge, the doctors and nurses in the IPP-V Santhome corporation hospital informed me in 1995 that IPP-V hospitals throughout Tamil Nadu stipulated that they would only perform an abortion if the woman accepts one of two family-planning methods: either an IUD after one child or sterilization after two or more.

The Medical Termination of Pregnancy Act of 1971 legalized abortion in India. In 1995 there were approximately 50,000 officially recorded abortions performed every year in Tamil Nadu.[30] The actual number would in fact have to have been much higher due to the fact that many women were getting abortions outside of biomedical institutions and many doctors who were not licensed to perform abortions were performing them unofficially. Abortions were being performed free of charge in 166 public hospitals throughout Tamil Nadu. Yet many preferred to go to private hospitals and pay for their abortions.

One of the reasons that women preferred the private clinics was that many of the public hospitals stipulated that they would only perform an abortion if the woman accepted an IUD or sterilization, as Chandira's case above shows. As stated in the *Year Book 1989–90* published by the Tamil Nadu Family Welfare Bureau, Directorate of Medical and Rural Health Services, "It has been found that 86 percent of women undergoing medical termination of pregnancy accept sterilizations, making it an effective intervention."[31] In 1995, most hospitals were advocating the use of an IUD as a spacing mechanism following an abortion. Some women who did not want the IUD still opted to go to one of these public hospitals for a free and safe abortion, knowing that they could easily have the IUD removed for a minimal cost at a private clinic. Others, however, refused to go to the public hospital for an abortion because of the strict family-planning policy attached. They would, therefore, either go to a licensed private clinic or get the abortion done more cheaply by an unlicensed person, often with serious medical consequences.

Moving Targets: Medical Practitioners' Views

The following excerpts of interviews in 1995 with hospital personnel who were working or had worked in hospitals where routine insertion was practiced reveal that many of them did not give a second thought to the fact that they were inserting IUDs without women's consent. As they saw it, they were just doing their jobs, meeting the targets laid down for them.

Interview with a doctor from the IPP-V Thousand Lights Hospital, Madras (in English):

CVH: Do you usually put in a loop after the first delivery?

Doctor: A copper-T on the day they go home. Earlier we did it after the placenta was expelled. This way the patients are comfortable. Those who don't undergo sterilization get a copper-T.

CVH: Do they ask for it?

Doctor: We brainwash them from the start. One or two flatly refuse. We tell them after insertion and then get their signatures. They have to return after a week for a checkup.

Interview with a doctor from the Santhome IPP-V hospital, Madras (in English):

Doctor: Most women coming to the hospital are aware of family planning. Only about 10 percent are resistant. We will not routinely insert an IUD. We try to get women to accept an IUD on the fifteenth day after delivery when they come for their first postnatal visit. Actually we are supposed to do it before they are discharged, but to avoid the risk of expulsion [i.e., the risk that the IUD will fall out] we do it on the fifteenth day. This is possible now as it is only now that women themselves are motivated. In the government hospitals they routinely insert IUDs. Sometimes they even insert two without realizing it—one in the delivery ward and one in the postnatal ward! I know because I have done it myself, when I was working as a doctor there. The patient doesn't know about it. . . . This was three years ago. Why? Because we are given targets. Patients who have an IUD inserted in Gosha Hospital often get referred to Santhome if they have problems. At Santhome we will check and correct the IUD but we will not remove it unless there is a problem. For removal we tell them they should go back to the government hospital but they won't go back to the government hospital because they know they will not remove it there. Instead they go to a private clinic to have it removed. . . . Problems do happen with IUDs because women often don't come for checkups.

Interview with a public health nurse from the IPP-V Santhome hospital, Madras (in English):

Nurse: Every woman who delivers at Santhome will get an IUD inserted immediately after birth if they are not getting sterilized. This is compulsory. Many women will then get them removed at a private hospital because they don't like the idea of having a foreign object in their body.

Interview with a maternity assistant (nurse) from IPP-V Santhome hospital, Madras:

Nurse: At delivery time we try to compel women to get the "loop" put in, at least within forty-five days after delivery. At Kasthurba Gandhi Hospital they put the "loop" immediately after the delivery before the woman goes to the maternity ward, while she is still on the delivery table. This is because there are so many patients at Kasthurba Gandhi Hospital so there is no time to ask ahead of time so they just put it. Sometimes it will fall out. Some people then come to the Santhome corporation hospital saying that their "loop" is causing them to have stomach aches and causing their body to be

> weak, so they ask to have the "loop" removed. Often it has already fallen out. At Santhome hospital we put the "loop" on the third day after delivery. We ask the woman if she wants it. If not we say okay, but we follow up with MPHW motivation to try to get them to accept it within forty-five days. This is another difference between the corporation hospital approach and government hospital approach. For those women who deliver at government hospitals there is no follow-up visit to try to motivate women after they leave the hospital. So there is a sense that they just need to insert the IUD right away because there will be no second chance. Whereas at the corporation hospitals we have MPHWs to do follow-up work.

Interview with a doctor from the Chengalpattu Medical College Government Hospital (in English):

Doctor: When I worked at Gosha Hospital we always put a loop in as soon as the baby was delivered. In some cases we would even put in two loops by a mistake! Here it is not possible to put in the loop without the woman's permission because here in the *mofussil* [rural districts] the families will complain. We are more restricted here than in Gosha or the other large government hospitals in Madras where they don't have to worry about what other people will say.

It is important to note that there is variation among hospitals regarding the extent to which they insert IUDs without consent. Women in both Madras and Kaannathur-Reddikuppam, as well as NGO and government health workers in Madras and other cities throughout Tamil Nadu, informed me that in general it was the largest government hospitals under the control of the director of medical education in the largest urban centers, such as Madras, which had a reputation for these practices. Women using the smaller IPP-V corporation hospitals in Madras as well as the primary health centers outside of Madras, and even the larger government hospitals located in smaller cities such as nearby Chengalpattu, did not complain of routine insertions as frequently as did those women who used the large government hospitals in Madras.

In fact, when I broached this issue with doctors and nurses working in these other types of hospitals they often spoke with envy about the fact that the staff working in the government hospitals in Madras *could* routinely insert IUDs without consent because the government hospital staffs did not feel accountable for their actions to the communities they served. These other hospitals placed outreach workers in the communities which they served, and these workers were in constant personal contact with the women who used the hospitals and with these women's families. The lack of an outreach system attached to the large government hospitals in Madras was also seen as a justification for routine insertion of IUDs immediately following birth, because of the fact that there was no mechanism by which these large hospitals could trace their patients and try to "motivate" them after they left the walls of the hospital. They viewed women who had left the hospital as "moving targets" which were difficult to reach. It was, therefore, the anonymity of the large institution as well as the anonymity of the population it served that led to more covert and coercive practices with regard to IUD insertions.

Although most of the patients and medical practitioners who told me of this routine practice were referring to hospitals in Madras, and particularly to Madras's Kasthurba Gandhi Hospital, two women's NGOs working in Tamil Nadu provided corroborative evidence that routine IUD insertion was taking place in other parts of Tamil Nadu as well. Based on their own study of the quality of family-planning services in three rural sites around the town of Chengalpattu, the Rural Women's Social Education Centre (RUWSEC) reported that:

> . . . the incidence of involuntary "acceptance" of a method of contraception—the epitome of lack of choice—was not uncommon. This was especially true in the case of IUD insertions . . . Vijayalakshmi, who had pain and heavy menstrual bleeding following insertion of an IUD without her knowledge after her first delivery, went to a private doctor, who charged 50 rupees to remove the IUD. "After some days, I had unbearable pain; my cousin took me to Madras for a checkup with a doctor . . . The doctor said that the T part of the IUD was stuck in the cervical canal."[32]

The Working Women's Forum collected data in Madras, Kanchipuram, Vellore, Dindigul and Adiramapattinam which point to widespread routine IUD insertion in cities and towns throughout Tamil Nadu. From April 1990 to March 1995, among women participating in WWF activities in these five cities, there were 15,704 women who "accepted" IUDs. Of the 8,770 women whose IUDs were inserted after their first deliveries, 5,714 (65 percent) had not known of the insertions. Of the 5,604 who accepted IUDs after their second deliveries, nearly 2,337 (42 percent) reported they had not been given a choice and would have preferred sterilization. From March 1995 to December 1996, 52 percent of the 2,343 women who reported they had had an IUD inserted (in the same five cities plus the town of Dharmapuri) said they had not been given any option.[33]

MEDICAL RISKS AND LOCAL CONCEPTIONS OF THE BODY

Many negative side effects are associated with the use of IUDs. Among the most serious complications is the possibility of developing pelvic inflammatory disease (PID) which can lead to infertility. PID can occur with an IUD when a preexisting lower tract infection is not treated; the process of IUD insertion carries the infection into the upper tract. PID can also occur if the IUD or the IUD inserter is not sterile.[34] Studies in Tamil Nadu and elsewhere in India suggest that the rates of genital tract infections are very high among low-income communities. Some researchers have documented that women are frequently not checked for lower tract infections at the time of IUD insertions, and their health is jeopardized as a result.[35] Because PID can lead to infertility, IUDs in the United States are generally only recommended as an alternative to sterilization for women who do not plan to have any more children. In Tamil Nadu, on the other hand, the IUD is advocated as a spacing method.[36]

Less-serious but more-common side effects of IUD use are an increase in menstrual bleeding, painful cramps, and backaches. I frequently heard women complain of these side effects. Many said that they had not been informed by the medical staff that such side effects or more serious complications might result from IUD insertions. Indeed many did not know they had had an IUD inserted until they began to experience such problems. Others said that they had simply been informed by the medical staff that for some women the IUD "does not agree" *(ottuvarātu),* but they were not told what the signs of "lack of agreement" were and what to do in the event that their IUD "did not agree." Indeed, there was a general consensus among the women I met that for some women the IUD simply "does not agree." And those women for whom it did not agree usually opted to have it removed if their bodies had not already rejected it. As noted above, women sometimes faced barriers to having IUDs removed in a public hospital, and they sometimes had to pay to have them removed in a private clinic or by a less-trained person within the community for a reduced fee.

This notion of the IUD "not agreeing" with a particular individual is, I argue, an extension of a local concept of the uniqueness of each body in a given place and time.[37] Ayurveda and Siddha systems of medicine, which are closely related to one another and are widely practiced throughout Tamil Nadu, include humoral theories of the body based on three humors, or three "defects," known collectively as *tridosa.* In Siddha medicine (which is unique to Tamil Nadu) these three *dosas* are: *vatham* (corresponding loosely to the Greek humor of "wind"), which is the source of motion in the body; *pittam* (corresponding loosely to the Greek humor of bile), which is the source of heat, cooking the body; and *kabam* (corresponding loosely to the Greek humor of phlegm), which is the connective *dosa* in the body.[38] In Siddha theories of medicine a healthy body should generally have the following ratios of these *dosas: vatham:* 1, *pittam:* 1/2, and *kabam:* 1/4. The ratio can be detected through the pulse, but it fluctuates throughout women's reproductive life cycles.[39] In Tamil Nadu theories of *tridosa* are combined with cultural notions of "hot" and "cold" qualities, creating a conception of each body as a unique composition of *dosas* and of "hot" and "cold" qualities based on numerous factors such as caste, native place, sex, life cycle, diet, mental and moral attitude, and astrology.[40] Within this conceptualization, health *(cukam)* is understood as the state of balance between *dosas* and between "hot" and "cold" qualities. Each person's means of attaining and maintaining *cukam,* such as the diet one takes, will therefore vary. Illness is caused by a lack of balance because one *dosa* becomes dominant, or "angry,"[41] or because the body becomes overly "hot" or overly "cold." As Srinivasmurthi states:

> It seems the *tridosha* theory looks at the question from the standpoint of the soil, while the germ theory looks at it from the standpoint of the seed.
>
> "Keep out the seed—away with all germs and you are safe"—that is the slogan of the germ enthusiast. "It seems impracticable to keep out germ seeds which are ubiquitous. Therefore keep the soil in such a condition that no seed can grow, even if it gets there." So urges the Ayurvedist.[42]

Since each person has a unique composition and since illness is caused by the predominance of one *dosa* or of either "hot" or "cold" qualities, each individual's treatment must be compatible not only with that individual but also with the particular time and place within which the individual is situated. While biomedical conceptions of the body also include a notion that each body is unique, that uniqueness is usually attributed only to biology itself rather than to other social, environmental, and cosmological factors.

In his book *Fluid Signs: Being a Person the Tamil Way,* Valentine Daniel suggests that this "person-centric" concept and the search for compatibility of substances (between people, places, houses, etc.) is a fundamental part of "Hindu culture." As he writes in his discussion on the concept of *conta ūr* (native place):

> This person-centric definition of space is in keeping with the person-centric orientation of Hindu culture. For instance, there is no *dharma* (code of conduct), no unit of time, no food or soil that is moral or good for all persons. Even as moral laws are not universal and vary according to *jati,* stage of life, individual life circumstances, and so on, so there is no universal rule for what kinds of food are most compatible with all people.[43]

Although I find the term "Hindu culture" to be highly problematic for its being simultaneously overly inclusive and overly exclusive, I did find that women and men whom I met in Tamil Nadu, both rich and poor, Hindu, Muslim, and Christian, did hold this conception of the self and health while simultaneously holding many other conceptualizations, including allopathic notions of health.

In my discussions with women they almost always conceptualized their experiences with IUDs within this framework of compatibility or lack thereof. Sometimes women specifically said that IUDs are "hot" and therefore may cause problems for women who are already "hot" or for women who may become "hot" while the IUDs are inside their bodies. Other times, the connection between *dosas* or "hot" and "cold" was not made so explicitly, but the overall conceptualization of "not agreeing" was employed. And yet, when I asked a Siddha practitioner at the Tamil Nadu government's Anna Hospital for indigenous medicine, in Arumbakkam, Madras, about the "heating" quality of IUDs, he told me that this was all "psychological." The real problems which women faced from IUD use, he explained, were due to improper care.

When women conceptualize IUD problems within this framework of compatibility, the medical risks of IUD use do not become generalizable. Too often women come to know of problems associated with IUDs after it is too late, after they have tried the IUD to see if it would be compatible with their unique bodies in a given time and place. As Kasthuri said, "It is good. But for some people it becomes difficult. For some people it does not agree." Furthermore, this framework is not conducive to collective action against routine insertion. This is not simply a matter of culture preventing effective forms of resistance. Despite the Siddha doctor's critique of applying *tridosa* theory to IUDs, many of the medical staff I met used this logic when trying to "motivate" women to accept IUDs, thereby exempting themselves from criticism when problems arose. I am not suggesting that the health staff are strategically using this cultural conception of the body as a means to prevent resistance. For they themselves often hold the same cultural conception along with allopathic models of the body. What this demonstrates is that particular cultural conceptions do come to serve political purposes even when the actors are not consciously selecting them and using them to achieve those ends.

IMPACT OF THE REPRODUCTIVE HEALTH CARE POLICY

Women's NGOs in the region, such as the WWF and the RUWSEC, however, have taken the initiative to lobby against routine IUD insertions. In 1994, for example, representatives from the WWF met with the national secretary for health in Delhi to discuss the problems of routine and sometimes forced IUD insertions in Tamil Nadu under the target policy. And in September of 1995 the WWF called the Tamil Nadu health secretary to a state advisory committee meeting at the WWF to discuss these issues and to provide a forum for the health secretary to hear women voice their complaints based on their own experiences of routine IUD insertions in government hospitals.[44]

The NGOs' critiques of the target policy were both echoed and influenced by the consensus at the 1994 UN international conference on population held in Cairo that target approaches to reducing population had been ineffective. A crucial mandate set by lobbyists at this conference was that the government move away from narrow demographic approaches to population issues toward a focus on issues of gender inequality as a key factor contributing to problems of population growth in many parts of the world.

Furthermore, the women's NGOs' concerns over human rights abuses associated with the target approach in India were reemerging in the 1990s at the same time that feminist organizations were waging a campaign against the human rights abuses associated with the Depo-Provera and Norplant trials, particularly in North India.[45] The government of India's family-planning program was thus being criticized from many angles.

In March of 1995 the minister of health and family welfare for Tamil Nadu declared that from April 1995 onward the target approach to family planning would be stopped.[46] And in December of 1995 the central government announced plans to end the system of targets by the following April.[47] The national, "target-free" reproductive health care (RHC) program was officially inaugurated in 1996. This is an India-specific multidonor program involving the World Bank, USAID, UNICEF, DANIDA, and Swedish SIDA, along with the government of India. New training manuals for health workers were developed, and fifteen-day workshops to reorient health workers began in March of 1997. Each state was given a mandate to phase in this program in one or two districts at a time. In May 1997 I carried out research in Chennai (formerly Madras) and Delhi to assess the nature and impact of this new policy.

The RHC program was designed to replace the previous child survival/safe motherhood (CSSM) initiative. One question I asked of people engaged in the RHC program was *why* this shift had taken place and what the nature of this shift was. In response to the question of why, there was a general consensus that the previous CSSM approach had been both ineffective and prone to abuses. The new RHC approach was expected to rectify these flaws by emphasizing both a decentralized approach to planning as well as a more comprehensive vision of women's health throughout the life cycle.

The impetus behind decentralized planning in the RHC approach was a consensus at the 1994 Cairo conference that local outreach health workers should be active in the planning process, since they are in a position to analyze the health needs of the specific communities within which they work and sometimes live. With India's new RHC program, therefore, MPHWs and VHNs are expected to assess a community's health needs and to design new targets based on these needs. Goals are thereby to be established primarily at the district level rather than at state and central-government levels.

It is therefore a misnomer to call this a "target-free" approach, since health workers were still establishing targets. Yet, in addition to modifying the locus of target production, the goal was to also alter the *kind* of targets being set. Family-planning targets for a certain number of contraception "acceptors" were to be replaced by targets which could serve as indicators of the quality of health care needed and provided. How such indicators would be defined and standardized, however, remained unresolved in May 1997. There was a sense of apprehension within central-government agencies that the fallout of abolishing numerical family-planning targets would be a short-term reduction in contraception "acceptors," particularly in the northern states. In South India, however, rates of contraception "acceptors" continued to rise despite the new policy, since many women in South India had begun to voluntarily opt for family planning.

Although the RHC policy called for an end to numerical family-planning targets and such targets were no longer generated at the state level, we must not assume that this practice and its effects are extinct. In May of 1997 women in Nochikuppam and in Kaanathur-Reddikuppam told me that MPHWs and NGO health workers were no longer chasing targets with the same vigor as they had in the past. And yet governmental and nongovernmental health workers told me that despite the new RHC policy they were still directed to reach numerical family-planning targets. A doctor in the Santhome corporation hospital informed me that she told MPHWs attached to the hospital that despite reports to the contrary, the policy still required them to establish and meet numerical family-planning targets. She explained to me that she was concerned that without such targets to meet, the outreach health workers would have no motivation to work. This opinion was in fact voiced by many policy planners in both Chennai and Delhi.

The extent to which this RHC approach had altered the coercive tactics in postpartum wards described in this chapter was similarly varied. Within the framework of this policy there was no longer a 70-percent "acceptance" target set for postdelivery contraception. And the government had passed orders that IUDs must *not* be inserted immediately postdelivery and that sterilization or IUD acceptance must *not* be required of people seeking abortion in government hospitals. During my research in May of 1997 I found that these new policies were indeed being implemented in some of the corporation hospitals. A nurse at the Santhome corporation hospital explained that under the new policy they were only inserting IUDs forty-two days following delivery. MPHWs attached to that hospital were required to go to the communities to make follow-up visits with postpartum women forty-two days after their deliveries to "motivate" them to return to the hospital to have an IUD inserted. The nurse said that MPHWs were finding it difficult to convince women to accept IUDs at that time. If women refused the IUDs, the MPHWs advocated using condoms and distributed them free of charge, and the acceptance rate for condoms was high. This nurse also concurred that the hospital was no longer stipulating that women seeking abortions accept sterilization or IUDs because the government had recognized that such stipulations were forcing some women to seek the potentially dangerous services of untrained abortionists, or else to simply have larger families than the women themselves wanted.

However, women in both Chennai and Kaannathur-Reddikuppam reported that in Kasthurba Gandhi government hospital, routine postdelivery IUD insertions were still taking place and women with four or more children were being pressured to undergo sterilization. Some people speculated that this was because many doctors in Tamil Nadu felt that it was only due to their efforts to pressure women to accept family planning that the fertility rate had come down so far in the state. Most women I met, however, felt that the fertility rates had come down because women themselves were choosing to use contraceptives for economic reasons.

Clearly this policy was taking effect in different sites at different rates. MCH policies throughout India have been dominated by family planning and driven by numerical targets for so long that it will take time for a fundamental reorientation to transpire. Policymakers and health workers alike said that in 1997 the policy remained abstract and had not yet taken root in people's consciousnesses at the local level.

There was, however, also a concern that this was not simply an issue of time. Several people working in the nongovernmental sector felt that although international agencies were committed to a real philosophical reorientation in women's health to include both life-cycle and socially embedded perspectives, in the implementation of the policy, the government was simply linking together preexisting family-planning, CSSM, reproductive tract infections (RTI), STD (especially AIDS), and abortion services. And family planning remained the dominant force in the equation.

As of 1997, attitudes toward this new policy included a healthy mixture of guarded optimism and cynicism. It will take more time before anyone can adequately assess the effects of the RHC policy. The discourses embedded in this policy—"participatory planning," "target-free," "life cycle," and "social health"—are not merely top-down instruments of propaganda but in fact have long been brewing at the local level, as evidenced by the local critiques of earlier policies. Therefore, regardless of whether or not the governments involved are now capable of and committed to implementing a policy that reflects a fundamental reorientation toward women's health, the rhetoric of the policy resonates with the local concerns of the women who are the recipients of health services. As mentioned above, local NGOs in Tamil Nadu have already begun and will continue to respond to these local concerns and to push governments toward real change. Furthermore, as women are increasingly entering the political arena at the local *panchayat* level, there is hope that they will be committed to active participation in and successful implementation of the new policy at the local level.

CHAPTER 6

"Baby Friendly" Hospitals and Bad Mothers

Maneuvering Development during the Postpartum Period

> This is a "baby friendly" hospital, you see. So we are insisting that these women give mother's milk as soon as the baby is born. And we force them to eat some nutritious food right away. The women who come here are mostly illiterates, you see. So they don't know what is best for them. They have very superstitious beliefs and will starve the mother and baby for three days after the delivery. Women will do what they are told while they are here on the board [delivery table]. It is after they go home that the problems begin.
>
> Doctor, IPP-V Thousand Lights Corporation Hospital, Madras (in English)

The words of this doctor are testimony to the fact that in Tamil Nadu the postpartum period is a key site within which discourses of development are maneuvered. I use the expression "maneuvering development" in two senses. First, it refers to how development apparatuses maneuver individuals and groups to adopt new sets of ideas and practices in an attempt to fashion modern subjects. Second, it refers to how the people who are the targets of development maneuver within and around these discourses in ways which collude with, resist, or alter the discourses.

As the anthropologist Arturo Escobar has argued, the transnational discourse of development, in its myriad forms, has been a central element in the modernizing process and in the construction of social and cultural difference in the post–World War II era.[1] James Ferguson writes that "development" is to the post–World War II era what "civilization" was to the nineteenth century.[2] Both "development" and "civilization" are discourses of evolutionary progress which serve to reproduce and legitimate differential positions of power between and within nations or empires. Although at its inception the agenda for international development emphasized the economic transformation of so-called less-developed or Third World nations through the replication of the Western model of industrialization and urbanization,[3] by the 1970s the agenda had shifted to a broader goal of fulfilling "basic human needs," or "minimum needs," to improve the "quality of life" for those living in the Third World.

Within this new framework the provision of biomedical MCH care has become a central component of the development process and a key indicator for determining levels of development. Based on this criterion in combination with demographic statistics, such as maternal and infant mortality rates, Tamil Nadu is considered one of the more-developed states in India. Nevertheless, the development apparatus in the area of MCH care in Tamil Nadu is still highly active, and women using public maternity hospitals, as well as women who make up the target populations for female MPHWs, are the object of its projects. Governmental and NGO development workers in the field of MCH care in Tamil Nadu construct these women as "less developed" and attempt to reform their minds and transform their bodily practices. By referring to "development workers in the field of MCH care," I include both those people engaged in policy and administration as well as allopathic practitioners working for government and NGO hospitals. What all MCH development workers have in common is their target, by which I mean not the abstracted numerical targets of population policies, but rather the "less-developed" women. It is generally lower-class women who are the objects of this development project, though some middle-class women who make use of public maternity hospitals may also find their maternal health practices being condemned by health workers. MCH development workers view the postpartum period as a particularly opportune time to achieve these reforms because women who deliver in the hospital are a captive audience. As the doctor quoted above said, "Women will do what they are told while they are on the board. It is after they go home that the problems begin." Here, "board" refers to the delivery table, which in most government hospitals is a long, narrow metal table which is cut out at one end to catch the baby.

Arturo Escobar has proposed that development is first and foremost a discourse, a coherent system of representation that creates the "reality" of its objects and exerts control over them. He writes:

> Foucault's work on the dynamics of discourse and power in the representation of social reality, in particular, has been instrumental in unveiling the mechanisms by which a certain order of discourse produces permissible modes of being and thinking while disqualifying and even making others impossible. . . . Thinking of development in terms of discourse makes it possible to maintain the focus on domination—as earlier Marxist analyses, for instance, did—and at the same time to explore more fruitfully the conditions of possibility and of "stand[ing] detached from [the development discourse], bracketing its familiarity, in order to analyze the theoretical and practical context with which it has been associated" (Foucault 1986, 3). It gives us the possibility of singling out "development" as an encompassing cultural space at the same time of separating ourselves from it by perceiving it in a totally new form.[4]

This Foucauldian approach accomplishes a radical relativization of development discourse by showing it to be a distinctively modern and Western formulation. It suggests, as well, that the logic of development discourse is fundamentally cohesive. Ethnographic research, however, highlights the gaps in what appears to be a totalizing development discourse. The perspectives and experiences of both the people who are constituted as the "objects" of development as well as the people in the institutions that implement development locally point to a much messier and often contradictory experience of development. Akhil Gupta describes this experience as the "complex border zone of hybridity and impurity."[5] In short, we cannot assume that the logic of development discourse as produced by official reports, studies, and programmatic statements necessarily structures the way that development is used and experienced at the local level.

In this chapter, I analyze the discursive interactions between MCH workers and lower-class postpartum women in order to focus on how development discourses become localized and on the contradictions which permeate those discourses in *practice*. I do this through an analysis of the discursive interactions between MCH workers and the women who are their targets as the health workers attempt to transform women's postpartum practices. In particular, I examine discourses on the diet of the new mother, the diet of the baby, and the bathing practices for both mother and baby.

This chapter's critique of how development discourses serve to construct and reinforce social hierarchies of class and, to some extent, caste, does not reflect a conscious malevolent intent on the part of health workers who deploy such discourses. Indeed, most of the doctors, nurses, and MPHWs genuinely believed that they were helping postpartum mothers. And in many cases, their medical advice could and did benefit postpartum women. The point here is rather to understand how social relations are shaped in the process and, therefore, to comprehend how these attempts to be helpful can backfire and lead to resistance.

NEW MOTHER'S DIET

The First Three Days

Most of the women I met in Nochikuppam, Kaanathur-Reddikuppam, and other regions of Tamil Nadu believed that for the first three days following delivery, the new mother should not eat much at all. Many would only take coffee or tea and bread or *roti* for those three days. They would drink the coffee and tea mixed with milk and sugar but would only drink them once they had cooled to room temperature. Several types of explanations were given in support of this initial dietary taboo. One woman in Madras explained why they didn't eat food for the first three days:

> When they are in the hospital they bleed. So in order to ensure that the "blood" will come out, they won't give rice. After delivery the *vayiṟu* will have small sores or wounds *[puṇ]* all over it. When we give rice to the woman who has just delivered she will not be able to take it because of all these wounds in the *vayiṟu*. So as far as possible, she should not be given rice until three days have passed and the wounds have begun to heal.

Three important notions are revealed in this passage. The first is that the part of the body evoked here is the *vayiṟu*, which is usually translated as "stomach." Here, however, the term describes a body part which is both stomach and uterus in its functions. Second, there is a concern that eating rice—a viscous food—will inhibit the flow of blood from the *vayiṟu*. A steady flow of postpartum blood is considered critical to the new mother's health. Third, there is the notion that the rice will aggravate the "wounds" in the *vayiṟu* and thus prevent them from healing. Several women told me that these wounds are muscular tears in the *vayiṟu* which are caused by the force of the baby descending in birth. Some expressed a concern that these open wounds would become "infected" if the rice were to come into contact with them. The initial postpartum food and drink should be given cool or at room temperature because the intake of warm foods and drink would prevent the wounds from healing.[6]

Another frequent explanation given for the initial three-day dietary taboo was the need to keep the new mother's body "dry." In particular her *vayiṟu* should be kept as "dry" as possible. This refers to oppositional cognitive categories of "hot" and "cold" and "wet/watery" and "dry" in reference to bodies and foods. These categories are prevalent throughout much of the Indian subcontinent. Postpartum bodies are generally thought to be both "cold" and "wet" *(nīr uḍampu),* and both these states render the postpartum mother vulnerable to colds and fevers. On the other hand, a "dry" body, which is often called a *kal uḍampu* ("stone body"), is said to be strong and impenetrable to disease. The "wetness" of the postpartum body was associated in part with the postpartum blood. But there was also concern that taking food at this time would cause diarrhea, and a fear that this would render the bodies even more "wet." There are other dangers associated with diarrhea. As one woman in Madras said: "If we have had stitches during the delivery[7] and we eat something on the first day which causes diarrhea, then the stitches might come out. I am afraid of that. So that is why we don't eat for the first three days."

These explanations for the initial food taboo reflect a concern for the new mother's own body. Some women, however, explained this taboo in terms of the effect of food on the newborn. They said that if the mother ate food during the first few days after delivery, it would affect the mother's milk when it came in and would result in the baby's getting a disease known as *māntam.*[8]

If a woman delivered in a public hospital she would typically remain in the hospital for three to five days following a normal delivery and for five to seven days following a cesarean. During the hospital stay there were ongoing negotiations and debates among the medical staff, the postpartum mother, and the mother's family members regarding what constituted an appropriate postpartum diet. Generally, doctors and nurses in these hospitals said that women should begin to eat regular food within a day of delivering their babies. They advocated a regular diet based on nutritional theories. Many doctors and nurses saw as one of their missions educating postpartum women about the value of nutrition following delivery and convincing them to take regular food soon after the delivery.

The following comments by a nurse at the Santhome IPP-V corporation hospital elucidate the tensions, contradictions, and strategies which are common to the negotiation between allopathic and non-allopathic models of health within a development discourse. They demonstrate how social differences—in this case class and race—are mapped onto bodily practice in development discourses:

> The doctors and nurses say that new mothers should eat everything right away after delivery. We try to get them to eat *iḍlis*—something soft—and spinach or other greens. But women don't always listen. They think if they eat food their system will not get cleaned out of blood. They think they should keep their bodies dry *[kāy]* and if they eat food their bodies will not be dry. But we nurses and doctors tell them that the "digestive system" and "reproductive system" are separate systems so that the food they eat will not have an effect on cleaning out the blood from the "uterus." We say that it is important to eat for strength. But many won't listen. Some people won't even drink water, which nurses say is important for breast milk. On the third day women will always eat *racam* and *cātam*[9] without fail. But *racam* has no nutritive value, only water. This problem is better now. Those people who live in the "streets" now eat more. If some new mother eats good food in the hospital and others see, then she will serve as a "model." There was an Anglo-Indian woman who was eating normal food after her delivery. We pointed this out to the other women and when the others saw her they, too, ate. Similarly most women won't do "abdominal exercises," but when they saw the Anglo-Indian woman doing "exercises" others did them as well.

Allopathic practitioners, like this nurse, often conceived of the body as being composed of distinct anatomical systems; in this case the "reproductive system" and the "digestive system" are emphasized. These "systems" are presented as not only distinct but wholly unrelated to one another "so that the food they eat will not have an effect on cleaning out the blood from the 'uterus.'" The irony is that in attempting to critique the postpartum dietary taboos, the nurse employs this compartmentalized view of anatomical systems while simultaneously promoting regular food intake by using a nutrition model which is itself based on a more holistic view of the body. Furthermore, she glides from one sentence in which she condemns the lack of water intake based on the effect that this will have on producing breast milk to the very next sentence in which she scoffs at the nutritious inadequacy of *racam* taken after the third day because it is "only water." The fact that allopathic practitioners employ multiple models of the body in varying contexts is not in and of itself problematic. Indeed, a multitude of models and explanations are employed to explain and justify non-allopathic practices as well. Rather, the problem, as seen in this particular passage, lies in the social claims which are employed to justify the shifting allopathic models and to denigrate what are perceived as local systems of knowledge. These kinds of shifting epistemologies and differential posturing in the name of "the scientific method" suggest that in many of these contexts the development discourse may be more concerned with constructing and reproducing social difference than with improving individual women's health.

In this passage, class distinctions are constructed and hierarchically organized on a continuum of more developed to less developed, as exemplified by the statement that those who "live in the 'streets' now eat more" food after delivery. The people living in buildings facing "the streets" here are implicitly ranked above those living in the "slums" (like Nochikuppam) made up of government housing-board complexes or clusters of huts which are connected by footpaths rather than streets (i.e., this phrase does not have the same connotation as "street people" in the United States). And racial distinctions are evoked when the body of the Anglo-Indian woman, symbolizing a tie to the "civilizing" process of British colonialism, stands as a "model" for the modern body—a body which is self-consciously fortified by nutrition yet disciplined by the "slimming" craze of the transnational beauty discourse, as evidenced by the "abdominal exercises" that women are encouraged to do to return to their pre-pregnancy body shapes.

This nurse had faith in development's narrative of progress and believed that given the right role models women from the "slums" would change their dietary practices. Others, however, were discouraged and felt that it was an uphill battle to convince "these women" to change their ways. As a doctor from the Santhome corporation hospital sarcastically remarked (in English), "These women won't ask questions about food or diet and they don't listen to what we have to say about it because they are masters regarding diet. We tell them but they don't listen." The sarcastic implication is that they are "masters" insofar as they have power to refuse advice, but ultimately they are slaves to a "traditional" way of life. The representation of the relationship between these women's "less-developed" status and their agency was ambiguous and fluctuated in different contexts. At times they were constructed as victims, which, as Chandra Mohanty suggests, has been the case for the construction of "Third World women" more generally.[10] Specifically, they were viewed as victims of "tradition." Yet at other times they were represented as immoral mothers and even criminal actors endangering the health of themselves and their children and thus obstructing development. As the doctor quoted at the beginning of this chapter said, "[They] will starve the mother and baby." This ambivalence with regard to the construction of a mother's agency is reminiscent of a similar ambivalence in the late-nineteenth- and early-twentieth-century constructions of the *dai,* who was sometimes viewed as dangerously mired in tradition and at other times as a self-serving, stubborn, even evil actor.

Day Three Onward

Pattiya Cāppāḍu From the third day after their delivery onward, women often selectively introduced other foods to their diet. This diet after the third day was called *pattiya cāppāḍu.*[11] After the third day, the postpartum mother would eat a rice-based meal with *racam* and a vegetable *kuṛampu* (a sauce) only once a day. She would usually take this meal in the late morning, around 10 A.M., or in the early afternoon, around 3 P.M. She was not supposed to eat the meal in the evening since it would not be properly digested at night. Some said that if a postpartum woman lay down soon after eating a full meal, the liquid from the undigested food would flow and converge in her head or brain. This, along with several similar comments discussed below, points to not only the fluidity of the cultural construction of the self in terms of relations among people and between people and objects, as Valentine Daniel has demonstrated,[12] but also a cultural construction of fluidity *within* one's own body, which differs from allopathic understandings of the body.

Unlike an ordinary *cāppāḍu,* this meal should not contain any *kāram,* or peppery spices.[13] Turmeric should be avoided until the ninth day. Coriander powder, on the other hand, was reintroduced after the third day because it was said to aid digestion. Some mothers would eat only boiled food so as to avoid all oil or fat. They were concerned that if they consumed fatty foods, the fat would pass to the baby through their breast milk and lead to a condition called *karuppu* (blackness), in which the baby's skin develops blackish spots. Many feared that the baby might die from this condition and believed that if they limited the mother's intake of fatty foods they could either prevent or reverse this condition.

Certain kinds of vegetables which were frequently included in normal *cāppāḍu* were to be avoided in this *pattiya cāppāḍu.* For example, all vegetables which are considered "watery" should be avoided because they might cause *cītaḷam*[14] in both the mother and child. *Cītaḷam* is a condition of coolness and dampness that can cause colds *(caḷi)* and/or fevers accompanied by fits *(jūram).* As mentioned above, people tried to keep the postpartum mother's body as "dry" as possible. "Watery" vegetables included such things as pumpkin, snake gourd, and Bangalore *brinjal* (eggplant). Smaller varieties of *brinjal* were often used as the base for the *kuṛampu* of this *pattiyam,* but they had to be used only when they were young and tender. Similarly, only small, young drumsticks and tender beans could be eaten during this time. Younger vegetables were preferred since they do not contain many seeds. The fear was that the seeds might pass through the breast milk to the baby and get stuck in the baby's stomach, causing diarrhea or *māntam.* Furthermore, ripe vegetables with seeds are fibrous and might cause diarrhea for the mother. Some said that women should avoid fish with lots of bones at this time, since the bones, too, might pass to the baby through the milk and cause indigestion.

Cītalam is caused not only by "wetness" in the body but also by "cold" foods producing "cold" bodies. Whereas a pregnant woman's body was thought to be very "hot" with an increase in the *dosa pittam,* a postpartum woman's body and a newborn's body were usually said to be "cold" and therefore susceptible to *cītalam.* Therefore, "cold" foods were avoided;[15] "hot" foods might be given not only to counteract the "cold" quality of the postpartum body but also to dry the body out. Yet I was also told that women should avoid eating some "hot" foods, particularly fruits such as papaya and mango, during the postpartum period, just as these foods were avoided during pregnancy. During pregnancy "hot" foods were avoided to prevent the risk of miscarriage. During the postpartum period "hot" foods were believed to cause excessive bleeding for the mother and diarrhea for both mother and baby.

Most non-Brahmins whom I met also said that nonvegetarian food *(kavicci)* should not be included in the *pattiya cāppāḍu* until after the ceremonial day of *tīḍḍukkaṛittal* (on the ninth, eleventh, or thirteenth day after delivery). In general nonvegetarian food was considered to be very fatty, and fatty foods should be avoided, first, because they are associated with *karuppu;* and second, because the fat which passes through the breast milk is difficult for the baby to digest. Fatty foods were also considered "heavy," and one Siddha doctor explained to me that "heavy" foods should be avoided in the postpartum diet because they might cause constipation, and the straining due to constipation could result in a prolapsed uterus.

In addition to the various restrictions placed on the postpartum *pattiyam,* women were encouraged to eat certain kinds of foods, particularly foods which were believed to enhance the mother's milk supply. These included such things as garlic and *paṛayatu* (the previous night's rice reheated with warm water). Among nonvegetarian foods introduced at a later stage, soups made with chicken, mutton liver, or the chest bone of the goat as well as particular kinds of fish such as *kārappoḍi* and *pālcuṟā* were said to enhance mother's milk. Jasmine flowers, on the other hand, were known to inhibit the flow of breast milk, so women refrained from adorning their hair with jasmine while breastfeeding.

International development agencies which are engaged in the promotion of allopathy often divide "traditional" practices into three categories according to their effects on health: "positive," "harmless," and "harmful." According to the first major World Health Organization report on traditional birth attendants, "diet restrictions" fall into the category of "harmful."[16] In Tamil Nadu MCH development workers frequently complained that postpartum dietary taboos were depriving mothers and children of essential nutrition. Some went so far as to say that these "superstitious" practices resulted in starvation.

In practice, however, women in Tamil Nadu did consume many foods which fell into the various taboo categories. A similar disjuncture between structure and practice with regard to postpartum dietary practices is described by Carol Laderman in her ethnography of childbirth in Malaysia. As Laderman writes, "The richness of ambiguity and variability of interpretation of Malay systems of food avoidance, at the practical level do not allow us the liberty of formulating a simple cause-and-effect relationship between traditional food beliefs and nutritional health."[17] In fact, she argues, there is a great deal of dietary experimentation at the individual level, and the rules restricting certain foods must be seen as models on which people can draw to explain individual problems and not necessarily as rules which dictate practice. This is precisely the way in which postpartum dietary rules in Tamil Nadu must be understood as well. In the region of Malaysia where Laderman worked and in most parts of Tamil Nadu, the humoral theory of the body was prevalent. As discussed in Chapter Five, the humoral theory of the body in the Tamil context is based on the concept of compatibility with bodies which are unique in time, space, and social context. Thus, these dietary restrictions served to predict, prevent, and explain the lack of compatibility of certain foods with particular postpartum bodies.

There is indeed a serious problem of malnutrition among many women in Tamil Nadu, particularly during their childbearing years, as MCH development workers claim. But cultural conceptions of the postpartum body and postpartum diet are not responsible for these problems of malnutrition because they are used in a flexible way. The problems of malnutrition stem more directly from structures of class and gender discrimination.

In an attempt to combat the problem of malnutrition during women's childbearing years, the government provided pregnant and lactating women with *cattu uṇavu,* or "nutritious food," free of charge through its ICDS program, as described in Chapter Two.[18] This food came in the form of a powder and the ingredients included wheat, ragi (a cereal grain), soya, fried gram, and jaggery. A doctor who was very active in public health research and administration in Tamil Nadu told me that state and nongovernmental organizations were trying to convince pregnant and lactating women to consume more ragi. As she explained, due to a patriarchal cultural ethic of self-sacrifice among women in Tamil Nadu, women were not willing to take much food for themselves, even during pregnancy and the postpartum period when they needed it most. In particular, women refrained from taking extra rice, since rice was a highly valued food in Tamil culture. Ragi, on the other hand, was as nutritious as rice but was associated with low social status. By eating ragi instead of rice, the doctor explained, women would not feel as though they were depriving their husbands and children of their share of rice. According to this doctor (in English), "Only by working within the cultural context of the sacrifice of women to their husbands and children can you achieve better nutritional status for pregnant and lactating women." This comment is typical of the ways in which development discourses attempt to be "culturally appropriate." It is at this level that applied anthropology has often been viewed as useful to the development apparatus. Frequently, the goal of development seems to be to get people to change a practice which is perceived as deleterious without changing the social structure which leads to that practice in the first place. In this case it is the structures of patriarchy which lead women to forfeit their share of food. The impact of this structural inequality on poor women's health can be extreme. The promotion of ragi as a good substitute for women may be a helpful stopgap measure, but it is clearly a Band-Aid solution to grave structural problems. A similar kind of development maneuvering at work is evident in the discussion below on breastfeeding.

Piracava Maruntu In addition to the *pattiya cāppāḍu,* many women began to take a special medicine known as *piracava maruntu* (delivery medicine) from the third day following delivery onward. This medicine was sometimes made at home by older women or by a *maruttuvacci.* Increasingly, however, people were buying it ready-made in shops which sell Siddha and Ayurvedic medicines. It usually came in the form of a *lēkiyam.*[19] The ingredients varied somewhat from community to community and from family to family. Yet throughout Tamil Nadu I found that the main ingredients in this particular *lēkiyam* were dried ginger, asafoetida, and black jaggery.[20] The asafoetida was to help clear the blood out, and the dried ginger was to help with digestion. One woman described this *lēkiyam* to me:

> It will be very tasty as well as very strong for the *iḍuppu* [hip].[21] If we take this, they say the dirt *[aṛukku]* after the delivery will come out. After brushing the teeth in the morning, the first thing you have to do is eat that. I took it for six months after my first child was born. They say that only if you take that will you have the "power" to carry and deliver the next child.

Some women take this *lēkiyam* as frequently as three times a day. Shahida in Kaanathur-Reddikuppam explained that in addition to cleaning out the blood and aiding digestion, this *lēkiyam* was also effective in reducing the *cuṇḍu vali,* or "pulling" pains usually associated with pulled muscles and nerves, of the *vayiṟu,* which continue for three days following delivery. Shahida advised women to begin taking this *lēkiyam* immediately after giving birth to alleviate these pains.

Some people took the *piracava maruntu* in the form of a powder which they ate plain or mixed with the *sambar* or *kuṛampu* . In this form it was often called *piracava maruntu celavu.* The ingredients were often similar to those used in the *lēkiyam,* without the jaggery and ghee. In addition to cleaning out the postpartum blood, this *celavu,* taken in combination with the *pattiyam,* was supposed to enhance the quality of the mother's milk. Kaveri from Kaanathur (whose prolonged labor was described in Chapter Four) took this *celavu* for one month. Her family purchased it from an Ayurvedic medical shop. The cost for the entire month was about Rs. 200, a big investment for a family of few means. Her mother explained how and why they gave the *celavu* in combination with the *pattiyam:*

> First I mix tamarind with the *piracava maruntu celavu* and then mix that together with tender eggplants to make a *kuṛampu.* Then I give that *kuṛampu* with rice to my daughter. She should eat this twice daily for three months and should not eat anything else—no milk, no greens, no eggs, nothing. Everyone else does this so we also do it. We give this *pattiyam* and *celavu* so that the mother's milk will be healthy and will not harm the baby. If the mother is not breastfeeding we let her eat whatever she wants. But while she is breastfeeding she must follow this *pattiyam* for the first three months. After that the baby will be strong enough so she can eat regular food. There are a few other things which we will give her occasionally in

> small quantities during the first three months. Sometimes we give a little rice with the husk on it. We roast this until it becomes fluffy. Then we winnow it and give it. Or she can take very small amounts of groundnuts *[mukkaḍalai]*. If she eats too much of these other things the baby will get stomach pains. In this house we give the new mother the *celavu* with eggplant. Some other people in this area give "brandy." If they give "brandy" they shouldn't give the *celavu* with eggplant and if they give the *celavu* with eggplant they shouldn't give "brandy." Both the "brandy" and the *celavu* will be very hot.

Although it is not quite accurate that "everyone else does this" in this community, this description provides a sense of the extent to which postpartum diets *may* be regimented in Tamil Nadu.

In my discussions with MCH development workers in Tamil Nadu I found that the use of *piracava maruntu* in the postpartum period held ambiguous and shifting positions with respect to the categories of "positive," "harmless," and "harmful." Shahida was recommending this to women. Most of the other allopathic doctors, nurses, and MCH policymakers, however, considered these medicines to be ineffective but "harmless" and thus ignored use of them in order to avoid confrontation. Yet they strongly opposed the use of *lēkiyams* and *celavu* following either a cesarean or sterilization because, they argued, these medicines could cause diarrhea and could therefore result in complications with the stitches. Most postpartum women I met who had undergone such surgical procedures were quick to abide by the doctors' advice in this case. Even if they had used these medicines to their satisfaction following previous deliveries, they would not do so following a cesarean or sterilization. It seems they readily accepted this advice because they were already keenly aware of the dangers of diarrhea in the postpartum period as evidenced in the explanations for many of the food taboos.

What is interesting here is the fact that in one context, the MCH development workers discredited local concerns about the connection between certain foods and diarrhea in their attempt to promote a nutritional model of postpartum health. And yet, in other contexts, they pointed to the potentially harmful effects of local medicines which may cause diarrhea. MCH development workers are, of course, not the only ones to employ multiple models of the body in varying contexts and to shift their position on what constitutes the means and ends of healthy practice. As I have shown, the practices and knowledge of the women who are the targets of development are in a similar state of flux. But what seems unique to MCH development workers is how they presented each of their shifting models uncritically as if it alone were correct, both scientifically and morally. Ashis Nandy and Shiv Visvanathan have attributed this lack of reflexive skepticism to the methodological premise of "modern medicine" itself, namely the "principle of falsifiability." As they write:

> It is possible to argue that modern medicine, which was one of the last sciences to grow out of the traditional sciences in Europe and consolidate itself as a "proper" science in the nineteenth century, was the first major system of healing to try to do away with this element of scepticism and self-criticism. Some amount of scepticism and criticism survived in the popular culture, but it did not easily translate into philosophical doubt within the system. The Popperian principle of falsifiability, so central to the positivist self-concept of science, does not include within its scope any scepticism towards the basic philosophical assumptions or culture of post-seventeenth-century science. Once medicine became a positivist science, it also became philosophically and culturally less self-critical.[22]

In the context of the interactions between MCH development workers and their targets, however, my sense is that the lack of self-critique has to do with the relations of power in these person-to-person interactions and is rooted more in the discourse of development itself than in the structure of "modern medicine" per se.

BABY'S DIET

Breast Milk

The women I met in Tamil Nadu who took many of the postpartum dietary precautions mentioned above did so in part because they viewed the infant's body at this time as a *pacca uḍampu,* which literally means a "green body." The sense here is that the body is weak and vulnerable like the tender shoot of a plant. And just as a tender shoot is nourished by water, this *pacca uḍampu* is nourished by mother's milk and is highly sensitive to fluctuations in the content of the milk.

Immediately following delivery many women in Tamil Nadu did not put the baby to the breast to drink the colostrum, which in Tamil is called *cīmpāl.*[23] They feared that the *cīmpāl* would cause diarrhea and nausea for the baby. A few women also told me that because the *cīmpāl* was thick it was too hard for the baby to suck. Furthermore, some believed that colostrum is derived from menstrual blood which ceases at conception and which has been stagnating during pregnancy.[24] It is, therefore, viewed as "polluting."

Often women waited three days until the milk came in before putting the baby to the breast. This coincided with the period during which the mother was drinking only coffee and eating only bread. During this time many would give their babies sugar water. There was some debate among Ayurvedic medical practitioners as to whether or not this taboo against the consumption of colostrum is in accordance with Ayurvedic texts' discussions on what constitutes healthy mother's milk.[25] Biomedical doctors today, however, argue decisively that colostrum provides newborns with essential antibodies. I am not judging these divergent explanations from two different medical systems of knowledge. Rather, what interests me here is how the MCH development workers promoting allopathy negotiated what they perceived to be "harmful" cultural practices surrounding breastfeeding. Within the MCH development discourse, concern over the refusal to give newborns colostrum was part and parcel of a general anxiety about a perceived global decrease in breastfeeding.

Concern over the decrease in the prevalence and length of breastfeeding throughout the world emerged as a public development issue in the early 1970s.[26] This alarm was triggered both by the "second wave" of American feminism and its "natural childbirth" movement and by the popularity of the world-systems dependency theories of the time. Dependency theorists criticized multinational corporations for creating a dependency on baby formulas and processed baby foods in the Third World.[27] Third World communities were thought to be particularly vulnerable and crippled by the shift from breastfeeding to bottle-feeding because conditions of poverty in the Third World, it was argued, would mitigate against sanitary uses of bottles and formulas and would thus lead to an increase in infant disease and mortality. Rather than change the social conditions which prevent people from using formulas in a safe fashion, or which were forcing many women in the Third World into urban industrial labor that did not provide the time and space for breastfeeding, there was a tendency to fixate on the value of breastfeeding alone, particularly in poor communities. And there was a tendency to romanticize and reestablish "cultural traditions" of long-term breastfeeding as though the desire to identify oneself as "modern," or the fact that women were duped by multinational corporations, were the sole reasons for women to adopt bottle-feeding practices.

The Human Lactation Center was established in Westport, Connecticut, in 1975. It was initially funded by a grant from USAID for the purposes of investigating the relationship between breastfeeding practices and infant mortality and the social and political factors influencing breastfeeding worldwide, particularly in the Third World. Part of this grant went into funding the first International Conference on Human Lactation in New York in 1977. The proceedings from this conference were compiled and published as a book entitled *Breastfeeding and Food Policy in a Hungry World* (1979), edited by Dana Raphael. One of the chapters, co-authored by Ben Gaynes and Lucinda Hale, is entitled "Political-Economic Factors of Breastfeeding." The opening of this chapter aptly demonstrates how the "marketing" of breastfeeding was brought into the development campaign:

> If one starts with the proposition that breastfeeding, for well-proven reasons, should be maintained in the Third World, then the real questions become (1) can it be, and (2) will it be? It certainly can be, and with the obvious talents demonstrated in this volume, probably will be. In fact in the Third World the future has been born again for the believers in and the proponents of breastfeeding. Macroeconomic and political factors have combined to present a unique and optimistic opportunity to market breastfeeding. The use of the word market is deliberate. Whether it is a religion or Coca-Cola, whether it is a product, service, or idea, the item must be sold. The social, political, and economic climate of the marketplace must be able to accept the idea without that acceptance upsetting its infrastructure. Therefore the idea cannot be in direct conflict with the planning concepts under which that market operates. It seems to us that events of the last three years have altered social, economic, and political processes in the Third World for what (depending on the efforts) should be the benefit of those programs. At the very least, there will be a slowdown in the erosion rate of the utilization of the human lactation process.[28]

The commodification, "marketing," and "utilization" of the practice of breastfeeding by Gaynes and Hale as well as their commodification of "religion" provide a particularly disturbing example of what Escobar calls "the pervasive economization of subsistence."[29] Most significantly, Gaynes and Hale say that breastfeeding as a commodity should be marketed without "upsetting" the market's "infrastructure." "Therefore," they say, "the idea cannot be in direct conflict with the planning concepts under which that market operates." In short, just as the promotion of ragi consumption for pregnant and lactating mothers should be done in a "culturally appropriate" fashion, the marketing of breastfeeding by international development agencies should not "upset" the "infrastructure" of the "marketplace." Both are stopgap measures that address the symptoms rather than the causes of social problems that impact negatively on women's health.

The more recent UNICEF- and WHO-sponsored Baby Friendly Hospital Initiative (BFHI) to promote breastfeeding was first implemented in India in 1992 in collaboration with the national Ministry of Health and Family Welfare as part of a global movement formulated at the World Summit for Children in 1990. The primary goals of the BFHI as reported in its task force pamphlet, distributed by UNICEF in Madras, were to end the free and low-cost distribution of infant formula in maternity wards and to encourage hospitals to follow "baby friendly" practices, including the "ten steps to successful breastfeeding."[30] According to Dr. Srilata in the Madras UNICEF office, in 1995 70 percent of all certified "baby friendly" hospitals nationally were in Tamil Nadu and Kerala, with approximately 400 certified hospitals in each of these states.[31] Throughout Tamil Nadu posters promoting the benefits of breastfeeding adorned the walls of public maternity hospitals, ICDS *balwadis,* and NGO offices. And the government frequently ran television and radio programs about the values of breastfeeding. VHNs and MPHWs organized marches, rallies, and entertainment shows to spread the word about breastfeeding to the public.

An eighty-year-old woman from Nochikuppam expressed consternation about the fact that breastfeeding had become so public in recent years. She was not referring simply to the propaganda about the benefits of breastfeeding, but also to the fact that women were increasingly breastfeeding *in* public. Shaking a bony, bent finger at me she explained:

> In those days women would not breastfeed in front of men, not even in front of our husbands. In those days we thought that we should be discreet when breastfeeding. We thought that husband and wife shouldn't even see each other at all for five to six months after the delivery. At the very least, the husband shouldn't see us breastfeeding during that time because if he sees us he might get aroused. For the same reason, in those days women would not wear a *poḍḍu*[32] during those months. Sometimes we would even wear nose powder to deter our husbands. Even with all those precautions, still we were having babies within one year of each other. Since I refused my husband during this period, he went off and had an affair with a Maliyali woman [from Kerala]. I saw this going on right in front of my own eyes. But was I going to bring all that out into the streets? Certainly not! Nowadays it's not like that. Now people will bring everything out into the streets and make a big scene. I didn't want to say anything about this affair because I was afraid that it would bring a bad name to my husband. I never blamed my husband for that. It was the other woman who is to blame, don't you think?[33]

This woman's concern was that many things which used to be kept private in order to protect the family in various ways were increasingly brought into a public arena, threatening the integrity of the family unit. She clearly saw this as a general modernizing process involving the disintegration of women's sense of propriety and a dismantling of the extremely tenuous ways that propriety provided protections for women against the unwanted sexual demands of men.

Doctors, nurses, and MPHWs, on the other hand, claimed that middle-class women had abandoned the "tradition" of long-term breastfeeding in an effort to be "fashionable." They thus view modernity as a culprit in the loss of this "Indian tradition." In the early months of my research I was discussing my project with a doctor who was at the center of this campaign. When she found out that I had a seven-month-old baby myself she wanted to know if I was breastfeeding. I explained that I was but that because of the demands of my research I had begun to introduce Lactogen formula during the day. She shook her head disapprovingly and said (in English), "You must stop the formula immediately. I will teach you how to express milk into a *pālāḍai*[34] so that someone can give it to your daughter while you are away. It is the Indian way. And I will teach you which foods to give your baby. *Iḍli,* rice and dal, ragi . . . Our Indian food is perfectly suited for weaning babies. Next time when you come I will teach you all these things. Let the research begin at home!" I went home that day feeling humbled but somehow exhilarated about the opportunity to learn some wonderfully natural "Indian way" to combine work with breastfeeding without the humiliation of the mechanistic electric breast pump I had used back in America. It was a moment where I was swept away by the romantic rhetoric of a "natural India."

Several months later I watched this same doctor conducting a workshop for a group of women who were being trained to become MPHWs. When the doctor discovered that one of the women had a five-month-old baby who was sick, she began publicly interrogating and humiliating the woman for giving her baby Lactogen. The trainee meekly explained that since she had started this training program she had begun to give the baby formula a few times in combination with breast milk. The doctor replied, "In your role as a multipurpose health worker you are telling other mothers to breastfeed continuously at least up to six months. Are you so mighty that you don't have to practice what you preach?" She went on reprimanding this woman and saying that she should bring her baby with her during the training courses. A few other trainees tried to speak up on behalf of the woman to say that it was not possible to bring their babies with them to the training, but the doctor cut them off. Finally, the doctor told the woman that she would have to discontinue the course until her baby was older. And she sent her off. The woman left, biting her lip to hold back her tears. It was then that I realized that the tenor and fervor of this breastfeeding campaign seemed to be at times more concerned with legitimizing state and NGO development institutions' apparent commitment to a prochild, "baby friendly" approach, giving them the moral high ground, than with providing the social and economic framework within which long-term breastfeeding would be both acceptable and feasible.

For women working in the organized sector, the government of India's highly progressive Maternity Benefit Act of 1961 established legal paid maternity leave for women who had been working for a particular employer for at least 160 days prior to delivery.[35] This act provides women with up to three months' paid leave following delivery if they work for the government or for a company which is large enough to have a workers' insurance scheme. The act also stipulates that employers must allow women "nursing breaks" at least two times daily. Young babies, of course, need to nurse more frequently than that. A more significant problem, however, is the fact that many women working in the organized sector work far enough away from home that such "nursing breaks" are not feasible. In 1995 some companies were beginning to establish day care on their grounds to deal with this problem. In Tamil Nadu the M. S. Swaminathan Foundation was actively promoting this cause.

Most of the women whom I met for my research, however, worked in the unorganized sector. For these women there was of course no paid maternity leave. In fact, as discussed in the Introduction, I found that most women stopped working out of their homes during their childbearing years, even if they were extremely poor. For example, most women in fishing communities engaged in the sale of fish before and after their childbearing years but not while their children were very small. Those who did resume paid work in the informal sector soon after their children were born tended to work in or near their own homes so that they, too, were able to continue breastfeeding while working. So, many of them did continue to breastfeed for one to two years. Indeed, lower-class women in Tamil Nadu are often rhetorically glorified by MCH policymakers for their long-standing "tradition" of breastfeeding children for up to two years. Yet, as with so many public health campaigns, the breastfeeding campaign targeted lower-class women and claimed that these women are being led astray by middle-class women's example.

The women who had stopped breastfeeding early on usually explained that they did so because they had insufficient milk, or because they themselves got sick, or because their milk was sour.[36] Many felt that if the mother were separated from the baby for up to eight hours, their breasts would get engorged and their milk would go sour. Rather than switching to expensive formulas, however, more often women from very poor communities began to substitute cow or water buffalo milk, partly due to the high cost of formulas and partly due to the fact that the animal milk was often already available at home. Many simply stretched the milk that was available even farther to feed the infant as well as other family members. The dangers associated with this practice may have compromised children's health more than drinking formula would have if the government had provided it.

Another contradiction between the discourse of a "baby friendly" approach and the procedures implemented within this approach was apparent in how Madras's largest government hospitals provided breast milk to infants in the absence of their mothers. In some of these hospitals, such as the Kasthurba Gandhi Hospital, some babies born by cesarean or with forceps as well as some preterm babies were kept in the pediatrics ward of the hospital while their mothers remained in the maternity ward. The hospital staff would then collect expressed milk from all the mothers in the maternity ward, even those who had their babies with them, and gave the collective milk to the babies in the pediatric ward. One middle-class new mother whose baby was born by cesarean in Kasthurba Gandhi Hospital explained to me (in English):

> Every morning the nurses come from the pediatric ward to collect the milk and go. They ask everybody to express the milk. Even if some are not willing they force them. When the nurse came and asked me the first time they said, "It is for your child; you have to give it." So I gave it to them thinking it was only for my child. Then after that I saw her collecting milk from everyone else in the same bottle. Then I thought it is going for all the babies in general. The next day when she came and asked me to give it I said, "No, no, I can't give it." So she went off. But what I think is that with other people, with illiterate people, they just force them and tell them, "You have to give." They won't talk back to them you see. So they get scared and give the milk. My baby came to me twenty-four hours after delivery and after that I started to feed him.

This collective breast milk was also given to newborn babies who were referred from other, smaller hospitals for intensive neonatal care. In such cases the mothers remained in the hospitals where the babies were born because the larger government hospitals could not accommodate them due to the expense and overcrowding. The collective breast milk is in some ways a very positive and creative way to facilitate a "baby friendly" approach in the context of complicated births and emergency referral situations. But it can also be viewed as a solution which legitimizes the separation of mother and baby for the sake of medical "efficiency" and which legitimizes the economic rationalizing of MCH care in a system in which public high-tech emergency care is concentrated in very few institutions. Increased governmental spending for MCH care and greater distribution of such spending could prevent the scenario in which women and children are being transported sometimes long distances to those few hospitals with tertiary care.

Donkey's Milk

Some people in Tamil Nadu gave babies small amounts of donkey's milk during their first few days of life.[37] With the increase in motorized vehicles, donkeys' labor was no longer utilized for much. *Dhobis* (laundry workers) continued to use donkeys to transport clothes, but even this was becoming less common. Consequently there had been a decrease in the number of donkeys and thus in the availability of donkey's milk, particularly in urban areas such as Madras. People complained that donkey's milk was harder to come by and that the cost had been inflated due to the scarcity. It cost about Rs. 30 for two spoonfuls (the amount given at one time).

Donkey's milk was believed to both cure and prevent the disease *karuppu,* or *karuppan.* Both words refer to darkness and the color black. If a baby is born with a very black and slightly bluish complexion, it is said to have *karuppu.* Some people call this disease *civappu,* referring to a reddish color. One sign that a baby might have *karuppu* is the presence of small "wounds" *(puṇ)* on the skin. Often these wounds or blemishes are dark in color. Some people told me that this symptom can be confined to one part of the body. For example, those who get *kāl karuppu* (leg *karuppu*) have dark wounds from the knees down to the feet. Other signs that a baby might have *karuppu* include the absence of crying and difficulty breathing. People said that *karuppu* (and *civappu*) could sometimes be fatal. Donkey's milk was sometimes given if any of the above symptoms were present. It could also be given once as a preventative. Some said they gave the donkey's milk to ensure that their baby's voice would be clear and loud.[38]

I was told that *karuppu* could be caused by eating a dark purple berry known as *nākappaṛam*, and sometimes palm fruit *(panampaṛam)*, during pregnancy. Pregnant women, therefore, often avoided eating these fruits. Although most of the women I met took only *nāḍḍu maruntu* (country medicine) after delivery, a few also said they took special medicines during pregnancy which would help prevent disease in their children. One middle-aged woman in Adiramapattinam said that in the fifth month of her pregnancy she took *añcu nāḍḍumaruntu* ("five country medicine"), which consisted of five ingredients: curry leaves, *pūvaracam paḍḍai* (the bark of the portia tree),[39] *koḍikkaḷḷi* leaves (from the moon creeper),[40] *pannāḍaiyappan taṇḍu* (the stem or stalk of a palm tree), and *mūkkirattai vēr* (the root of spreading hogweed).[41] These were ground together as a paste. The juice was then extracted from the paste and consumed. This juice, she explained, protects children from all disease, particularly from *karuppu*. As she said, "These days we have immunizations, and these days if a baby is born with *karuppu* they can put it in an incubator. But in those days we had *nāḍḍu maruntu* for the same purposes." People trained in allopathy, however, often scoffed at these ideas. They felt that the taboo against eating *nākappaṛam* was one more example of the "harmful" ways that superstitious beliefs prevented women from getting adequate nutrition. Furthermore, allopathic practitioners contended that *nāḍḍu maruntu* was ineffective and that donkey's milk could be dangerous for the baby.

Several of the doctors and nurses I met dismissed the existence of *karuppu*. Others translated it into allopathic terms, calling it hypoxia, hypothermia, sinusitis, and asphyxia.[42] One allopathic doctor said that *karuppu* was caused by congenital heart disease and required heart surgery. A Siddha doctor told me that *karuppu* was the same thing as asphyxia and would result in immature brain development. However, he said that this condition was caused by one or more of the following factors: allopathic drugs taken during pregnancy; viral infection; the effect of eclipses; drugs taken to induce abortion; or marriage among relations. And one health worker suggested that *karuppu* was a disease which "backward" people had fabricated to cover up acts of female infanticide.[43] Attributing symptoms of *karuppu* to a baby, she said, was an indication of criminality. Once again, therefore, we see the conflation of "superstition," "backwardness," "criminality," and "immorality" in the development discourse as it is played out in the context of maternal and child health.

It is, however, important to underscore the fact that this development discourse on maternal and child health was not simply a top-down discourse used by those trained in allopathy or by members of a particular class. As Foucault has pointed out, whereas juridical power is a top-down, coercive form of power, discursive power is diffused throughout the social body and internalized within the psyches of individuals of *all* social classes.[44] The story of Chitra demonstrates this point well. I met Chitra in the postpartum ward of the Community Health and Development (CHAD) Hospital in Baghayam, which is affiliated with the well-known Christian Medical College of Vellore. This private, philanthropic hospital caters to a low-income clientele. Chitra's baby was five days old when we met. She had been planning to go home two days after the child was born but, she said, the doctors told her that there was a problem with her blood so they were keeping her in the hospital to give her injections. She said the problem was that her blood was very dark *(karuppu)*. As is often the case, Chitra's mother had brought her to the hospital for the delivery and was staying with her in the postpartum ward. Chitra's husband was coming to visit once a day and then reporting back to his own parents, who lived too far away to visit.

Her husband's parents insisted that if Chitra's own blood was dark, then surely the baby must have *karuppu*. So they had instructed their son to take donkey's milk to the hospital for the baby. The husband brought two teaspoons of fresh donkey's milk daily. Chitra explained to me that while she was pregnant she did not eat *nākappaṛam* or *panampaṛam* because her husband's family had warned against it. Despite the fact that she and her husband lived alone, the wishes of her husband's family generally prevailed. Chitra's mother explained that in their own family they did not believe in the taboo against eating *nākappaṛam* and they did not believe in the disease of *karuppu* for babies. As she put it, "These things are all superstitions *(mūḍanampikkai)*." When Chitra's husband brought the donkey's milk to the hospital, Chitra and her mother would thank him for bringing it and put it aside on the shelf, saying they would give it to the baby in the evening before going to sleep. Each day, after the husband had left, Chitra's mother promptly disposed of the donkey's milk by tossing it into the bushes just outside of the maternity ward. She explained that they pretended to give it to the baby in order to avoid any conflict. "But, why," she asked me, " should we give such backward things from those days, when 'modern science' can do so much?" Here, then, is a case in which one family has discursively set itself above another by accepting the development discourse's dichotomies between "science" and "superstition," and between the "modern" era and "those days." And yet, whereas medical staff in a hospital were often in a position to openly denigrate "backward" practices because of their institutional position of power, Chitra and her mother had to do so surreptitiously because of the patriarchal structure of family relations in which the wife was expected to abide by the wishes of the husband's family. The common practice of having a new mother remain in her own parents' house for a long period following delivery of course gave her family a certain amount of leverage over her husband's with respect to postpartum care. Several people, however, commented that in the space of the hospital it was even easier for them to assert their views on postpartum care if those views were in accordance with the hospital staff's views. For some women, this meant that the hospital provided them with a legitimate space in which to circumvent not only the demands of their in-laws but also those of their own parents.

But Chitra's story was further complicated by the fact that her mother did not allow Chitra to go to the hospital to get a blood test to confirm her pregnancy. Her mother had heard that such a test might cause a miscarriage and did not want to take this risk. Perhaps in the circulation of rumors, the risks of amniocentesis had gotten transferred onto the test to confirm pregnancy. However this fear came to be, it clearly demonstrates that discourses and systems of knowledge such as "allopathy" or "biomedicine" are never whole entities in practice, but rather they are made up of shifting constitutive parts that are constantly being put together in new ways at multiple levels of the "local."

Baby Food

According to the MCH policy in Tamil Nadu in 1995 women should give their babies mother's milk exclusively for three to four months. After that they should begin introducing foods to their children little by little for taste. Beginning in the sixth or seventh month, policymakers said that mothers should give all foods to their children with the intent of providing good nutrition. Within a year the child should have tried all types of food. In practice, people were increasingly giving their infants processed powdered baby foods such as Nestum and Cerelac. These were considered high-status foods. Because of the expense of these processed foods (approximately Rs. 70 per packet), some government agencies were trying to combat this trend.

Despite the MCH recommendations, many people restricted certain foods from their children's diet during the first few years, just as they restricted foods from the mother's diet directly following delivery. Rather than discussing the dietary taboos for children at length, I provide Priya's story as an example of the nature of the MCH development discourse as it maneuvered to change people's practices and as it was maneuvered by those it sought to change. Priya was a twenty-nine-year-old Brahmin woman who was nine months pregnant with her second child when I met her at the Santhome corporation hospital, where she was coming for her prenatal checkups. Her first child, a girl, was five years old at the time. The following discussion took place among Priya, her mother, a hospital nurse, myself, and Annette. The nurse had just explained the MCH recommendations for baby food to Priya.

Priya: We will not give banana until three years of age because it's a cold food. For my daughter I didn't give banana until she was three years old. There was no problem because of it. Now she is eating everything.

Nurse: Will you not give it for this child [in utero] either?

Priya: [Shakes her head to indicate "no."]

Nurse: Aiyeyo! Will you *still* have this superstition *[mūḍanampikkai]?*

Priya: Nothing goes wrong because of that belief, does it?

Nurse: You are doing wrong *[tappu].* You are not giving what you *should* give for the child and yet you are saying that you are not doing anything wrong.

Annette: In a "joint family" you can't say anything. You should listen to whatever they say.[45]

Priya: After three years you can give anything. Now my daughter eats four bananas a day!

Nurse: Then your child will never grow in those three years.

Priya: Why won't it? It grows well.

Nurse: The "maximum growth" . . . the "period" when the child grows well is in those three years only.

Priya: Instead of that we are giving lots of milk, curd . . .

Nurse: You can't get all the "nutrients" in milk and curd.

CVH: Do you give dal?

Priya: Yes, we give dal from the tenth month on. We boil dal separately, add ghee, and give it. There is "health" in all those, isn't there?

Nurse: There is . . . I am not saying no. But for the "brain development," for the "brain cells" . . . I'm saying don't restrict certain foods. Why are you restricting "particular foodstuffs"?

Priya's mother: My daughter was very nice in her childhood. She was fat and nice to look at. Only after growing and becoming older has she become thin. We will not give mango, banana, or jackfruit for three years because these are cold foods. They have a lot of cold effect.

Nurse: After three months, along with breast milk you should give "substitute" food.

Priya: Until I stop feeding the child I myself shouldn't eat such kinds of foods.

Nurse: Aiyeyo!

Annette: When will you do the *annapirāsanam*?[46]

Priya: Only after completing one year we will do the *annapirāsanam* with *homam* and give rice. The maternal uncle should feed the child.

Nurse: Won't you give the child rice before one year?

Priya: No, we won't. For my daughter I didn't give it. Not even *iḍli.* We will give only milk, *kanji* . . .

Nurse: Will you not give for this child [in utero] either?

Priya: If it eats I will give.

Nurse: It will eat. It won't say, "I won't."

Priya: Maybe we can look for a good day [i.e., astrologically auspicious day] in the sixth month and start giving.

Just at that moment, Priya's daughter came skipping into the room wearing her blue and white school uniform and carrying her bookbag on her back. She asked her mother who I was, and when her mother explained, she began to speak to me in her perfect schoolgirl English. "I have put her in an 'English medium' school and she is doing very well in her studies," her mother explained proudly, as if her daughter were living proof of the efficacy of the family's dietary practices.

Several interesting moves can be gleaned from this discussion. We hear the nurse's amazement and outrage that despite her advice regarding the proper diet for the child, Priya "still" believes it is better not to feed babies bananas and does not intend to change her practice with the second child. For the nurse there is a sense of progress disrupted. After repeated inquiries about what she will do for "this child" in utero, in the end Priya concedes and says that "maybe" she will feed rice to the second child as early as the sixth month. Priya seems to be extricating herself from an uncomfortable conversation rather than being convinced of the nurse's claims.

Annette's point that Priya does not have a say in the matter because she lives in a joint family is an interesting intervention. She is clearly trying to defend Priya against what she perceives as the nurse's overly antagonistic manner. And yet the implication is still that given the right social conditions, i.e., a nuclear family arrangement, Priya would be free to accept the MCH advice and progress would prevail. But Priya does not accept this characterization of her lack of agency, and she continues to defend her position: "Why won't it? It grows well." Her statements are based on her own experience, seeing her own daughter grow.

Unable to adequately respond to this question, the nurse draws on the notion that the "maximum growth" (in English) of the child takes place in the first three years, and that what is most significant about this growth and what is most at risk from these food restrictions is the development of the "brain cells" (in English). Here, once again, the discourse reveals itself to be fundamentally about creating social difference. Nowhere does the nurse explain *why* the absence of bananas or rice specifically will harm the development of the child when it is clearly being fed other foods. Rather, as soon as there is mention of restricting any foods and when humoral theories of "hot" and "cold" are evoked, a red flag goes up and Priya is accused of doing something wrong *(tappu)*. When the "wrong" is being done to the baby, the tone of the discourse becomes saturated with a sense of immorality and criminality: "You are doing wrong. You are not giving what you should give the child and yet you are saying that you are not doing anything wrong." Even Priya's own mother feels that her mothering techniques are being attacked, and she is compelled to say that Priya herself was a "fat," i.e. healthy, baby. By evoking the notion of stunted brain development without elaborating at all on this process and the effects of specific foods on this process, the implication is that a general lack of knowledge on the part of the mother will be biologically and irrevocably reproduced in the child if the mother does not accept the modern MCH system of knowledge being offered. It was because of the nurse's accusational tone that Priya's daughter's stellar English performance seemed to carry such a sting of vindication.

It is important to note Priya's class and caste status here. The fact that she has placed her daughter in an "English medium" school, requiring extra fees, reveals her middle-class status. And, as mentioned above, she is from the Brahmin caste. Yet, because she has chosen to seek MCH care from an IPP-V hospital which has been established to provide services for the urban poor, she finds herself being subjected to the same kinds of developmentalist critiques as lower-class and lower-caste women using the same services. Unlike many other interactions I witnessed between patients and medical staff in public hospitals, however, Priya and her mother continued to defend their postpartum practices in the face of an ongoing critique. Their staunchness might be due to their class and caste position. Most of the very poor women in these hospitals conceded more rapidly to the medical staff's recommendations, though their concessions were often more in speech than in practice.

This conversation emphasizes the degree to which the MCH development discourse in Tamil Nadu reproduces unequal power relations, constructing mothers as not only backward, uneducated, and superstitious but also criminal. Elsewhere (see Van Hollen 1998a) I have argued that the national and international media attention given to the contemporary practice of female infanticide, which was said to have been first "discovered" in Tamil Nadu in the mid-1980s,[47] has contributed to the criminalization of poor mothers in the development discourse. This media attention was partially responsible for the shift in the Tamil Nadu government's MCH policy from an emphasis on the mother to the child, especially the girl-child, in the early 1990s while Jayaram Jayalalitha was the chief minister of the state.[48] In short, the media's attention to female infanticide in Tamil Nadu has created a localized version of the MCH development discourse which tended to criminalize poor mothers by constructing them as always potential "murderers" of their girl-babies. It was especially poor women who were said to practice female infanticide, since those who could afford amniocentesis or private ultrasound "scans" had the option of sex-selective abortions. Although sex-selective abortion was also highly condemned by the media, it was not criminalized to the same degree that female infanticide was. This was true even in 1997, despite a national law banning prenatal sex-determination tests in January of 1996.

It was in this context that I could understand why the health worker mentioned above went so far as to tell me that *karuppu* was a disease which "backward" people had fabricated to cover up acts of female infanticide. If a mother says her girl-baby has *karuppu,* this health worker warned me, it is a sure indication of the mother's criminal intent. Therefore, the health worker explained, from then on she would make it her mission to take any baby who reportedly died of *karuppu* immediately to the hospital for a postmortem check for poisoning. Her plan was to deceive a mother into letting her take the dead baby by telling the mother that the doctors would try to revive the baby's life. In her zealous imaginings of this crusade, it never occurred to her that this presumption of criminality could leave parents holding on to a fragile, false sense of hope, further prolonging their grief.

BATHING OF MOTHER AND BABY

Tīḍḍukkaṛittal *and Ritual "Pollution"*

Following the delivery of a baby, many lower-class women in Tamil Nadu followed strict rules regarding when and how to bathe both mother and child. Most Hindu women I met told me that prior to the ceremony of *tīḍḍukkaṛittal* (which usually took place on the ninth, eleventh, or thirteenth day following delivery), the mother and baby should only have body-baths, without getting their heads wet. On the day of the *tīḍḍukkaṛittal* the mother and baby were given their first head-baths. For Muslims the ceremonial equivalent of the *tīḍḍukkaṛittal* took place on the fortieth day after delivery, when special head-baths were given.[49] However, Muslim mothers and babies were given head-baths prior to the fortieth day, and, like Hindus, they generally took their first head-baths on or around the eleventh day after delivery. Many Christians in Tamil Nadu performed the special ceremonial head-bath on the thirtieth day after delivery when the baby was baptized. As did Muslims, Christians also gave the mother a head-bath two or three times prior to the thirtieth day, beginning on or around the eleventh day. Among all religious communities, and particularly among people living in rural and semirural areas, these head-baths were frequently given to the mother as she sat outside on a small stool on top of the spot where the placenta was buried.

Great significance was placed on giving the first head-bath *(talaikku ūttuvāṅka)* to the mother and baby. For Hindus the ritual of *tīḍḍukka-ṛittal* marks the passing off or removal of the *tīḍḍu*. *Tīḍḍu* is often translated as "defilement" or ritual "pollution" and is associated not only with childbirth and menstruation but also with death. There is much debate in the anthropological literature on South Asia about the nature of the relationship between permanent (e.g., caste) and temporary (e.g., birth and death) states of "pollution," on the one hand, and the nature of the relationship between the conceptual axes of purity/pollution and auspiciousness/inauspiciousness, on the other hand.[50] It is not my intent to delve into the details of these debates in this chapter. What is interesting to me is the fact that the participants in these debates assume that there is a pan-Indian, or at least pan-Hindu, conception of the significance of "pollution" attached to birth. Based on my research in Tamil Nadu, however, my sense is that there is more variation in the way in which the "pollution" of birth is experienced and expressed than is usually acknowledged. Susan Bean's semiotic analysis of the categories and meanings of "pollution" within India also points to this variation.[51] Overall, I would argue that this "pollution" may have less significance in Tamil Nadu than, for example, in parts of Uttar Pradesh, where Jeffery et al. conducted their study of childbirth.[52] In particular, physical seclusion from men and other members of the family, and separation from cooking and sharing vessels with other family members, seemed to be less pronounced. Kalpana Ram's work among the Mukkuvar fishing community in southern Tamil Nadu seems to support my argument.[53] And certainly within Tamil Nadu the conventional notion of "pollution," which includes strict rules about touching vessels, cooking, and eating food, was more prominent among Brahmins than among other caste groups and other religious communities. Gabriella Ferro-Luzzi's study of women's "pollution" periods in Tamil Nadu suggested that there is regional variation in postpartum pollution periods within Tamil Nadu itself, arguing that restrictions were significantly more pronounced in southern Tamil Nadu than in the northern parts of the state.[54] Yet Ram's study in southern Tamil Nadu seems to reflect a similar pattern as my own work based in northern Tamil Nadu. Ferro-Luzzi also points out that economic status influences the degree to which pollution restrictions are applied, since the poor may not have the luxury of abstaining from cooking and other household interactions. This is certainly an important factor to consider in my own research. Yet, even among the poor, I often found great value placed on postpartum rest, diet, and bathing without great concern with ritual impurity.

In Tamil *tīḍḍu* refers not only to the state of "pollution" associated with birth, menstruation, and death, but also to the actual blood of birth and the postpartum period as well as menstrual blood. This blood was often distinguished from other kinds of blood, which were called *rattam* or sometimes *utiram.*[55] For Hindus in Tamil Nadu the ceremony of the *tīḍḍukkaṛittal* very literally marked the end of the heavy postpartum blood flow. It is for this reason that the ceremony usually took place on the ninth, eleventh, or thirteenth day after the birth. Sometimes, however, if a woman was still bleeding heavily, her relatives would forego the ceremony, wait for the blood to subside, and then choose a new day for the ceremony. Women said that this was because as long as the mother was bleeding heavily, her health was in a highly vulnerable state. It was only once the postpartum blood flow had subsided that a women could tolerate a head-bath without risking her health.

It is not a coincidence that the day of the *tīḍḍukkaṛittal* marked the end of the strictest *pattiyam* and the return to a somewhat normal diet for many women. It was on this day that many non-Brahmins resumed eating nonvegetarian foods. If the ceremony was postponed due to continued bleeding, the dietary changes would be postponed correspondingly because the continuation of heavy bleeding indicated that the mother's body would not be strong enough to accept a normal diet. In India, from a Brahminical perspective, nonvegetarian food is associated with ritual impurity. Therefore, one could argue that the fact that women waited until after the *tīḍḍu* had subsided to consume meat indicated more of a concern with maintaining a healthy body during the period of *tīḍḍu* than with merely isolating and containing the ritual impurity of the postpartum mother.

Indeed, when the *tīḍḍukkaṛittal* ceremony is viewed within the context of the strict dietary and bathing prescriptions and the cultural construction of the body which underpins these prescriptions, it becomes clear that the meaning of the ceremony and of the "removal of *tīḍḍu*" was more concerned with a rite of passage out of a state of extreme vulnerability of the mother and newborn's health than with the vulnerability of those who might come into contact with the mother's body as a "polluted" space.

In the fishing communities of both Nochikuppam and Reddikuppam women performed a special *puja* to the goddess Desamma once in the evening during the "ninth month" of pregnancy (sometimes on the same day as the *cīmantam*) and then once again in the evening on the day of the *tīḍḍukkaṛittal.* Desamma is specifically associated with the health and well-being of mother and child, so these two *pujas* lay like two banks of a wide and turbulent river. On one side, the *puja* served as a wish for a successful crossing; on the other, the *puja* was done to give thanks to the goddess for bringing mother and child safely to the other shore. Between these parallel *pujas* lay a space of danger, not of pollution.

On the chosen day for the *tīḍḍukkaṛittal* an elder female relative (usually the new mother's own mother, elder sister, or mother-in-law) would bathe the new mother early in the morning. If such a person was not available or able to help, the local *maruttuvacci* might be called. First, the elder woman would apply oil all over the hair and body of the mother. Sesame oil was most commonly used for this but some used coconut oil instead. All the water used for this bath must be heated on a stove or over a fire; no cold water should be mixed in. The elder woman would pour buckets of this heated water over the head, waist, and entire body of the new mother. As one woman explained, "When we pour this water all over the woman, if there is any blood clot it will come out." After splashing the hot water the woman might apply oil on the abdomen, pelvis, and buttocks to soothe the mother. The elder woman would wash the new mother's hair with *cīyakkāy* powder.[56] After the new mother's body and hair were patted dry, the elder women in the family would smoke her hair with *cāmpirāṇi* (frankincense heated over coals) in order to "dry" her body, and thus avoid *cītaḷam, caḷi,* and *jūram.* Women were not permitted to sleep during the day of the *tīḍḍukkaṛittal,* because of a concern that the water from the bath might flow and converge in the brain. Once again this points to a notion of fluidity within the body which is quite different from the allopathic view of the body.

An elder woman would bathe the baby as part of the *tiḍḍukkaṛittal* in much the same way as she would bathe the new mother. Bathing the baby was considered a specialized skill, and often a *maruttuvacci* was summoned. In addition to applying warm oil to the baby's body and hair, the *maruttuvacci* typically poured small amounts of oil into the baby's ears and sometimes into its eyes and nose in order to prevent the body from getting too "dry." The baby would then be vigorously massaged before the oil was rinsed off with hot water.[57] Many people washed the baby with specialty baby soaps, such as Johnson's Baby Soap, following the oil bath. After the bath the *maruttuvacci* often would give the baby its first taste of *piḷḷai maruntu* (children's medicine), which she had prepared herself and which she would give with each subsequent oil bath. Although there was some variation in the way this medicine was prepared, many people included dried ginger, asafoetida, and roasted garlic. This medicine was given to ensure that the baby would have regular bowel movements. After giving the baby the medicine, the *maruttuvacci* would dry the baby with *cāmpirāṇi* smoke. And using a thick black paste known as *mai,* she would dab black marks on key points of the baby's body. The *mai* used for the *tīḍḍukkaṛittal* should always be homemade. It is made by burning *vasambu* (sweet flag) over a fire until it becomes charred, and then mixing that with either the mother's milk or castor oil heated on a hot knife. The *maruttuvacci* in Nochikuppam (Nagamma) dabs the *mai* to numerous parts of the baby's body: the umbilical cord, the center of the chest, the palms of both hands, the center soft portions of the bottoms of both feet, the "third eye," and finally the top center of the forehead *(nethri).* These marks were to protect the baby from being afflicted by the evil eye *(drishti)* and malevolent spirits *(pēy picācu).*

On the day of the *tīḍḍukkaṛittal* Hindu families typically gave the baby its first new clothes and ornaments, and named the baby for the first time. Prior to this day, the baby would remain unnamed and would be dressed in second-hand clothes. This practice points out again that in Tamil Nadu, the significance of this *tīḍḍukkaṛittal* day is tied more to crossing over a threshold from extreme vulnerability to greater security of health than to moving from ritual "pollution" to "purity" in a hierarchical sense. For it was only after crossing over this liminal period that the baby became a member of society with its own identity.

There are some practices which *do* point to the fact that this day marked the end of the period of ritual "pollution." From the day of delivery until the day of the *tīḍḍukkaṛittal,* women were not supposed to worship because of their ritual impurity. Hindu women were not allowed in the *puja* area of the house; Muslim women did not read the Koran or do *namaz* until the fortieth day; and Christian women would not go to church until thirty days after delivery. The rituals of *tīḍḍukkaṛittal,* the "fortieth day," and the baptism, therefore, included worship, symbolizing that a woman was once again in a pure state.

Many Hindus in Tamil Nadu purified their houses on this day by sprinkling sea water, turmeric water, and cow's urine around the walls, floors, and doorways. These were referred to as the "three waters," and each was thought to be sacred. One woman explained, "We use these to remove the *tīḍḍu.* We use cow's urine because the cow is associated with

Laksmi so the cow's urine has the quality of Laksmi. The sea water is sacred because it is made up of all the different waters from all the different rivers mixing together. And turmeric water is sacred because we use turmeric for *puja* so it is considered auspicious *[maṅkaḷakaram]*. By mixing all three of the waters together we believe that we can drive all the impurities out of the house." As this comment suggests, these "three waters" were said to be cleansing as well as sacred. Many people told me that these "three waters" have "antiseptic" qualities, the implication being that *tīḍḍu* was also associated with a state of sepsis.

Sometimes a Brahmin priest would come to the house on this day to give his blessings and recite Sanskrit verses. The priest's presence further symbolized that the period of ritual impurity was over. As many anthropologists have pointed out, Brahmin priests are often in the position of receiving the ritual "pollution" of others.[58] In Tamil Nadu this was also true of the *dhobi* (laundry) women, who in Tamil are called *vaṇṇātti*. In some families, the *vaṇṇātti* played an important role following the birth of a baby. The families who employed a *vaṇṇātti* said that the very first thing that should happen on the day of the *tīḍḍukkaṟittal* was that the *vaṇṇātti* should come to the house to collect the *tīḍḍu* clothes. In exchange for the *tīḍḍu* clothes the *vaṇṇātti* would leave clean clothes which had been given to the *vaṇṇātti* by other families and would be returned to their owners after they had been washed again. People said that the sight of the *vaṇṇātti* leaving the new mother's house on the morning of the *tīḍḍukkaṟittal* signifies to others that the house is now pure and rid of the *tīḍḍu*. After washing the *tīḍḍu* clothes, the *vaṇṇātti* would return to the house to exchange the now-cleaned *tīḍḍu* clothes for the other people's clothes.[59] Although Gloria Raheja argues that in Pahansu in Uttar Pradesh, impurity (unlike inauspiciousness) cannot be removed through exchange,[60] in Tamil Nadu the *vaṇṇātti* clearly assisted in a *process* of removing *tīḍḍu*. (This does not mean that all *tīḍḍu* was removed through this exchange alone, however.) Much has been written about the "polluted" status of the *dai* in the context of childbirth in India.[61] In Bijnor, where Jeffery et al. conducted their study, if anyone outside of the family was to wash the new mother's clothes it would be the *dai* and never the *dhobi*.[62] In parts of Tamil Nadu, however, the "pollution" of childbirth seemed to be more commonly transferred to the *vaṇṇātti* than to the *maruttuvacci*.

The abstinence from worship, along with the ritual cleansing of the house and the roles of the priest and *vaṇṇātti*, all support the commonly made point that in Tamil Nadu, as in many parts of India, there is indeed a concern about the ritual "pollution" associated with postpartum blood. But this point does not explain everything about the cultural understanding and experience of *tīḍḍu* and of the removal of the *tīḍḍu*. In fact I would argue that for most of the women I met the removal of ritual "pollution" in the *tīḍḍukkaṛittal* was secondary to marking the end of the flow of blood and its implications for the health of the mother and child.

"Pollution" and MCH Policy

Nowhere is the emphasis of the cultural concern with childbirth "pollution" more pronounced than in discussions about the role of the *dais* in India's MCH services. The 1918 report of the Victoria Memorial Scholarship Fund demonstrates how the *dai* was represented by colonial allopathic medical practitioners, and purportedly by local people throughout India, as a low-caste, filthy, "vermin-ridden" woman whose main function was to deal with the "pollution" of childbirth rather than to impart specialized knowledge of the reproductive body. The Victoria Fund report suggested that because of a cultural conception of childbirth as polluting, only low-caste women would stoop to doing this work, and these low-caste women were highly unsanitary. The result is that cultural notions of "pollution" are thought to be major threats to women's health during delivery and the postpartum period and serve as obstacles to "modern" notions of sepsis and sanitation. Jeffery et al.'s account of birth in rural Uttar Pradesh in the 1980s suggests that local views of both childbirth and *dais* as polluting continue to prevail in contemporary North India. As they write, "Village *dais* are not considered to have esoteric knowledge or specialized techniques; their distinctiveness rests on their willingness to accept payment for cutting umbilical cords, unpalatable defiling work that no ordinary woman values or wishes to perform."[63]

Following the lead of the Victoria Fund in the colonial era, after independence the government of India included provisions for *dai*-training programs in its Second Five-Year Plan in 1956, and these programs have continued up to the present. Like the earlier Victoria Fund, these government *dai*-training programs are seen as a temporarily necessary, though ultimately inadequate solution to the problem of poor MCH care in rural areas.[64] Jeffery et al. argue that these government *dai*-training programs are, however, destined to fail because they do not adequately address local notions of caste and childbirth "pollution" which mitigate against any kind of respect for the *dais* within society.[65]

I do not deny that an androcentric cultural construction of women's *tīḍḍu* as impure and a discriminatory caste system which forces some people to do "polluting" work combine to stigmatize the role of the *dai*. Yet once again, in Tamil Nadu there was much more concern with the ways in which blood, food, and water interact to ensure a healthy mother and baby during the postpartum period than with the "polluting" nature of the *tīḍḍu*. The *maruttuvacci* as well as elder female relatives all played active roles in monitoring this interaction. Their knowledge of the postpartum body of mother and child was often valued, and their advice regarding treatment was given careful consideration alongside that of local MPHWs and other allopathic medical practitioners. In Bijnor, on the other hand, Jeffery et al. report that the *dai* gave little or no postpartum care or advice.

Furthermore, it is important to note that although the cultural concern with childbirth "pollution" is sometimes constructed as a "traditional" custom which is an obstacle to "modern" notions of sepsis, the division of labor in allopathic hospitals replicates this concern. Women who worked as *ayahs* in hospitals during my research were always members of lower castes, and they were responsible for disposing of the blood, feces, and urine during birth. Due to a long-standing caste reservation policy for Tamil Nadu's medical education institutions, women from a range of caste groups worked as doctors and nurses in maternity wards. However, I never came across higher-caste women working as *ayahs,* or "sweepers," in these maternity wards.

Although the women I met seemed less concerned with issues of ritual impurity surrounding childbirth than with protecting the health of the mother and child, they did evoke the concept of cleanliness when discussing the merits of hospital versus home births. Many women said that the hospital was a cleaner and more hygienic place for a delivery than the home. This was no doubt partly a result of public propaganda campaigns against home deliveries with *dais* and in favor of hospital deliveries, dating back to the colonial period. But in some cases it was also a result of the reality of the conditions of poverty in which many of these women lived. Women in the low-income urban communities of Madras, such as Nochikuppam, were particularly convinced that the hospital was cleaner than the home, since their homes were often severely overcrowded and swarming with flies and the clean-water supply was such a chronic problem. In addition to the cleanliness of the delivery site, many people said that a distinct advantage of the hospital was that the medical staff would wash all the sheets and clothes. This was work which was laborious if done by one's own family members, or costly if a *vaṇṇātti* was engaged.

MCH Policy on Bathing the Baby

The MCH policy regarding the postpartum bathing of newborns and new mothers in public maternity hospitals had been shifting over the years prior to my research in 1995, and medical staff in hospitals were often uncertain about what the new orders were and what they "should" do. Generally, the shift seemed to be away from a policy of bathing all newborns immediately after delivery to a policy of not bathing babies for at least the first three days due to the risk of hypothermia. Often nurses said that apart from a sponge bath, the babies were not bathed during their hospital stays, and that the families would give the babies their first full baths on the ceremonial bathing days at home. Yet in other public hospitals, nurses would give the newborns baths immediately after delivery unless the baby's birth weight was low. Not only were there discrepancies among hospitals with respect to bathing procedures, but there was not always consensus *within* a given hospital about what should be done. My questions often elicited heated arguments among nurses and doctors about what the latest government orders were. Arguments for and against the immediate bathing of babies were always couched in terms of the "scientific method." This situation was a good example of the kind of confusion which can ensue when policy is made from the top down without the provision of sufficient explanations for changes.

The ambiguity surrounding this practice seemed to be partly due to the fact that not much emphasis was placed on this question within the development discourse. Unlike the practices surrounding the diets of mother and child, there was not a sense that some "traditional" bathing practice had to be stopped. On the contrary, there was an awareness that in this case, a new MCH policy was aligning itself with "traditional" practice. And thus several nurses commented that this new hospital approach demonstrated that the "traditional" method was "scientifically" proven.

In the context of this shifting policy, hospital nurses explained that in recent training workshops they had learned that if a baby was born with the coating of vernix still on its skin, the vernix should not be washed off.[66] The explanation one nurse gave for this was that the vernix gave the baby "immunity power" and that it had "antibiotic power." Both expressions were given in English embedded in a Tamil conversation, and, according to her, both amounted to the same thing. In Tamil, this vernix covering is called *māvu* (flour), and most people insisted on wiping it off the baby because it was considered to be *aciṅkam* (disgusting or unseemly). If family members insisted on washing the vernix off despite the nurses' explanations about its medical benefits, the nurses were quick to oblige the families' wishes and did not press the point too much.

What the allopathic medical establishment *was* strongly opposed to, however, was the application of oil when the baby was finally bathed. The danger, they said, was that when oil is applied to the eyes and poured into the ears and nostrils of infants it can cause infections.[67] One doctor told me that oil applied even on the surface of the skin was harmful because the oil mixed with soap would somehow enter the baby's lungs, block the air in the lungs, and thereby lead to an infection. She said that when she had worked in Kasthurba Gandhi Hospital in Madras ten years before, she had seen many cases like this but that in her work at a the Santhome IPP-V corporation hospital in recent years the number of cases had subsided because of government campaigns to stop this practice. Many people commented that mothers and *maruttuvaccis* were endangering the lives of innocent babies by continuing with this practice. Instead of oil, they recommended that people use specialty baby soaps, such as Johnson's Baby Soap, which were available in most provision shops and were widely advertised in women's magazines. Despite the high cost of these baby soaps many people, even in extremely poor communities, had begun to use them and believed that regular soap would be too hard on the baby's skin. What was happening was that many people were using both oil and specialty baby soaps simultaneously.

DEVELOPMENT AND THE "SCIENTIFIC METHOD"

The same MCH workers who were being directed to advocate against the use of formulas and baby foods in favor of *some* "traditional" feeding practices were simultaneously actively promoting the use of expensive baby soaps and actively opposed to "traditional" oil baths. At the same time, they were in favor of the "traditional" practice of delaying the baby's first head-bath. What is interesting is that in one case the development discourse assumed that women were straying from the beneficial practice of breastfeeding, while in another case the discourse assumed that women were clinging to the "harmful custom" of oil baths. In both cases, therefore, it was the development worker who knew what was best, and who presented this knowledge as "scientifically" proven. In the case of the delayed head-bath, there was a convergence of what was thought to be a still widely followed "traditional" practice and the "scientific method." Part of the confusion surrounding the rules of bathing the infant lay in the fact that "tradition" and "science" were converging in uncomfortable ways. As mentioned above, the development discourse often seemed to be predicated on and to reify notions of social evolutionary difference, whereas here the *difference* was not so obvious.

Nevertheless, in all these cases it was the knowledge of the "scientific" underpinning of a certain practice which was thought to reflect development or modernity rather than the practice itself. Breastfeeding, in and of itself, was not viewed as a symbol of development, but the knowledge that breastfeeding provides a baby with essential nutrients without the risk of bacterial infection through unhygienic bottle use *was* a symbol of modernity. Waiting until the ninth, eleventh, or thirteenth day to give the baby its first head-bath was not a symbol of development, but the knowledge that immediately bathing an infant may cause hypothermia was. The mere use of the language of allopathy with its English terminology ("nutrients," "infection," "hypothermia") and the assumed knowledge that undergirds this language thus constructs social difference such that the wielder of this language is viewed as developed, as "one who knows" *(teriñcirukkiṟavaṅkaḷ)* and "one who has studied *(paḍiccirukkiṟavaṅkaḷ),* while the "other," "these women," are rendered less developed, sometimes in spite of their actual practices. It is in this context that a nurse could tell me that "immunity power" and "antibiotic power" are the same thing since both are paradigmatic tropes in the language of "science."

In her discussion on development discourse and the construction of "the village" in Nepal, Stacy Pigg remarks, "Development discourse creates a paradox: It locates villages on the periphery of development, yet its ostensible aim is to make villages developed."[68] Although a similar construction of the urban/rural divide was also operative in the development imaginary in the Indian context, I found that with respect to the development agenda of spreading allopathic MCH care, class, particularly as understood in terms of levels of education, was the dominant category evoked to explain the contradictory need for and obstacle to national development to which Pigg points. Furthermore, because this discourse revolved around reproduction and the bodily production of new citizens (i.e., babies), the obstacle (i.e., the lower-class, uneducated mother) was constructed not only as "backward" but as one who could potentially endanger the life of these future citizens. MCH development discourse was thus infused with the opposition between criminal mothers and innocent babies with the state and allopathic medicine allied with the innocent. The presumed potential criminality of poor mothers may have been particularly striking in Tamil Nadu, since the state had been singled out by national and international media reports as the place where contemporary practices of female infanticide were first "discovered." On one occasion, just after I had introduced myself to a woman in Kanchipuram and told her about my interest in childbirth, she turned to my research assistant and asked, "Has she come here, like the other American doctors, to ask if we kill our girl-babies?"

The "scientific" grounds for MCH policy at any given point in time and in any given context are always shifting, yet the balance of moral power remains the same. The irony is that some lower-class women in Tamil Nadu chose not to use government allopathic MCH care services, particularly in-hospital services, in part because of the forms of condescension, blame, and discrimination which they experienced surrounding their postpartum practices. Rather than development discourses inadvertently serving the interests of the state as Ferguson has shown,[69] in this case the discourses sometimes undermined state interests by inadvertently discouraging women from coming to the hospital in the first place.

CONCLUSION

Reproductive Rights, "Choices," and Resistance

During the United Nations' Fourth World Conference on Women, held in Beijing from September 4 through 15, 1995, the largest Madras-based newspaper, *The Hindu,* ran a series of articles covering the event and the parallel NGO meeting held in Huairou, China. I was struck by the logo which this newspaper used for the series: the silhouettes of two figures hoeing on a hillside. Only by examining the small photo closely could I make out the drapes of the saris which hung on the two figures and thereby know for sure that they were both women. It was the weight of the wooden hoes which seemed to be highlighted and not the femaleness of the bodies.

The image of the woman as a wage laborer carrying out heavy manual work is not one which we see often in mainstream media representations of the women's movement in America. The comparisons, articulated in these *Hindu* articles, between the concerns which Indian and American women were bringing to the UN conference made it clear that the anomaly of this logo within the context of American feminism was itself one of the most critical issues debated at the conference. As it was presented in the Indian press, this debate pitted the "developing countries" against the "rich countries" in several ways. First, Indian delegates stressed the need for and responsibility of "rich countries" to provide economic resources to improve the position of women in "developing countries." Members of the South Asian Caucus attending the NGO conference highlighted the negative impact of external debts, structural adjustment, and other development policies on the lives of many poor women in the "developing world" and argued that members of the "rich countries" should take steps to prevent such policies which are harmful to women.[1] In short, the major issue which Indian representatives brought to the table was economics. First and foremost their agenda was to address the crisis of the increasing "feminization of poverty" and to call for an international commitment to reverse this process. The main agenda which the "rich countries" were trying to push through, on the other hand, was ensuring human rights, as universal rights, for women. The point that women's rights are human rights had previously been established during the UN Geneva Conference on Human Rights. Above all, representatives from the "rich" countries wanted to reiterate the importance of women's reproductive rights. In order to stave off the clashes with the Vatican and Islamic fundamentalist groups which stalled the 1994 Conference on Population held in Cairo, the committee drafting the *Beijing Declaration* chose to reproduce exactly the texts on reproductive and sexual rights, including abortion, from the Cairo conference.

Many Indian women's groups also advocated the need to strive for women's rights, including reproductive rights. India's involvement in drafting the Beijing conference's *Platform for Action* was lauded as a sign of India's commitment to upholding women's rights in the face of opposition from the Vatican and some Islamic fundamentalist organizations, both of which were claiming that the human rights approach was too individualistic and as such it was emblematic of a form of cultural hegemony which values the individual above society.[2] Yet the consensus among the Indian women's organizations seemed to be that socioeconomic changes, not rights, should be the priority of the Beijing conference. In fact, there were some who agreed with the opposition groups that the rights issue placed too much emphasis on the individual. But their reasons for critiquing this approach varied radically from those of the Vatican and the Islamic fundamentalists. Rather than argue that an individualistic approach reflects a form of cultural hegemony, they suggested that the individualistic and legalistic nature of the human rights approach deflects attention away from the global and local social, political, and economic structures which serve to deny women all sorts of rights in the first place. As S. Swaminathan wrote, "The more forceful the attempt to formulate an agenda for women's empowerment on the basis of human rights, the more diluted becomes the programme for action."[3] Reflecting on an earlier meeting entitled Rethinking the Women's Movement, which was held in Delhi in 1992, Ratna Kapur voiced similar concerns about the use of the human rights discourse in the women's movement. As she wrote:

> The women's movement has been aware of the underlying factors responsible for dowry, the unequal economic relationships between men and women, and the patriarchal relationships on which the family is based. Yet the law precludes such an analysis. It only permits the issue to be addressed in terms of individual rights and remedies, rather than in terms of power relationships within the family as well as the broader socio-economic context that deny women access to property and wealth. . . . The use of rights and rights discourse in the courts can and does depoliticise women's claims and can be used by groups with opposing political agendas to undermine feminist agendas.[4]

My research interests emerged out of the confluence of these two feminist agendas represented at the Beijing conference. The research was driven by a commitment to women's reproductive rights *and* guided by a desire and need to understand how women's reproductive rights are shaped by specific local and global political-economic and socio-cultural structures. I strongly agree with many anthropologists that "'rights' are always historically and culturally located."[5] This anthropological perspective on "rights" enables a conjoining of these two feminist agendas which are otherwise viewed as competing. Anthropologists today recognize that it is critical that we do not allow a relativistic stance on human rights to prevent us from seeing how the "cultural" is constituted within the context of relations of power.[6]

It was from this politically engaged anthropological position that I tried to understand how the reproductive rights of poor women in Tamil Nadu were structured and how such structures impacted the ways in which these women made decisions about the kind of care they sought during childbirth. The material presented in this book makes it clear that, in addition to many socio-economic and cultural factors which contribute to women's reproductive decisions, we also need to understand the prominent role that the discourse of modernity has in shaping poor women's reproductive "choices." Once again, I use the word "choice" in quotation marks to highlight the fact that these decisions are never made in a power vacuum by totally "free" individuals.

The community of Kaanathur-Reddikuppam serves as the most useful example through which to understand this issue of choice, for it was there that I encountered the greatest variation in childbirth practices.

Since this was a community going through rapid transformation, the issue of choice with respect to reproductive health was being openly debated. In Madras, on the other hand, there was a much greater consensus about where one should go to seek maternal and child health care, and options were generally restricted to either large government hospitals, such as the Kasthurba Gandhi Hospital, or smaller IPP-V hospitals, such as the Santhome hospital. There is a tendency to glamorize the proliferation of "choices" in the modern world, and thus some think that those communities where multiple "traditional" medical practices exist side by side with "modern" practices are inherently more fortunate than communities with fewer options. In reality, however, we must always consider what is gained by such "choice" and how these choices are structured by such things as political-economic inequalities.

DISCOURSES OF MODERNITY AND REPRODUCTIVE "CHOICE"

Many of the women from Kaanathur-Reddikuppam who had gone to the hospital explained that "these days everyone goes to the hospital." When I asked why everyone was going to the hospital some would say that it was because "these days we are *navīnamayam* [modern]," whereas in the past everyone was calling the *maruttuvaccis* because "in those days everything was *paṛakkam* [tradition/habit]." Using the term "*navīnamayam*" is somewhat of an erudite way of talking about modernity, of naming it as a thing. More commonly, women referred to modernity as a process of coming to know. Those who are modern, therefore, are *teriñcirukkiṟavaṅkaḷ* (those who have come to know); those who are not modern are *teriyātavaṅkaḷ* (those who do not know). This process of coming to know which makes one modern is usually associated with formal education. So some referred to people whom they considered to be modern as *paḍiccirukkiṟavaṅkaḷ* (those who have studied). And people speaking in English almost always used the term "illiterates" to refer to all those people whom they considered to be unmodern and "backward."

Several health workers whom I met who were from the communities in which they worked described their training as a kind of conversion experience from not knowing to knowing. The knowledge gained was not confined to health issues alone, but implied a knowledge of the world at large. As Muttamma in Reddikuppam explained:

> I went to the VHS health course in 1984. Before that I had just lived at home according to my in-laws' wishes. I was married when I was only thirteen years old, just after I had attained age. I married my mother's sister's son. I had all my children before 1984. Six children. Four of my children were born at home. One child is retarded and I think it is because the *maruttuvacci* spread ash on the umbilical cord after she cut it. It was only once I took this training that I came to know the world. Had I known now what I know today, I would have stopped with two children and I would have gone to the hospital for my deliveries. Ever since I took the training I have been involved in social work and volunteering.

This passage reveals how people equated education with the use of modern maternal health-care services and family planning, and the spirit of volunteering. Just as social work and volunteering were associated with good citizenship, so, too, was going to the hospital during childbirth and using family planning. So the fact that one "now knows" was explanation enough for why one went to the hospital for a delivery. "Choosing" to deliver a baby in a hospital, like "choosing" to limit the number of babies one has, was a way of identifying oneself and/or one's family as modern and "developed." This was a message that international, national, state, and NGO organizations were actively promoting. And it was a concept that was indeed internalized by most women I met.

Yet, at the same time, women often had reservations and fears about delivering in hospitals: they were afraid of being all alone without any family or friends around; of being scolded and/or beaten for expressing pain; of having to accept family-planning measures against their will; and of being hassled about their postpartum beliefs and forced to adopt the hospital's postpartum practices. These fears were most tangible when women talked about the large government hospitals and were exacerbated in part by political-economic constraints that structured the nature of care given in large government maternity hospitals. More significant, these fears were rooted in international, national, and local discourses of modernity which legitimize practices that discriminate against poor, often low-caste women. There was a widespread attitude among medical staff in these hospitals, and among some MCH policymakers, that "these women"—i.e., lower-class, lower-caste women using public maternity services—were *not* modern; they were *teriyātavaṅkaḷ,* "illiterates" who didn't know what was best for them and were not capable of making good decisions. Therefore, many doctors and nurses felt that it was their responsibility and prerogative to not only propagate the benefits of modern MCH care but enforce this kind of care, since they said that this was the only way that "these women" could become *teriñcirukkiṟavaṅkaḷ* (those who have come to know).

Lower-class women were told to come to the hospital in order to be modern, but upon entering the hospital doors they were viewed as unmodern and sometimes treated with condescension, derision, and disrespect because of their "backward" status and their "backward" practices. The hospital staff's condescending attitudes served to construct and maintain social and cultural structures of hierarchy between MCH health workers and maternity patients. For women in Tamil Nadu the connection between maternity and modernity was thus riddled with contradictions. In communities like Kaanathur-Reddikuppam, where both institutional and noninstitutional options were available, discourses of modernity simultaneously compelled and repelled poor women from seeking maternal health care in allopathic institutions.

CALLING SHAHIDA: A HAPPY MEDIUM?

Based on VHS and ICDS records for 1994–1995, thirty-one women from the community of Kaanathur-Reddikuppam (including Bilal Nagar) had their deliveries in a hospital, and twenty-nine remained home for their deliveries. Only twenty-four of the home deliveries had records of who attended the delivery. Of these twenty-four, fourteen were attended by Shahida (the privately practicing MPHW) and ten were attended by Chellamma or Karpagam (the midwives). Considering the fact that Shahida had moved to the area and begun seeing deliveries only in 1994, her popularity was very impressive. When I returned to the area in May of 1997, all the VHS health workers in the area confirmed that Shahida was seeing an even larger percentage of the home births than she had been in 1995. What could account for the appeal of this newcomer on the scene in Kaanathur-Reddikuppam?

Shahida represented for many a happy medium between their desire to have what they viewed as a modern birth and their fears of being discriminated against in hospitals for their lack of modernity. One advantage that Shahida had over the midwives was her air of professionalism, a result, in part, of the simple fact that Shahida was of a different class and caste than the midwives. While Chellamma and Karpagam were both "scheduled caste" women who worked primarily as wage laborers, Shahida was a middle-class Muslim MPHW who worked exclusively in this profession. While Chellamma and Karpagam wore cotton saris, Shahida wore polyester, a symbol of middle-class status. Though Shahida had received only MPHW training, many people in fact referred to her as "doctor," and once or twice I noticed that she had signed papers using this title. She had a clinic attached to her home. The clinic had a sign out front and was located inside the compound of the *panchayat* president, Murugesan. Some people referred to this clinic as a "hospital." One woman even told me that she had decided to have Shahida assist with her delivery since she had been led to believe that the clinic was a hospital and she would therefore have her delivery in a hospital, overseen by a "doctor." She was surprised and a bit disappointed, therefore, when Shahida came to her own house for the delivery.

Shahida not only had an air of professionalism and professional training, but, unlike Chellamma and Karpagam, she also had medicines and technologies which people associated with a modern birth. She gave enemas, glucose, and oxytocin drugs on an almost routine basis, and she also carried with her an array of basic first-aid medicines, should they be required. As discussed in Chapter Four, many women in Tamil Nadu had come to feel that the use of drugs to induce labor was a fundamental and appealing component of a modern birth. Also, Shahida told women to assume the lithotomy position during the final stages of birth.[7] The lithotomy position was also routinely used in hospitals, which further helped to distinguish Shahida from Chellamma, who, like many *maruttuvaccis* in Tamil Nadu, encouraged women to deliver in a squatting position (sometimes squatting on two bricks) or while sitting on Chellamma's outstretched legs on the floor, facing her.

Shahida used those elements of a modern birth which women had come to see as positive. At the same time, they felt they could avoid those aspects of "modern" childbirth, as practiced in the government maternity hospitals, which they viewed as negative. At home, they felt relatives could be with the birthing mother (though, as we saw with Kaveri's delivery described in Chapter Four, Shahida did not always allow this). At home women would not be beaten and scolded for expressing their pain to the extent that they were said to be in the large government hospitals. At home they would not be pressured to adopt family-planning measures that they may not have wanted at all or may not have wanted immediately after delivering. And at home, they would be able to follow the postpartum practices which they deemed beneficial to mother and baby without being criticized, and even criminalized, for doing so.

At the end of the twentieth century births in allopathic institutions were by no means hegemonic in India as a whole, and not even in Tamil Nadu, which was viewed as one of the model states with respect to the provision of allopathic MCH care. The mere fact that a large percentage of births in both India and Tamil Nadu continued to take place in the home with the assistance of a *dai* was testimony to the fact that allopathy was not hegemonic. The large number of home births obviously cannot be viewed as a form of resistance, as home births in America are considered today, since many home births in India take place in rural areas where limited access may rule out allopathic MCH care as a "choice." But the individual decisions of some women in Kaanathur-Reddikuppam to stay home and have Shahida attend their deliveries *can* be viewed as a kind of resistance. For if Shahida had *not* had her practice in the area, those women who called her said they would have gone to the hospital rather than remain home and have their deliveries overseen by one of the local midwives.

The form of resistance in Kaanathur-Reddikuppam was strikingly different from the forms of resistance embodied in the home birth movement in America, since the form of modern birth has been so radically different in these two contexts. In America, where biomedical birth has become hegemonic and has historical associations with male medical dominance, women feel that a hospital birth denies them of a "natural," woman-centered experience. Male doctors have been criticized for being distant and unable to empathize with the birthing woman's experience. The technology employed and the medical staff in American hospitals are said to deny women control over their bodies. What is lost, in short, is the individual's experience. Since biomedicine is hegemonic in the American context, resistance is counterhegemonic, attempting to circumvent the hierarchy of professionalism and do away with modern technological interventions.

Modern birth has taken on a very different structure and meaning for poor women in Tamil Nadu than that described by feminist scholars of the medicalization of birth in the West. The biomedicalization of childbirth throughout the globe, therefore, cannot be viewed as a monolithic process. Because of the nature of the *particular* rendering of modern birth described in this book, poor women in Tamil Nadu never voiced a concern that allopathy was denying them a full-bodied, spiritual, woman-centered experience of natural birth. Rather, their criticisms were waged against the multiple forms of discrimination which they faced as *poor* women at the hands of *ayahs* trying to exert their professional dominance and higher-class and usually higher-caste doctors and nurses. And women complained about the corrupt and heavy-handed practices of state institutions in which bribery and family-planning pressures were chronic. Rather than criticizing the overuse of technology, women sometimes complained that they were being denied technological interventions which they felt they needed and to which they felt entitled. And rather than feeling as though the individual phenomenological knowledge of their bodies was being discredited, many women felt as though the collective knowledge of their bodies and of the bodies of their babies was being not only discredited but ridiculed and deemed dangerous, even criminal. Their critique was not so much a lament over the loss of the individual's experience as it was a condemnation of how their *collective rights* were being denied.

Their resistance, therefore, did not involve a rejection of allopathic birth as controlled by a male-dominated professional science; but, rather, their resistance took the form of the search for some access to the professional and the technological aspects of modern birth outside of the institutional structures which they felt had not served them well and which had attempted to eradicate what they viewed as viable collective cultural practices. In short, despite the fact that the feminist agendas of the "rich" versus the developing countries at the women's conferences in Beijing and Huairou were represented by many as competing—with the former portrayed as concerned with women's reproductive rights and the latter with the impact of the structures of poverty on women—poor women in Tamil Nadu viewed the struggle for women's reproductive rights and the struggle against global and local structures of poverty and of class- and gender-based discrimination as inextricably linked.

Epilogue

While I was writing my dissertation, on which this book is based, people used to ask me: "And you, Cecilia? What about your own birth experience? Won't you write about that as well?" But I did not feel compelled to do so.

With the reflexive turn in anthropology, we are called upon to be conscious of and to reveal our social, cultural, political, and even emotional positions vis-à-vis our research topics and the people whom we study. We recognize that culture is not a "thing" which exists objectively out there in the world, but rather it is a process which is continuously constructed and reconstructed through social interactions, within and against relations of power. Anthropologists, as cultural analysts, are actively engaged in this process of culture making through our social interactions in the "field" and through the act of writing ethnography. It is precisely because writing culture is a creative endeavor that it is important to make our relationship to the research as explicit as possible so that the reader can better understand the creative process that went into our analysis and has the opportunity to come to different conclusions than our own. I do think that I inhabit my writing and that my relationships to my work and to the people who are the subject of this book are made clear. But I also felt, and still feel now, that out of respect for the women who shared their stories with me there should be limits to the extent to which I inject myself and my personal experiences into this ethnography. To include my own birth story, I felt at the beginning of my research, would be too self-indulgent. This is, after all, a book about birth among poor women in South India. But since then my life has changed radically such that I can no longer *not* include my own stories when telling the birth stories of other women.

While I was writing my dissertation I was pregnant with my second child. The dissertation was to be submitted in early May 1998. My baby's due date was June 1. The race was on. I joked about the fact that the gestation time for one was nine months while for the other it was nine years!

On April 30, 1998, I gave birth to a stillborn baby, Charlotte Van Hollen Rodgers. Born just one month before her due date, she weighed a full seven pounds, seven ounces. In the hospital room we cradled her in our arms and kissed her. We swaddled her and put on her little hospital cap. We wept and wept and wept. My mother came to see her. Our four-year-old daughter, Lila, came to give Charlotte the pictures which she had been drawing for her baby sister. And when Charlotte became too blue, we said our goodbyes and let her go. We sent Lila's pictures off to be cremated along with Charlotte. And we buried her ashes in Vermont in a beautiful hand-carved box from India.

A generation ago in America it would not have been culturally acceptable for us to name this baby or to utter her name in public. We would not have been able to hold her and stroke her fingers. We would not have a photo album by which to remember her and grieve. She would not have become a member of our family as Charlotte has. But today in America counselors are telling parents who lose their babies to acknowledge them as part of the family. To "say hello and goodbye." At the same time, in anthropology we are encouraged to inject the personal into our public writing. And so it is, at this particular juncture in history in which we are urged to bare our souls for the sake of therapy and of ethnography, that Charlotte must inevitably become a part of this book, albeit sequestered in the pages of an epilogue.

I can no longer *not* tell my story because this experience has altered my relationship with my work. It has changed the way I understand the women whom I met in Tamil Nadu, and has intensified my sense of commitment and urgency to my work. It made me realize some of the most crucial questions which remained unasked during my fieldwork. And the research I had done also influenced the way I dealt with my own loss, particularly during my subsequent pregnancy and the birth of a healthy baby boy. Having a stillborn baby blurred all distinctions between my work and my personal life, not only making the personal political and public, but also making the political nature of my work personal in a deeply emotional and embodied way.

Many of the women I met in Tamil Nadu had experienced the loss of one or more babies at birth or shortly thereafter. This was particularly true of older and middle-aged women but also of some younger women. They would list the number of babies they had had by highlighting those who had lived rather than those who had not made it, as if it was the survivors who were remarkable and not those who had died: "Eight born; five living"; "four born; two living." The deaths seemed to be routine, in part because I had come to expect them from the copious demographic literature on infant mortality in India, and in part because of the way these women themselves did not emphasize the deaths. These deaths never really shocked me. I would express my condolences through the tone of my voice or the look in my eye. I would dutifully jot down notes in my notebook and fill in the appropriate spaces in my questionnaire. How many died? When? Of what cause? But I didn't press for too many details. And I never asked women to elaborate on the meaning of these losses and how they coped with them. With all my interest in modernity and childbirth, this now seems like a glaring gap in my research. Future research should explore how modernity has transformed the cultural experience of infant and fetal loss in India. I have focused on cultural variations in modern child*birth* but we also need to understand variations in modern child death, particularly since birth and death have been so intimately woven together in Indian religious cosmologies.

When Charlotte died I was in shock. Naïve as it may sound, I honestly hadn't believed that a woman in America who had access to high-quality biomedical care could ever have a stillborn baby. Through my research I had come to the conclusion that the only real life-threatening risks in maternal and child health care were those associated with global and local structures of class and gender inequality, and I did not feel that these issues had contributed to the loss of my own baby. It was as if I had lost sight of the fact that, although "nature" is always shaped by socio-cultural processes, it nevertheless must be reckoned with as a powerful, unpredictable player. It was as if I had bought into the biomedical myth of the possibility of conquering death.

I had not, however, uncritically embraced biomedical models for my own pregnancies and births. I had read enough of the feminist literature on the subject to know that childbirth does not always require biomedical intervention and that such intervention can at times *cause* medical complications requiring more interventions than would have been necessary if things had been left alone. During my first pregnancy, I made arrangements to give birth in a free-standing birth center, assisted by a midwife. I battled with my insurance company to earn that right. But in the end I was diagnosed with gestational diabetes and the midwife and my obstetrician agreed I would be better off birthing in the hospital. Even in the hospital I was still determined to have as little technological intervention as possible. When my due date came and went and the doctors were recommending induction with pitocin, I objected and made them do a nonstress test to verify what I already knew, that my baby was still kicking strong. But when my water broke and no contractions followed, it became medically necessary to induce. And over the course of a long and exhausting labor (as most first labors are), my hopes for a technology-free delivery were further chipped away. I was immensely relieved when, after three hours of the final pushing stage, my doctor offered to help my baby out with vacuum extraction, and she also did an episiotomy. My one victory in my struggle to have a "natural" birth was that I managed to give birth with no anesthesia. My husband said the nurses viewed my birth as some kind of a freak show and some came just to sit and watch; to give birth with pitocin and no anesthesia was not an everyday occurrence at Marin General Hospital as it was at Kasthurba Gandhi Hospital.

When I was pregnant the second time, with Charlotte, I still wanted as little intervention as possible but I was not as dogmatic as I had been the first time around. I decided right away to deliver in the same hospital since I was familiar with it and had a good relationship with my obstetrician. Furthermore, due to the contentious politics of midwifery in America today, the new midwife at the birth center where I had planned to deliver my first baby was not assisting deliveries there; that was no longer an option. Part of the reason I was not so determined to stay away from the hospital and all its associated technology as I had been before was the research which I had conducted between these two pregnancies. During my research I had met many women who were tremendously grateful to have access to biomedical care and the technological assistance it could provide in times of need, and I met others who lamented the fact that they had been denied that access. I, too, had come to feel fortunate for having access to good medical care, should some problem arise. And I did not feel I would be subjected to the kinds of problems in hospitals of which poor women in Tamil Nadu were critical, since those problems were primarily associated with forms of class discrimination.

It didn't really occur to me that even with the best of biomedical care during pregnancy and birth, something could go so terribly wrong.

So when my own baby died, I had to confront the fact that poverty was, of course, not the only cause of infant death. But then again, and more significant, it made me that much more saddened and enraged that class discrimination on a global scale *does* put women and children at greater risk of suffering such losses. If I had to grieve for the loss of a baby whose life could not have been saved, how much greater the tragedy for a mother to have to grieve for the loss of a baby who could have lived if she had not been denied access to better nutrition and health care because of grave inequalities or because she faced so much discrimination in medical institutions that she shied away from them?

Charlotte's death shattered my faith in many ways and taught me that there are things far beyond my control. Yet when I was pregnant for the third time, I found myself trying to gain more control, or at least more foresight, through some of the new technologies which biomedicine now had to offer. At a routine prenatal checkup in the ninth month of my pregnancy with Charlotte my doctor detected that my baby (whose sex had still not been identified, by my choice) had a severe case of hydrocephalous. I was rushed off to see a specialist who confirmed that the condition was extreme. Charlotte had virtually no brain left intact. There was only a remote chance that she would live and if she had lived, she would never have developed at all beyond breathing and sucking. Breathing and sucking her whole life long. A genetic test undertaken at this time revealed that she did have a genetic problem, and later genetic tests indicated that this problem was unique to her; neither my husband nor I was a carrier of the trait.

So when I was pregnant the third time we knew that there was almost no chance that this would happen again. But we also knew that the chance of it happening in the first place had been equally remote. Statistics become meaningless in the face of lived experience. And by now I had read up on all the things that can result in stillbirths and had heard many sad and gruesome stories from parents in support groups who had been through similar experiences. With my third birth, I wanted to use whatever technology was available that I did not consider risky. For me, this meant I would do an alpha-fetoprotein (AFP) blood test, which I had chosen not to do with my first two pregnancies, but I would not have an amniocentesis because of the potential risk of miscarriage. For me this also meant that I had twice as many prenatal checkups as was normal, frequent high-resolution ultrasounds (for my first pregnancy I never had a single ultrasound by my choice), and, toward the end of the pregnancy but well before my due date, I found myself frequenting the doctor's office for nonstress tests by my choice. Perhaps most shocking of all, I *elected* to have my labor induced with pitocin a full ten days before my due date came around. This was certainly a new me.

The convergence between my request to be induced and the same request made by so many of the women whom I met in Tamil Nadu did not elude me. What had appeared to me to be a major cultural *difference* between women in America and in Tamil Nadu seemed to be evaporating by my own example. Of course I did not embody all the culturally specific notions of *vali* and *sakti* which informed Tamil women's desires to be induced. But there were many similarities. Like the women in Tamil Nadu who told me that a fast labor was best to reduce risks to the baby and mother, I, too, felt that the sooner my baby was born, the smaller the chance that he would simply and mysteriously stop living in utero, as had happened to other women whose stories I had now heard. I knew this was not scientifically "rational," but it was emotionally very potent. And, like the women in Tamil Nadu who felt they no longer had the same *sakti* to give birth unassisted by technology, I, too, felt that much of my emotional power and confidence had been drained out of me after Charlotte's death and that I would welcome any help in quickly bringing this baby into the world alive. But, again like the women in Tamil Nadu whom I met, and like my old self, I was still determined to give birth without anesthesia, and during this labor I, too, felt that the waves of pain were bringing the baby closer and closer to life.

What, then, am I to make of the *difference* about which I wrote in my ethnography? Do women in Tamil Nadu imbue the *vali* of birth with a fundamentally different meaning than women in America do? Or does the difference lie primarily in the fact that most women in America, like myself in an earlier incarnation, never really anticipate the possibility of infant death, even if they may have other worries associated with pregnancy and birth? I think there is probably a bit of truth to both these explanations. And I think, too, that the cultural meanings of *piracavam, vali,* and *sakti* in Tamil Nadu had seeped into me, informing my response to my own loss and transforming my own understanding of my body and my aspirations. Just as there is always an autobiographical bent to how ethnography is conceived and written, so, too, autobiography becomes punctuated by ethnography.

APPENDIX I

Sample Interview Questionnaires

I developed the following questionnaires at the beginning of my research; questions changed somewhat during the course of the research to accommodate data. Apart from the general sociological data, these questionnaires served as general guidelines for interviews, rather than texts that had to be strictly followed. These questions were translated into and asked in Tamil.

1. GENERAL SOCIOLOGICAL DATA

Name:
Code name and number:
Address:
Date:
Place of interview:
Also present:
Translator:
Sex:
Age:
Marital status:
Date of marriage:
Relation to spouse (kin/nonkin):
Religion:
Caste:
Educational background:

Occupation:
Income:
Location of employment:
Spouse's educational background:
Spouse's occupation:
Spouse's income:
Native place:
Where were you born?
Number of children:
Age, sex, and place of birth of children:
Who is living in your house now?

2. INTERVIEWS WITH POSTPARTUM WOMEN

Interviews with pregnant women were similar to the interviews with postpartum women except geared toward expectations for the future and comparisons with past experiences.

Pregnancy

Can you describe the experience of your pregnancy?
Did you have any difficulties during your pregnancy?
If so, how did you treat these problems?
Did someone check your health during your pregnancy?
Who? How often? What did they do during these checkups?
Was it difficult for you to carry out your daily chores while you were pregnant? Did anyone help you with your work?
Are there special foods that are good to have during pregnancy? Did you have these foods?
Are there some foods you should avoid eating during pregnancy?
Did you take any indigenous medicines during your pregnancy?
Did you take any allopathic medicines during your pregnancy?
Did you have any special foods or medicines during your earlier pregnancies?
Did you make any special prayers or offerings to god or do any special ceremonies while you were pregnant? Please explain. Did you have any special ceremonies during your other pregnancies?
Did you stay in your husband's home throughout the pregnancy or did you go to your parents' house? When did you go? Is the distance between your husband's house and your parents' house great?
Where were you staying during your earlier pregnancies?
Were there any other differences between this pregnancy and your earlier pregnancies?

Delivery

When was your baby born?
Where was your baby born?

Is your baby a boy or a girl?
How much did your baby weigh at birth?
Who assisted you with the delivery?
How did you find out about this person? About this hospital?
Please describe your experience with this delivery from the time you realized you were in labor until the baby was actually born.
How did you know when to call someone for help?
Whom did you call first?
What did they do?
Did your labor pains begin on the date that was predicted by the doctor/*dai* or were they early or late?
If late, did you do anything at home to induce the labor? Did they do anything in the hospital to induce the labor?
If your delivery was in a hospital, who took you to the hospital?
If your delivery was in the home, who came to your home to help?
If you went to the hospital, what were the first things they did in the hospital? Describe the room you were in and the other people in the room. What were the other people doing? Did they allow anybody to come into that room or were some people supposed to stay out of the room? Did you stay in the same room throughout the delivery or did they move you to another room?
If your delivery was at home which part of the house were you in? Who was in the room with you and what were these people doing? Did they allow anybody to be in the room or were some people supposed to stay outside?
Was the delivery painful?
Can you describe how those pains felt?
Did you do anything to reduce the pain?
Did you take any indigenous medicines or did they give you any medicines in the hospital to reduce the pain?
Did you shout out during the delivery?
Did you walk around during the delivery or were you lying down? What positions did you find most comfortable?
Did you or someone in your family make any special prayers during the delivery?
Did you have anything to eat or drink during the delivery?
How long did your pains last?
When did you first feel the pains? When did you start to push the baby out? And what time was the baby born?
Was it difficult to push the baby out?
What position did you use for this?
How did you feel when the baby came out?
Did the baby cry out?
What did the doctor/nurses/*dai* do as soon as the baby came out?
Who cut the umbilical cord?
How long did it take for the placenta to come out?
What did they do with the placenta?
Did somebody note the time of the birth? Are there some times which are auspicious and some times which are inauspicious for a birth?

Did you put the baby to the breast immediately after it was born? If not, when did/will you begin to breastfeed?
Have you had any difficulty breastfeeding?
Did your baby have anything else to eat or drink immediately after the birth?
Did the doctor/nurses/*dai* examine the baby after it was born?
What kinds of tests did they do?
Has the baby been with you ever since he/she was born or did they take the baby into another room?
Where did you rest after the baby was born?
If your delivery was in the hospital, how long did/will you stay in the hospital before you went/go home?
Did you have anything to eat or drink immediately after the baby was born?
Are there some foods that are good to eat during this period? Are there some foods that you should avoid during this period?
Who provided the food at that time?
Was the experience of the delivery what you expected it to be or was it different than you expected? Please explain.
If you have another baby do you plan to have the delivery in the same place or in another place? Do you think you will do things differently for your next delivery?
Was this delivery different from your other deliveries? Please describe your other deliveries. Where were you? Who assisted with the birth? What did they do? Were there any problems? Was there much pain? Were those deliveries longer or shorter? Did you take any indigenous medicines or allopathic medicines during the other deliveries? Did you make any special prayers?
If you have had one delivery at home and one in a hospital, what has been the difference between these two experiences?
Are there any problems with delivering at home?
Are there any problems with delivering in the hospital?
Which place do you prefer?
Did your relations come to visit you immediately after the delivery? Who came? Did they do any special ceremonies or give any special gifts at this time?
Did you give the details for the birth certificate after the baby was born? Did you have to give a name for the baby at that time? What name did you give? Is that the same name you will keep for the baby? How did you choose the name?
What will you use the birth certificate for?

Postpartum

After the birth, whose house did/will you stay in?
If in your parents' house, how long did/will you stay there?
If in your parents' house, did/will your husband and in-laws come to visit? What did/will they do when they visit? Are there gifts exchanged?

If you go to rest in your husband's house, did/will your parents and relations come to visit? What did/will they do during these visits? Are there gifts exchanged?
Whose house did you stay in after your other babies were born? Who visited you and what gifts were exchanged?
How often do you breastfeed your baby?
How long do you think you will continue to breastfeed your baby?
When did you begin to breastfeed your other babies? How long did you breastfeed your other babies?
What foods do you eat after the delivery while you are resting at home?
Are there any foods that are good to eat during this time? Are these foods easily available?
Are there any foods that you should not eat during this time?
Do you take any indigenous medicines during this time?
Do you take any allopathic medicines?
Do you take any vitamins?
What did you eat or take as medicine after your previous deliveries?
After the delivery, how long do you rest without working?
Who will help you with your work while you take rest?
Will you be staying in a separate room or a separated part of the room during this time? Why?
When will you take your first head-bath after the birth?
When will the baby be bathed?
How long did you rest without working after your previous deliveries? Who helped you with your work at that time?
Do you need to protect your baby for several days after the birth? What do you protect the baby from? What will you do to protect your baby from these things?
Will you take your baby to see the doctor/nurse/*dai* after the baby is born?
How often?
What will they do during these visits?
Will you pay for these visits?
Did you take your other babies for such visits?
Will the doctor/nurse/*dai* check you also after the birth?
How often?
What will they do?
Have you had any problems with your health after the delivery?
Have you had any difficulties at home?
Did you have any difficulties after your previous deliveries?
Have you worshipped god or made any special offerings since the baby was born? What did you pray for?
Are there any special ceremonies you will do after the baby is born?
Are there any particular moments in the baby's development which are celebrated?
Naming?
Will the name depend on the horoscope?

First food?
First year?
Head-shaving?
Ear-boring?
Did you do these ceremonies for your other babies? Please describe these.
What ornaments do you put on your baby? Are the ornaments different for boys and girls?
Are you using any family-planning method now?
Do you plan to have another baby? If so, when do you hope the next baby will be born?
How many more children would you like to have? How many would your husband like to have?
Did you use any method of family planning after your other babies were born?

3. INTERVIEWS WITH TRADITIONAL BIRTH ATTENDANTS: *MARUTTUVACCIS/DAIS*

Many of these questions were also used in interviews with nurses and multipurpose health workers who assisted in various ways during home deliveries.

How long have you been helping with births?
How did you learn to do this?
Have you had training for this?
Where were you trained? When?
How long was the training course?
How did you find out about the training?
Did you receive payment to do the training? How much?
What did they teach you in the training course?
Did they provide you with a "kit"? What is in the "kit"?
How has the training changed the way you do your work?
Has the training changed the way people in your area treat you?
Has the training changed the way that people in the hospitals treat you?
On average, how many deliveries do you see per month?
Do you charge a fee for your services? If so, how much? If not, how are you paid?
Where do most of the women whose deliveries you see come from?
How old are most of these women? What is the range of ages?
What kind of economic background do they come from? What kind of work do they do?
What kind of educational background do they have?
What are their religious and caste backgrounds?
Do most women in this area prefer to deliver at home or in the hospital? Why?
Are there any dangers involved in delivering a baby at home?
Are there any dangers involved in delivering a baby in the hospital?

What are the most notable changes in the way childbirth is being carried out in this area today as opposed to one generation ago? What changes would you like to see in the future?
Are there younger women who are interested in learning how to see deliveries? Are there any women who are learning this from you now?
Where were you yourself born? In a hospital or at home?
Who assisted your mother during her delivery?
Do you know what your mother's experience was like?
Do you know whether your own mother was born in a hospital or at home and who assisted with the birth?
Do you do other work in addition to seeing births?

Prenatal

How often do women come to see you during their pregnancy?
How far along in their pregnancy will they be when they come for their first visit?
Do they usually come alone or accompanied by someone else? Who comes with them?
What do you routinely do during the prenatal checkups?
Will you tell them an estimated date of delivery? How do you determine this?
Do many women ask questions about proper nutrition, rest, and exercise during pregnancy?
What advice do you give them about these things?
Do you think they get adequate nutrition, rest, and exercise?
Do they get vitamin or mineral supplements? If so, how are they available?
Do they get any subsidized food supplements or money for food? Are there special foods or country medicines which women should take while they are pregnant?
Are there some foods which women should avoid while they are pregnant?
On average, how much weight do the women whom you see gain during their pregnancy?
Do you tell women about how a baby is conceived, what changes occur to the woman's body and to the fetus during pregnancy, and what happens to the body during the delivery? What do you tell them about this?
Do some women in this area get ultrasounds ("scans")? Why do they do this? Where do they go for this? How much does it cost?
Will women do any special exercises to prepare for delivery?
Do they learn any breathing techniques for delivery?
Do they ask about the signs for the onset of labor? What will you tell them about this? What will you tell them to do when their labor begins?
Do many women express worries about the pain of birth? What do you tell them about this?
Do they ask about techniques to relieve the pain? How will you advise them about this?
What are some of the risks you are able to detect during pregnancy? How will you handle these risks?

What are the most common complications that you tend to see during pregnancy? How do you handle these complications?
How many times have you detected risks during a woman's pregnancy and referred them to the hospital for their deliveries?
Are there any special religious ceremonies performed during a woman's pregnancy? Do you participate in these ceremonies?

Delivery

If the estimated date of delivery passes and labor does not begin, what will you do? How long will you wait before advising inducement? Why is it necessary to induce after a certain length of time has passed?
Are there any things you advise women to do at home to try to get labor started?
Are there indigenous medicines that women will take at home to induce labor?
What will you use to induce labor?
Will they sometimes go to the hospital to induce the labor? What will they use for this in the hospital?
Who will call you when a woman begins to feel the pains?
Will you go to the home of the woman when she begins to feel the pains?
What are the first things you will do when a woman starts to feel the labor pains?
Who will be in the room with the woman during the delivery? Are some people forbidden from coming inside?
What will happen during the early stages of labor?
Will the women be walking around? Where will they walk? Will they stay on the bed?
Will you give them anything to eat or drink during this time?
Do a lot of women shout out loud during delivery? Do you accept their shouting or do you ask them to remain quiet?
Do some women get very scared and frenzied during labor? What will you do in that case?
Do you advise them about breathing or about special positions for labor during this time?
If the pains are very severe will you give them anything to reduce the pain?
How do you know when a woman is ready to push the baby out? Do you do an internal exam?
What position will most women use to push the baby out?
Do you require women to use this position? Why?
Do you advise any special breathing techniques to help push the baby out?
If there are difficulties pushing the baby out what will you do?
Under what circumstances will you refer a woman to the hospital during her delivery?
How far away is the hospital? How will they go to the hospital?
Who will accompany the woman to the hospital?
Do you know the nurses and doctors in the hospital?

Of the deliveries you have seen, how many have been emergencies that required hospitalization?
What will you do immediately after the baby is delivered?
When will you cut the cord?
What will you do to the baby?
How soon will the baby be given to the mother?
Do the mothers begin breastfeeding right away?
Do some women feel it is better not to give mother's milk for the first few days?
How will the placenta be delivered?
What will you do with the placenta afterward?
Will the placenta be buried? Are there special ceremonies for this?
What kinds of records are kept about the baby?
How will they register for a birth certificate?
What are the most common complications that you see during delivery? How do you handle these complications?
What are the most common complications you see for the newborns?
What will you do if the newborn is a low-birth-weight baby?
Where is the closest hospital for babies if there is a problem after the birth? How will the baby be taken there? Will the mother go, too?

Postpartum

After the delivery, how long will the mother stay in the same room?
Will you give her anything to eat or drink at this time?
Who will help clean her up?
Will she be feeling hot or cold during this period? Why?
Who will be allowed in the room immediately after the birth? Will her relations come see her? Which relations generally come? Do male relations come?
Will the relations bring any gifts for the mother and baby? What will they bring?
Will they perform any religious ceremonies immediately after the birth?
How long will the mother and baby remain in the room?
What will the mothers be doing during this time?
Will the babies stay with them there the whole time?
What foods will the mothers take during this time?
Are there some foods or country medicines that are good for the mothers during this time?
Are there some foods or country medicines that the mothers should avoid during this time?
Will they give the babies anything to eat or drink besides mother's milk?
Will you give women anything to relieve the pain and to reduce the bleeding after the birth?
Who will help the mother to change her "napkins" and go to the bathroom during this time?
Who will give the mother a bath? How often?

Who will give the baby a bath? How often?
Do some women feel that the experience of birth is dirty? Are they ashamed or embarrassed by this experience? Why?
Is there *tīḍḍu* during birth? After the birth? How long does this last?
Will the woman rest without doing housework during the *tīḍḍu*? Who will help her with the work during this time? Will you help with this work?
Are there special ceremonies that are done on the day that the *tīḍḍu* is removed? How is it removed?
Are there dangers for the health of the mother and baby after birth? What do you do to protect them from these dangers?
Do you need to protect the mother and baby from the evil eye or other spirits? How do you protect them from these things?
After the baby is born, will you continue to check on the health of the mother and baby? How often will you check them?
What will you do during these checkups?
Do many women use family planning after their deliveries? Which method? Where do they go for that and when?

4. INTERVIEWS WITH ALLOPATHIC MEDICAL PRACTITIONERS

I interviewed practitioners including OB/GYNs, nurses, multipurpose health workers, and those who privately conducted deliveries.

How long have you been working in this profession?
What kind of training did you have for this? Where were you trained? How many years?
On average, how many deliveries do you see per month?
Do you charge a fee for your services? If so, how much? If not, how are you paid?
Where do most of the women whose deliveries you see come from?
How old are most of these women? What is the range of ages?
What kind of economic background do they come from? What kind of work do they do?
What kind of educational background do they have?
What are their religious and caste backgrounds?
Do you think that the process of childbirth always requires some degree of professional medical assistance?
If so, what is the most essential level of assistance required and what kind of medical training is necessary to provide such assistance?
What kinds of facilities, equipment, and pharmaceuticals are necessary?
Do most women in this city/town/village have access to the necessary services for childbirth?
Do you think these services can be delivered at home?
What are some of the dangers involved in delivering a baby at home?
What are some of the dangers involved in delivering a baby in the hospital?
Do most women prefer to deliver at home or in the hospital? Why?
Do doctors or nurses ever do home deliveries?

In what ways have modern technological innovations used in childbirth been helpful? In what ways can they be harmful?
What are the most notable changes in the way childbirth is being carried out in this area/Tamil Nadu/India today as opposed to one generation ago? As opposed to ten years ago? What changes would you like to see in the future?
Where were you yourself born? In a hospital or at home?
Who assisted your mother during her delivery?
Do you know what your mother's experience was like?
Do you know whether your own mother was born in a hospital or at home and who assisted with the birth?
Are most of the obstetricians and nurses involved in maternal health care women?
Will women feel uncomfortable seeing a male doctor for their deliveries?
Approximately what percentage of the doctors in this hospital are women and what percentage are men? Are there any male nurses? Is this changing?

Prenatal

How often do women come to see you during their pregnancy?
How far along in their pregnancy will they be when they come for their first visit?
Do they usually come alone or accompanied by someone else? Who comes with them?
What do you routinely do during the prenatal checkups?
Will you tell them an estimated date of delivery? How do you determine this?
What are the different roles for doctors and for nurses during these prenatal checkups?
Do many women ask questions about proper nutrition, rest, and exercise during pregnancy?
What advice do you give them about these things?
Do you think they get adequate nutrition, rest, and exercise?
Do they get vitamin or mineral supplements? If so, how are they available?
Do they get any subsidized food supplements or money for food?
On average, how much weight do the women whom you see gain during their pregnancy?
Will you tell women about the anatomy of conception, pregnancy and birth? What kinds of questions will they ask about this?
Do many women ask about the development of the fetus?
Will you use a Doppler [an instrument used to measure sound waves of the fetus] or an ultrasound? Will they request this? Is there a charge for these procedures? If you do an ultrasound, will they ask the sex of the fetus? Will you tell them?
Do you do amniocentesis? Do women request this? Will there be a fee for this?
Will they do any exercises to prepare for delivery?
Do they learn any breathing techniques for delivery? Who teaches them about this?

Do they ask about the signs for the onset of labor? What will you tell them about this? What will you tell them to do when their labor begins?
Do they ask about what to expect during the delivery? About the different stages of labor? Cervical dilation? Delivery of the placenta?
Do many women express worries about the pain of birth? What do you tell them about this?
Do they ask about techniques to relieve the pain? How will you advise them about this?
Do they ask about analgesics and the side affects? What will you tell them about this?
What are some of the risks you are able to detect during pregnancy? How will you handle these risks?
What are the most common complications that you tend to see during pregnancy? How do you handle these complications?
Do you ask women to come stay in the hospital/health center on a given date even if their labor pains have not started? Or do they only come once labor has started?
Will you tell women to bring anything with them to the hospital, e.g., clothes, food, etc.?

Delivery

If the estimated date of delivery passes and labor does not begin, what will you do? How long will you wait before advising inducement? Why is it necessary to induce after a certain length of time has passed?
Will you ask them to monitor their own fetal movements?
Will you do a nonstress test or a stress test to determine whether or not it is necessary to induce labor?
Are there any things you advise women to do at home to try to get labor started?
Are there indigenous medicines that women will take at home to induce labor?
What will you use to induce labor? How is this administered?
When a woman comes to the hospital to deliver, will she usually go to the temple or other religious shrine in your compound before she enters the labor ward?
What are the standard procedures when a woman arrives at the hospital for delivery?
Is there paper work to be filled out?
Who will usually accompany her to the hospital? Husband? Mother? Other relatives?
Will she be taken by a wheelchair?
Will she be shaved?
Will you give an enema?
Will she have to put on a hospital gown?
Will you take a pulse?
Will you monitor her contractions? How?

Do you do an internal exam?
Who will do all these things?
Where will the birthing woman stay during the early stages of labor?
Who will be allowed in the room with her? Will any of her relations be with her? If not, where will they wait?
Will there be other birthing women in the same room?
What will happen during the early stages of labor?
Will the women be walking around? Where will they walk? Will they stay on the beds?
Will you give them anything to eat or drink during this time?
Do a lot of women shout out loud during delivery? Do you accept their shouting or do you ask them to remain quiet?
Do some women get very scared and frenzied during labor? What will you do in that case?
Do you advise them about breathing or about special positions for labor during this time?
How do you determine whether it will be necessary to administer an analgesic? Will the women ask for this themselves? What will you give them? Does this have any side effects for the mother and the labor process? Does it affect the baby?
Who are the medical staff and service staff who will be in the labor room during these first stages of delivery and what are their various roles?
Once the woman is fully dilated and it is time to push the baby out, will she be moved to a different room?
How will she be moved? Who will accompany her? Where is this other room?
Will there be other women giving birth in that room as well?
Who is allowed to enter into this room?
What position will most women use to push the baby out?
Do you require women to use this position? Why?
Do you advise any special breathing techniques to help push the baby out?
If there are difficulties pushing the baby out what will you do? Will you use forceps? Vacuum? Cesarean?
What percentage of the deliveries you see require episiotomies?
What will you do immediately after the baby is delivered?
When will you cut the cord?
What will you do to the baby?
How soon will the baby be given to the mother?
What kinds of tests will be done for the baby? When will they be done? By whom?
How will the placenta be delivered?
What will you do with the placenta afterward?
Approximately what percentage of the deliveries you see are cesareans?
What are the main complications that lead to cesareans?
If a woman has previously had a cesarean will the following births also be cesareans?
If a cesarean is required, where will that be performed?

How will the woman be taken to the place to conduct the cesarean?
Who will do this operation?
Who will be allowed in the room at the time of the operation?
What are the most common complications that you see during delivery? How do you handle these complications?
What are the most common complications you see for the newborns?
What will you do if the newborn is a low-birth-weight baby?
Is there a neonatal intensive care unit here? Where is the closest intensive care unit? How will the baby be taken there? Will the mother go, too?
Approximately what percentage of the deliveries which you see are "natural," that is not involving drugs, forceps, or surgical methods of any kind?

Postpartum

What will happen immediately after the delivery?
How long will the mother stay in the same room?
Will you give her anything to eat or drink at this time?
Who will help clean her up?
Will she breastfeed her baby right away?
Who will be allowed in the room immediately after the birth? Will her relations come see her?
Will the baby be taken out of the room for any tests?
What kinds of records are kept about the baby?
Will the baby be taken out for the relatives to see?
Will the mother later be moved into a postnatal ward? How much later will this be?
How will she be moved?
How will the baby be moved?
Will there be other mothers in this ward?
Who is allowed in this ward?
Will relations be allowed to come? Which relations generally come? Do male relations come?
Will you give food and drinks in this ward? What will you give?
Will the relations bring food or drinks? What will they bring?
Will the relations bring any other gifts for the mother and baby? What will they bring?
Are any relations allowed to stay in the postnatal ward or are there strict visiting hours?
Will they perform any religious ceremonies in the hospital or in the hospital compound immediately after the birth?
What will the mothers be doing in the postnatal ward?
Will the babies stay with them there the whole time?
Will the mothers begin breastfeeding right away?
If it is their first baby, will someone show them how to feed the baby?
Will you give the babies anything else to eat or drink?
Do some women feel it is better not to give breast milk for the first few days?

Do you advise mothers about special nutrition needs while they are breast-feeding?
Do you advise their relations about this?
Do you provide them with any vitamin or mineral supplements at this time? Who pays for these?
Do you provide them with any supplemental foods during this time? Who pays for this?
Who will help the mothers to change their "napkins" and go to the bathroom while they are in the postnatal ward?
Will the mothers be bathed in the hospital? Who will help with this?
Will you give them anything to relieve the pain and to reduce the bleeding after the birth?
Will the babies be bathed in the hospital? Who will do this?
Who will dress the umbilical cord?
Will the mothers continue to dress the cord at home?
Will the mothers bring clothes for their babies or will these be provided by the hospital?
Do women feel that the experience of birth is dirty? Are they ashamed or embarrassed by this experience? Why?
Is this belief more common among certain communities?
What measures will be taken to confine women due to this feeling of dirtiness?
Will these measures be taken in the hospital or only in the home?
How would you describe the difference between the traditional Indian ideas of "pollution" associated with childbirth and the medical notion of germs also associated with childbirth?
Are some people worried about protecting newborn babies from the evil eye or other spirits?
Can you explain what these worries are about?
What do they do to protect their babies from this?
Will they take these precautions in the hospital or only in the home?
What will they do at home to protect the baby from such things?
How long will the mothers stay in the postnatal ward before going home?
Who will usually take them home?
How will they go home?
After they have gone home, will the mothers return to the hospital for postnatal checkups?
How often will they come for these checkups?
What will you do during these checkups?
Will you also check the baby or will they see someone else for that?
Do many women use family planning after their deliveries? Which method? Where do they go for that and when?

APPENDIX II

Official Structure of Maternal-Child Health Care Institutions and Practitioners in Tamil Nadu, 1995

RURAL SECTOR

I. Tertiary health care in government hospitals (attached to research institutions in major urban centers)

II. Secondary health care in *taluk* hospitals and district quarter hospitals

III. Primary health care for each development block of one million population.

  A. Primary health center (PHC)
  One for every 30,000 population
  Each PHC is staffed with:
    Two medical officers (one male and one female)
    Paramedics
    Pharmacist
    Health support staff
      Multipurpose health workers–male (MPHW—M), responsible for vertical public outreach health programs, such as those for tuberculosis, malaria, AIDS, and leprosy, as well as family planning
      Multipurpose health workers–female (MPHW—F), responsible for outreach programs for MCH care and family planning; some female MPHWs are sector health nurses (previously called lady health visitors), overseeing the work of the village health nurses

B. Health subcenter (HSC) attached to the PHC
Sector health nurse from each PHC oversees six HSCs
Each HSC is staffed with:
Village health nurse (VHN; previously called auxiliary nurse midwife [ANM]); VHNs can conduct deliveries in homes or in HSCs if the HSC has a building.

IV. Community level
A. Integrated Child Development Services (ICDS/*balwadis*)
Staffed with *anganwadi* workers providing pre- and postnatal nutritional supplements and immunizations, as well as care and meals for children
B. Traditional birth attendants (TBAs/*dais*), trained and untrained
C. Non-TBAs (family members, etc. who assist at births)
D. Nongovernmental organizations
For example, Voluntary Health Services (VHS)
VHS has mini-health-centers (MHCs) in some semirural communities, staffed with:
Two multipurpose health workers (one male and one female)
One lay first-aider (female)

URBAN SECTOR FOR MAJOR CITIES

I. Tertiary care in government hospitals

II. Primary care
IPP-V health posts
One IPP-V health post covers a population of 35,000–40,000
Some IPP-V health posts provide outpatient care only; others are maternity centers; some of the maternity centers are zonal health posts with operation theaters for cesareans
Each IPP-V health post is staffed with at least:
One female medical officer
One female health visitor
Several MPHWs, all female; each MPHW is responsible for a population of 5,000, providing pre- and postnatal care and family-planning education and supplies, and referring women to hospitals for deliveries
Link leaders (liaison between MPHW and community)—one from each community served by MPHWs

III. Community level
A. Integrated Child Development Services (ICDS/*balwadis*)
Staffed with *anganwadi* workers providing pre- and postnatal nutritional supplements and immunizations, as well as care and meals for children
B. Nongovernmental organizations
For example, Working Women's Forum (WWF) Reproductive Health Project

WWF health workers are women who live in the urban communities covered by WWF; they provide reproductive health information and collect reproductive health records, refer women to hospitals for MCH care, and provide family-planning information and some contraceptives

WWF health supervisors are women who were previously WWF health workers; they oversee the work of several health workers in a number of poor urban communities

Glossary

The following is a list of non-English words and English acronyms that appear frequently in the book.

ācai desire, wish
aciṅkam disgusting, unseemly, dirty
ANM auxiliary nurse midwife
ayah a woman who works as the lowest-level medical staff in maternity wards; *ayahs* prepare women for deliveries, assist doctors and nurses during deliveries, and clean and move mothers and babies following the delivery
Ayurveda traditional, pan-Indian system of medicine, based on ancient Hindu texts
balwadi a community center run by the government's Integrated Child Development Services (ICDS) program; the *balwadis* in Tamil Nadu serve as day care centers for young children as well as centers for providing some nutritious food for children as well as some pre- and postnatal care for pregnant and lactating women
cīmantam ritual performed during a woman's first pregnancy
cukku dried ginger
dai traditional birth attendant (pan-Indian term)
drishti the evil eye
harijan someone belonging to a low ("untouchable") caste; the term was coined by Gandhi and literally means "god's people"
IEC information, education, and communication

IMR infant mortality rate
IPP-V India Population Project-V
ja<u>n</u><u>n</u>i fever accompanied by shaking fits
karuppu blackness; refers to a disease in which an infant has dark spots on the skin; may be accompanied by difficulty with breathing
kaṣāyam herbal medicine
kōlam design made on the ground in front of the front door of the house and sometimes in the doorway; typically made with rice flour
kowravam prestige
lēkiyam a form of medicine made from a sweet base with things like white and brown sugar and jaggery; other ingredients are mixed with the sweet base and ghee is often added as a preserving agent; the final product is rolled into small balls which are taken by mouth
māman maternal uncle
māmiyār mother-in-law
maruntu medicine
maruttuvacci a traditional birth attendant in Tamil Nadu; often from the Barber caste
MCH maternal-child health
MHC mini-health-center
MMR maternal mortality rate
MPHW multipurpose health worker
mūḍanampikkai superstitions
nāḍḍu maruntu country medicine, traditional medicine
panchayat a body of local government, traditionally comprised of five members
paṛakkam tradition, habit
Pattinavar name of a fishing caste in Tamil Nadu
pattiyam a special diet
PHC primary health center
piracavam birth, delivery
piracava maruntu a medicine taken after delivery, usually in the form of a *lēkiyam* and typically containing dried ginger, asafoetida, and black jaggery
pittam (also *pitta*) source of heat in the body associated with humoral systems of knowledge in Siddha and Ayurveda medical theories
sakti divine female power associated with action and the generative force of the universe
scheduled caste (SC) official government term for low-caste ("untouchable") communities
Siddha a traditional form of medicine indigenous to Tamil Nadu
TBA traditional birth attendant
TFR total fertility rates
tīḍḍu blood associated with birth and the postpartum period; menstrual blood; ritual pollution
tīḍḍukkaṛittal ritual ceremony performed after birth to "remove the *tīḍḍu*/pollution"
uḍampu body
vācal threshold of the front doorway

vaḷaikāppu a ritual performed during a woman's first pregnancy that involves placing bangles on the pregnant woman's arms
vali pain, ache; strength, force
VHN village health nurse
VHS Voluntary Health Services
WWF Working Women's Forum

Notes

PROLOGUE

1. All names in this book are pseudonyms unless otherwise indicated. I have tried to substitute with names that are similar in kind to the real names (such as Sanskritic versus Tamil; Hindu versus Muslim versus Christian). Except where noted, all the quotes from my ethnographic interviews are translated from Tamil into English. English words used in Tamil conversations are in quotations.

The official name of Madras has recently been changed back to one of its precolonial names, a name often used by Tamil speakers: Chennai. While I was conducting my research in 1993 and 1995 the city was still officially called Madras, so I have chosen to retain that name for this book for historical accuracy.

2. In India, the equivalent of a high school diploma is referred to as a secondary school leave certificate (SSLC).

3. Daniel 1984: 130.

4. For more information on the sacred role of the *kōlam* and the threshold in Tamil Nadu, see Nagarajan 1993.

5. Although the private and public are never, in reality, distinct spheres of social life, I find this distinction to be heuristically useful for conceptualizing this movement from home to hospital. "Public" in this rendering refers to the space opened up by modern state institutions—in this case biomedical institutions—within which the state may exert control but which simultaneously creates a shared experience of the state and thus leads to collective reflection on and critique of the state. This latter aspect of the "public" as civil society has been the object of much recent interest among scholars studying "public culture" in South Asia. See for example contributions to the journal *Public Culture*.

6. Jolly 1998a.

7. Although I do take these "local" contexts to have empirical reality (though their boundaries can never be delineated), I am also aware of how the ideology of the "local" (or in anthropological practice, the "field") has played a central role in the modernizing projects throughout the world and in resistance to these projects (Gupta & Ferguson 1997; Nadel-Klein 1991).

INTRODUCTION. CHILDBIRTH AND MODERNITY IN TAMIL NADU

1. See Kay, ed. 1982.

2. Ginsburg & Rapp 1995; Davis-Floyd 1992.

3. Garro 1998: 325.

4. Sargent 1982: 12.

5. Clifford & Marcus, eds. 1986.

6. For discussions of medical pluralism in India, see Leslie, ed. 1976 and Leslie & Young, eds. 1992. Djurfeldt and Lindberg's (1975) study of medical pluralism and therapeutic choice in Tamil Nadu is particularly relevant to my own work, since they did research in the same general geographic area. In his study of medical pluralism in China, Arthur Kleinman envisions the multiple approaches of medicine as inhabiting three overlapping yet distinct spheres, namely the "popular," the "professional," and the "folk" (Kleinman 1980: 50). While similar types of categories are often employed in the discussion of medical pluralism in the Indian context, I avoid such typologies since I view these categories to be more reflective of the so-called professional medical practitioners' attempts to create hierarchies which assert their own authority over other medical practitioners'. As Leslie (1976) has pointed out, it is due to the power gained through such categorization that many Indian medical practitioners of Ayurveda, Unani, and Siddha felt compelled to professionalize their practices through the development of bureaucratic institutions which were modeled on biomedical institutional structures.

7. Ram 1994, 1998, 2001a, 2001b.

8. Gideon 1962; Freed & Freed 1980; Flint 1982; Jeffery et al. 1989; Patel 1994; Kolenda 1997.

9. Garro 1998: 320.

10. Geertz 1973.

11. Cohen 1998.

12. Ibid.: xvi.

13. Illich 1976: 132.

14. Mohanty 1991; Kleinman & Kleinman 1996.

15. Davis-Floyd & Sargent 1997: 3.

16. Browner & Sargent 1990: 217.

17. Spencer 1977; Freedman & Ferguson 1950; Ford 1964; Mead & Newton 1967; Hart, Rajadhon, & Coughlin 1965; Newman 1969, 1972; see also McClain 1982 for more discussion on these studies.

18. Mead & Newton 1967.

19. Frank 1992: 84.

20. Illich 1976; Foucault 1973; Madan 1980.

21. Scheper-Hughes & Lock 1987: 53.

22. Friedson 1970.

23. Lock & Kaufert 1998: 18.

24. Boddy 1998: 51.

25. Scheper-Hughes & Lock 1987.

26. For useful reviews of the literature on the anthropology of reproduction, including studies on the biomedicalization of childbirth, see McClain 1982; Browner & Sargent 1990; Ginsburg & Rapp 1991, 1995; Van Hollen 1994; and Davis-Floyd & Sargent 1997.

27. Gélis 1991; Martin 1987; Davis-Floyd 1992.

28. Rothman 1982; Oakley 1984; Martin 1987; Davis-Floyd 1992.

29. Ehrenreich & English 1973; Leavitt 1986; Martin 1987. For Foucault's concept of the "medical gaze," see Foucault 1973.

30. Oakley 1984; Jordan 1993; Duden 1993; Davis-Floyd 1992; Browner & Press 1995; Davis-Floyd & Sargent, eds. 1997.

31. Leavitt 1986; Reissman 1983; Rapp 1991, 1993; Franklin & Ragoné, eds. 1998; Lock & Kaufert, eds. 1998.

32. For a brief ethnographic account of this movement, see Anderson & Bauwens 1982.

33. See, for example, Kitzinger 1978, 1979, 1991 and Davis-Floyd 1992.

34. Kay, ed. 1982.

35. See, for example, Cominsky 1976; Sargent 1982; Kay, ed. 1982; Laderman 1983; O'Neil & Kaufert 1990, 1993; MacCormack 1994.

36. Jordan 1978.

37. For relevant studies on the United States, see Martin 1987; Rapp 1991, 1999; Fraser 1995; Lazarus 1997; and Becker 2000. For studies of other Western nations, see Oakley 1977.

38. See Leavitt 1986; Mitford 1992; and Apple, ed. 1990 for American history. See Gélis 1991 for European history.

39. Jordan 1993: 196.

40. Ibid.

41. Lock & Kaufert 1998: 16.

42. Ginsburg & Rapp 1995: 12.

43. Ibid.: 1.

44. See, for example, contributions in Ram & Jolly, eds. 1998 and Davis-Floyd & Sargent, eds. 1997, such as articles by Georges, Fielder, and Pigg.

45. Boddy 1998: 49. Boddy writes that infibulation is "a form of 'female circumcision' in which the midwife excises the girl's clitoris and inner labia and then pares her outer labia and stitches them together so as to 'cover' or 'veil' the vaginal meatus, leaving a pinhole opening for the elimination of urine and menstrual blood" (33).

46. Comaroff & Comaroff 1991: 23.

47. Scott 1985.

48. From *Child Survival and Safe Motherhood in Tamil Nadu* (Government of Tamil Nadu 1994: 36), published by the Directorate of Public Health and Preventative Medicine.

49. From the Government of Tamil Nadu's 1993 *State Plan for Action for the Child in Tamil Nadu.*

50. From the article "India and the World Bank," published in *The (Madras) Hindu,* Tuesday, February 23, 1993.

51. Personal communication with Dr. S. S. Kodimani, director, IPP-V for Madras Corporation, January 27, 1995.

52. Jejeebhoy & Rao. 1995: 125.

53. For some recent exceptions, see studies by Ram (1994, 1998) and Ravindran (1994, 1995b).

54. My trip in 1991 was funded by a grant from the Department of Anthropology, University of Pennsylvania. The 1993 trip was funded by a grant from the Dean of Arts and Sciences at the University of Pennsylvania.

55. This portion of my research was funded with the very generous support of a Fulbright-Hayes for Doctoral Dissertation Research Abroad Fellowship.

56. This trip was funded by a Lowie grant from the Department of Anthropology at the University of California, Berkeley.

57. In Tamil, *ellai* means "frontier" or "border," and *amman* means mother-goddess.

58. These are often referred to as "untouchable" castes. In some communities, members of these castes have followed Dr. Ambedkar's political movement and mobilized themselves within a pan-Indian *dalit* movement; they identify themselves as *dalits.* Most of the people in the communities where I worked, however, identified themselves using Gandhi's term, *harijan* ("god's people"), or the state bureaucratic label, "scheduled caste." I have chosen therefore to use these, their own categories of identity. The term "scheduled caste" refers to those castes that are entitled to certain benefits under the government's caste-based "reservation" policy. This is similar to the system of affirmative action in the United States.

59. This is her real name.

60. This systematic wage differential for men and women was first established within the colonial capitalist economy. Kynch reports that in the wage economy of Madras Presidency in 1872–1873 one man was systematically paid the equivalent of two women, which was also the equivalent of four children (Kynch 1987: 138). The Madras Presidency was a British colonial province that included the cotemporary state of Tamil Nadu as well as portions of the contemporary states of Andhra Pradesh, Karnataka, and Kerala. In postcolonial India, state boundaries were redrawn based on linguistic differences.

61. This town used to be called Mahabalipuram, and many still know it by that name. It was officially renamed Mamallapuram as part of a movement to revive Tamil names which had been changed or bastardized due to mispronunciations during the colonial era.

62. Other terms frequently used are "*kai vaittiyam*" (hand treatment) and "Tamil *vaittiyam*" (Tamil treatment).

63. *Ayahs* are women who work as the lowest-level medical staff in maternity wards. They prepare women for deliveries, assist doctors and nurses during deliveries, and clean and move mothers and babies following the delivery.

64. Female MPHWs are primarily engaged in outreach MCH work in the

surrounding communities. This work includes the provision of MCH education and prenatal care as well as the distribution of contraceptives.

65. While I videotaped, my research assistant asked questions and took notes. I then wrote down my own notes at home following the events. The video footage has been very valuable to me as I have tried to relive the events in order to transform memory into words. It was, however, somewhat limiting insofar as it narrowed my scope of vision and made the experience primarily a visual experience, shutting out other sensory experiences.

66. Pauline Kolenda (1997) has noted the same open enthusiasm for discussing these issues among women in the village of Khalapur in Uttar Pradesh.

67. For fruitful discussions of the role of childbirth in colonial discourses elsewhere, see Ram & Jolly, eds. 1998; and Boddy 1998.

CHAPTER 1. THE PROFESSIONALIZATION OF OBSTETRICS

1. See Sargent & Rawlins 1992; Boddy 1998; Manderson 1998; and Jolly 1998b for case studies.

2. Guha 1996: 25.

3. Mani 1990: 117. *Sati* here refers to the act of a widow's immolation on her husband's funeral pyre as well as to the woman who is immolated.

4. Bala 1991; Arnold 1988.

5. Stoler 1991.

6. For example see Guha 1996; Lal 1994; Arnold 1993; and Ramusack 1996, 1997, and 2000.

7. First All India Obstetric and Gynaecological Congress 1936: 13.

8. Selby 1999.

9. Jeffery 1988: 47.

10. Rozario 1995: 92.

11. Ibid.

12. For more discussion on the role of caste in *jajmani* socio-economic relationships, see Wiser 1936; Lewis 1958; and Fuller 1989.

13. Jeffery et al. 1989: 68.

14. Ehrenreich & English 1973; Gélis 1991.

15. Ehrenreich & English 1973: 13–18.

16. See Chawla 1994 for a discussion of the *dai* as ritual specialist; and Radhika & Balasubramanian 1990 for a discussion of the *dai*'s management of birth.

17. For the Jamaican case, see Kitzinger 1994; for the Sierra Leone case, see MacCormack 1994.

18. Jeffery & Jeffery 1993; Jeffery et al. 1989; Rozario 1998, 1995.

19. Pigg 1997.

20. See Jeffery et al. 1989; and Rozario 1995.

21. Jeffery 1988: 90.

22. Lal 1994: 34.

23. The Dufferin Fund's *First Annual Report*, 1886, p. 258, cited in Lal 1994.

24. Ibid., p. 13, cited in Lal 1994: 35.

25. Jeffery 1988; Arnold 1993; Lal 1994; Guha 1996.

26. This is often the preference of the woman's husband as well.
27. Government of Madras 1923: 5.
28. Arnold 1993: 258.
29. *Mofussil* refers to rural areas in India under the jurisdiction of district government bodies rather than city government bodies.
30. Iyengar is a Vaisnava Brahmin name.
31. Victoria Hospital 1904.
32. Borthwick 1984 cited in Lal 1994: 41–42.
33. Sargent & Rawlins 1992: 1226.
34. Arnold 1993: 258.
35. Lal 1994: 48.
36. Arnold 1993: 9.
37. Lal 1994: 39–43.
38. Borthwick, cited in Lal 1994: 40.
39. In those fields of medicine which recruited male medical students and which were not as directly involved in bodily practices deemed "polluting," members of higher-caste Hindu communities were often disproportionately represented. This was also true of the *bhadralok* castes in Bengal (Bala 1991, ch. 5).
40. Jeffery 1988: 84–90.
41. For examples of these debates see Government of Madras 1939a, 1939b.
42. Government of Madras 1939b.
43. The first individual *dai*-training school in India was established in Amritsar, Punjab, in 1866 by the civil surgeon Dr. Aichison (Arnold 1993: 259).
44. Victoria Fund 1918: 162.
45. Ibid.: 16.
46. Foucault 1977a.
47. Ram 1998.
48. Victoria Fund 1918: 40.
49. Chatterjee 1990.
50. Victoria Fund 1918: 124.
51. Burma was briefly part of British India until 1937, when it was administered as a separate British protectorate. Burma gained independence from Britain in 1948. See ibid.: 142.
52. Nandy 1983.
53. Victoria Fund 1918: 78.
54. Sargent & Rawlins 1992: 1227.
55. Jolly 1998a: 6.
56. From a 1923 memorandum by the director of public health; see Government of Madras 1923: 11.
57. See Government of Madras 1929.
58. For more discussion on the historical ties between these baby shows and other programs in the West and those promoted in colonial India, see Ramusack 1996 and 2000. Many of these pedagogical techniques of "mothercraft" continued to be used by state governments in India in 1995.
59. Victoria Fund 1918: 56.
60. Ibid.: 100.
61. Ibid.: 10.

62. Ibid.: 99.

63. Government of Madras 1923: 6.

64. Victoria Fund 1918: 2.

65. Government of Madras 1923: 8.

66. Government of Madras 1927. After independence and the breakup of the Indian states this came to be known as the Tamil Nadu Nurses and Midwives Act of 1926.

67. See Government of India 1928: 4.

68. Kynch 1987.

CHAPTER 2. MCH SERVICES IN THE POSTCOLONIAL ERA

1. Jeffery 1988: 112.

2. The concept of the primary health center first emerged in England in the 1920s. Although it was not widely implemented in England until the 1960s, it had already been put into place in many other parts of the world, including India (ibid.: 263).

3. Government of Madras 1938.

4. Jeffery 1988: 230–235.

5. These statistics and explanations of the official structure of public MCH care in Tamil Nadu were provided by Dr. Syed Fiaz, Tamil Nadu Department of Public Health, personal communication, February 2, 1995. Many of the same figures are published in the Government of Tamil Nadu's 1994 *Child Survival and Safe Motherhood in Tamil Nadu,* pp. 2–6.

6. "Development blocks" are officially designated regions within each state for the provision of a variety of governmental community development projects, including public health projects.

7. "Dr. Sanjivi" is a real name. Much of the information about the formation and structure of VHS was provided to me in private discussion with Dr. B. J. Krishnamurthy of VHS in February and March of 1993 at the VHS headquarters in Adyar, Madras.

8. Many of the construction workers in Tamil Nadu are women; and in a construction crew, it is the women who often do the most laborious jobs.

9. For example, he would recommend that postpartum women take two premade Siddha medicines known as *cowbākkiya cūnti* and *dasamūlārishḍam* to help the mother regain her strength and to heal the wounds of delivery.

10. From Government of Tamil Nadu 1995a: 2.

11. Much of the information on the origins, structure, and goals of the IPP-V projects was provided in discussions with Thangam Shankaranarayanan (IAS), director of the IPP-V project for Tamil Nadu, on January 25, 1995, and with Dr. S. S. Kodimani, director of IPP-V for the Corporation of Madras, on January 27, 1995.

12. When I returned in May 1997, most of the health posts which had received IPP-V funding were still operating under state-government funds. Due to the loss of World Bank funding, other health posts had been closed down.

13. "Eligible couples" means married couples in which the woman is between the ages of fifteen and forty-five years, i.e., in her "reproductive years."

14. From the India Population Project-V (IPP-V) *Health for All by 2000* pamphlet, p. 7.

15. Personal communication with Dr. S. S. Kodimani, director, IPP-V for Madras Corporation, January 27, 1995.

16. Personal communication with Dr. C. N. Sujayakumari, superintendent of Kasthurba Gandhi Hospital, March 5, 1993.

17. Personal communication with Dr. Sathiayavathy, zonal officer, Santhome Zonal Health Post, March 16, 1995.

18. Personal communication with the medical officer and public health nurse at the Santhome hospital, January 30, 1995.

19. Information about the origins, structure, and activities of the WWF has been culled from discussions with numerous members of WWF in March and April of 1993 and throughout the year of 1995. Both times, I was formally affiliated with WWF and they provided me with much assistance in all areas of my research.

CHAPTER 3. BANGLES OF *NEEM*, BANGLES OF GOLD

1. *"Talai"* means "head." And, as in English, this refers both to the body and to the notion of preeminence, as in the term *"talaivar"* (headman). It also means that which comes first in a sequence. So *talai piracavam* is not only the first delivery but also the most important, the preeminent delivery. The year following a marriage is marked by celebrating several other first *(talai)* events for the married couple, including the first time the couple celebrates key Tamil festivals together, thus the expressions *"talai Dipavali"* and *"talai Pongal."*

2. Wadley, ed. 1980: xiii.

3. For in-depth discussions on the concept of auspiciousness, its relationship to fertility, and how it is distinguished from the notion of "purity" in India, see Das 1977; Marglin 1985; Parry 1991; and Madan 1991.

4. Wadley, ed. 1980: ix-x.

5. See Menezes 1999.

6. See contributions to Breckenridge, ed. 1995.

7. Fuller 1996: 3.

8. Appadurai 1996: 6–7.

9. Meillassoux 1981; Jeffery et al. 1989.

10. Engels 1972 [1884].

11. Meillassoux 1981: xi.

12. O'Brien 1981: 165, 166.

13. Miller 1981; Dyson & Moore 1983.

14. Wadley, ed. 1980.

15. Jeffery et al. 1989, ch. 4.

16. The Arya Samaj was a late-nineteenth-century reform movement which was critical of many Brahminical Hindu practices but promoted Hinduism as a superior religion. See Freed & Freed 1980: 350–351.

17. Gideon 1962.

18. Patel 1994: 109.

19. *Nātasvarams* are long, oboe-shaped instruments commonly used to announce the commencement of a festival or marriage ceremony in Tamil Nadu.

20. Because the Tamil calendar is lunar, the correspondence between it and the solar calendar varies year to year. Nevertheless, we can say that in a general way there is the following correspondence: Cittirai (April 15–May 15); Vaikāci (May 15–June 15); Āni (June 15–July 15); Āḍi (July 15–August 15); Āvaṇi (August 15–September 15); Puraḍḍāci (September 15–October 15); Aippaci (October 15–November 15); Kārttikai (November 15–December 15); Mārkaṛi (December 15–January 15); Tai (January 15–February 15); Māci (February 15–March 15); Paṅkuni (March 15–April 15).

21. Kasthuri also told me that if a woman does not deliver within a week on either side of the ten-month period, people will say that she must have walked over a rope used to lead a cow or that she must be possessed by a malevolent spirit *(pēy)*.

22. It is considered especially inauspicious to be born during the peak of the hot season, known as "*kāttiri veyil.*"

23. As the Tamil proverb goes: Āḍi *paḍḍam tēḍi vitai* (look for the month of Āḍi, the suitable season, and sow).

24. Personal communication with Kausalya Hart, March 1998, Berkeley, California.

25. Turmeric plays an important role in Hindu ritual. In Tamil Nadu, Fridays and Tuesdays are considered to be auspicious days for Hindus. It is on these days that most people go to temple to pray, particularly to worship Amman, the mother goddess. Before going to temple on these days, it is very common for women to apply a layer of turmeric paste on their faces, which is perceived by many as a form of beauty, and the turmeric is supposed to be beneficial to the skin. Used in many food preparations, turmeric is not only valued for its flavor but is also believed to have great medicinal value.

26. *Sambhar* is a soup made out of dal and vegetables.

27. The number 101 is extremely auspicious in Tamil Nadu. The importance of this number reflects what Valentine Daniel calls the "rule of incompletion," in which no stage should be completed before the next stage begins (Daniel 1984: 131–132). In the case of ritual gifts the one in the number 101 implies a continuation of gifting rather than completion.

28. A round brown fruit with large black seeds.

29. A *pāvāḍai* is a long skirt with a wide embroidered border topped with a matching blouse, the formal dress for young girls.

30. Watching the children at this *cīmantum,* I could see that this sartorial gendering of tradition and modernity begins at a very young age. Partha Chatterjee (1990) has argued that in nineteenth-century nationalist discourse in Bengal, Indian women were represented as the upholders of "tradition" (versus modernity) and they were expected to continue to wear Indian clothes as a symbol of tradition, whereas Indian men were not enjoined to wear Indian dress to the same extent.

31. A *vesdhi* is a long white cloth wrapped around the waist. In North India this is known as a "*dhoti.*" A *tuṇḍu* is a small piece of white cloth which is draped over the shoulder.

32. For more in-depth discussion of the role of these men in Tamil society, see Mines & Gourishankar 1990.

33. See, for example, contributions in Wadley, ed. 1980. In fact, I was told that sexual intercourse during pregnancy is considered harmful to the fetus, especially during the later months of the pregnancy. Many women told me that their doctors told them to abstain from sex during pregnancy. Yet, when I said that in America doctors sometimes advise having sex in order to induce labor, I was told that some people make this same implication when they tease a woman by saying that it was only after her husband came to visit her in her mother's house that she suddenly got labor pains.

34. Radhika & Balasubramanian 1990, part 1: 27.

35. In Siddha the ratios of the pulse of the humors in a "normal" body are: *vatham:* 1; *pittam:* 1/2; *kabam:* 1/4. When a woman is pregnant, however, *vatham* and *pittam* are both one (personal communication with Dr. Kalyanasundaram, Anna Hospital, Arumbakkam, Madras, May 9, 1997).

36. A *mantiravāti* is someone who practices magic by reciting sacred hymns *(manthiram)* and can remove and/or inflict spells.

37. Gélis 1991: 53–58.

38. *Kuṅkumam* is a bright red powder used in most forms of Hindu worship; it is usually applied as a dot on the forehead.

39. The botanical name for the margosa is *Melia azidirachta indica.*

40. *Tāmpūlam* are also used to exchange gifts on other ritual occasions such as marriages and Saraswati Puja. The *vettilaipākku* is the common ingredient of the *tāmpūlam* on all such occasions.

41. Some people told me that if their families performed more than one *cīmantam,* they would only take the professional photos during the earlier ceremony in the fifth or seventh month of their pregnancy and not during the ceremony in the ninth month, because they felt that in the latter stages of the pregnancy their large bodies made them look unseemly *(aciṅkam).*

42. Brahmins also include a bangle made out of five types of metal that are thought to protect the mother's health.

43. Some people told me that gold is akin to god and that therefore women should only wear gold above the waist, where the body is pure. The body becomes increasingly polluted as you move down from the waist—the feet being the most polluted of all. Traditionally only silver is worn below the waist. There is, however, a new Kerala-inspired trend among some families to wear gold anklets.

44. Among lower-class communities in Tamil Nadu, elderly women may take betel nut publicly, as do men. Middle-aged women such as Vasanti may take it on special ritual occasions such as this *cīmantam.*

45. Wadley, ed. 1980: x.

46. Ibid.: ix–x.

47. Daniel 1980: 78–79.

48. Wadley, ed. 1980: 153.

49. Ibid.: xv, 153–170.

50. Egnor 1980: 15.

51. Ibid.: 2.

52. There should always be an odd number of *cumaṅkalis* participating in this ceremony, and there was a great deal of debate about how many that should be. The elder men in front argued with the women administering the ceremony on stage until finally all agreed that nineteen was the appropriate number for this evening's *cīmantam*. It is important that the total number of bangles be odd, so one *cumaṅkali* must be sure to place an odd number of bangles. The only color which cannot be used is black.

53. Although it is very common for the pregnant woman to return to her parents' house immediately following the *cīmantam* ceremony, she may have to wait a day or two in order to make the journey on an astrologically auspicious day at an astrologically auspicious time. This is particularly a concern among Brahmin communities.

54. In fact, one bomb was dropped in Madras near Parry's Corner.

55. Hobsbawm 1983: 1.

56. Appadurai & Breckenridge 1995: 8.

57. Agarwal 1994; Oldenburg 2002; and Kishwar 1984: 8. Oldenburg traces these changes only as they occurred in the Punjab, whereas Agarwal traces changes in various different regions throughout the subcontinent.

58. Oldenburg (2002) says that in the Punjab this occurred within the context of the *ryotwar* system, which gave land titles to the "tiller," and only men were tillers. We might suspect that since this *ryotwari* system was also implemented in Madras Presidency (Irschick 1994), it may have had similar effects on women's land rights in South India.

59. Oldenburg 2002.

60. Agarwal 1994, chs. 3 and 4; Upadhya 1990; Epstein 1973.

61. Srinivas 1989; see also Kapadia 1993. Srinivas says that this process cannot be viewed as "Sanskritization" since the modern dowry is not the same as the earlier Brahminical traditions of *kanyadan* and *stridhana*.

62. For in-depth discussion of precolonial, colonial, and postcolonial inheritance rules relating to gender, see Agarwal 1994, particularly chs. 3, 4, and 5.

63. Ibid.: 482.

64. Jeffery et al. 1989: 26.

65. Cross-cousin marriage refers to a particular kind of marriage alliance in which a young woman marries her mother's brother's son or her father's sister's son.

66. "*Kati*" is a polysemic and very inclusive term which means "ability, means, character, luck, fortune," as well as "refuge," as in "God is my refuge" (Cre-A Tamil-English dictionary). "*Kati illātaval*" means "she is one without *kati*."

67. *Pūri* is a kind of deep-fried bread.

68. Kapadia 1993: 46.

69. "*Orukai*" means, literally, "one hand."

70. One *aṇā* is equal to 1/8th of one paise (cent); these coins are no longer in circulation.

71. "*Cukam*" is usually used to mean health. Here it also means "pleasure," and particularly "sexual pleasure." In Ayurvedic and Siddha theories of health, sexual pleasure is considered to be central to good health.

72. "Pouring the water" here refers to the bath taken after the *tīḍḍu,* or blood/pollution, has subsided.

73. Another reason for not doing *cīmantam* is if a woman had a miscarriage in an earlier pregnancy; some will then not do *cīmantam* for subsequent pregnancies, but others do perform *cīmantam* even if they had a prior miscarriage.

74. The orthodox Brahmin communities are an exception here. According to orthodox Brahminical practice the *cīmantam* (as opposed to the *vaḷaikāppu*) is one of the forty *samskaram* ceremonies which must be performed during the lifetime of a Hindu. Therefore, if it is not done during the pregnancy it *will* be performed on the eleventh day after the delivery (personal communication with S. Venkatakrishnan, Madras, September 12, 1995).

CHAPTER 4. INVOKING *VALI*

A version of this chapter was previously published under the title "Invoking *Vali:* Painful Technologies of Modern Birth in South India," *Medical Anthropology Quarterly* 17, no. 1 (March 2003): 49–77.

1. See Martin 1987; Oakley 1984; Osherson & Amarasingham 1981.
2. Reissman 1983: 3.
3. Leavitt 1986; Miller 1979; Reissman 1983: 6.
4. Leavitt 1986, ch. 5.
5. Davis-Floyd 1992; Jordan 1993.
6. Becker 2000; Martin 1987; Rapp 1991, 2000; Reissman 1983.
7. See for example Martin's discussion on the relationships among class, race, and cesarean sections in the United States (Martin 1987, ch. 8).
8. See Robert Pear, "Mothers on Medicaid Overcharged for Pain Relief," *New York Times,* March 8, 1999.
9. Jordan 1978.
10. Jordan 1993.
11. Despite this heuristic distinction between culturally constructed ideologies and political-economic structures, we must, of course, keep in mind that political-economic structures are also always culturally produced.
12. Ginsburg & Rapp 1995: 2.
13. These are sample registration system (SRS) statistics taken from the Government of Tamil Nadu's *Statistical Handbook of Tamil Nadu 1994.* It is important to note that all IMR and MMR statistics are based on *registered* deaths and therefore are often lower than the actual rates.
14. Government of Tamil Nadu 1994b: 1.
15. For more in-depth discussion on the causes of and variations among infant mortality rates with particular reference to India, see Jain & Visaria, eds. 1988; Mahadevan et al. 1985; Sandhya 1991; and Gandotra & Das 1988.
16. From Government of Tamil Nadu 1993: 18.
17. From Government of Tamil Nadu 1993: 44, and 1994: 15.
18. From Ravindran 1995a: 176.
19. From UNICEF 1990: 6.
20. Mari Bhat et al. 1995, referring to Visaria 1971.
21. Bhatia 1988.

22. Jordan 1993: 47.
23. Shiva 1992: 273.
24. These statistics are from the *WHO South-East Asia Region: Regional Health Report 1996*, pp. 3–4. Note that statistics gathered in both India and Sri Lanka by WHO and UNICEF vary significantly from the nationally reported statistics.
25. From UNICEF 1990: 17.
26. From Gargi Parsai, "Tamil Nadu Family Planning Drive 'a Success,'" *The (Madras) Hindu*, May 4, 1995.
27. Ravindran 1995a; Srinivasa et al. 1997.
28. Srinivasa et al. 1997: iii.
29. Linguistically there is in fact no connection between the word *cāvu* (death) with a long *ā* and the word *piracavam* (birth) with a short *a*.
30. Egnor 1980: 17.
31. Horn 1994; Russett 1989.
32. Fraser 1995.
33. Ram 1998: 124.
34. Jolly 2002: 27.
35. For example, see Jeejeebhoy & Rao 1995: 140–145; Das Gupta & Chen 1995.
36. Many people also give barley water to facilitate urination during pregnancy. This is viewed as an antidote to edema.
37. Mukhopadhyay 1992: 84.
38. Government of Tamil Nadu 1990: 20.
39. Personal communication with the superintendent of Kasthurba Gandhi Hospital, March 5, 1993.
40. These figures were provided by a senior doctor and reader in OB/GYN at the Chengalpattu Medical College Hospital on August 4, 1995.
41. An episiotomy is a surgical cut in the perineum, the area between the vagina and the anus, to enlarge the opening through which the baby will be born. In large government hospitals in Madras episiotomies were performed routinely, as is often the case in American hospitals.
42. Sargent & Rawlins 1992.
43. Kalpana Ram's (1994) study of childbirth in the southern region of Tamil Nadu shows the same stock comments to be pervasive there as well.
44. Kitzinger 1994.
45. Patel 1994: 117.
46. Friedson 1970, part 2.
47. Ibid.: 115.
48. Goffman 1961: 122.
49. Ibid.
50. HRAF is a cultural anthropology organization founded at Yale University in 1949. HRAF has developed a classification of cultural information by subject in order to provide access to research materials.
51. Freedman & Ferguson 1950.
52. Sargent 1982: 124–125.
53. Trawick 1992: 101.

54. Desamma is an important goddess among the fishing communities in both Nochikuppam and Kaanathur-Reddikuppam. She is particularly associated with events connected to birth and the welfare of mother and child.

55. See Radhika & Balasubramanian 1990, part 2: 11.

56. The pounding stone *(ammikkal)* is a long rodlike stone which is usually held with two hands and used to pound paddy or other grains which are kept in the *padi* (measuring vessel).

57. Compounders are pharmacists. See Jeffery et al. 1989: 111–112.

58. Jordan 1993.

59. Sargent & Bascope 1997.

60. The lithotomy position, in which the birthing woman lies flat on her back with her knees bent up and her feet flat on the delivery table, has become routine in most American hospital births. This position is preferred by many doctors since it gives them greater ease of access to the baby. However, this position makes labor more difficult for the mother since it weakens and slows contractions and requires the mother to push the baby out without the aid of gravity. It also decreases the supply of oxygen to the fetus. Studies have shown that the use of the lithotomy position increases the need for forceps or a vacuum extraction and increases the likelihood of perineal tears. See Jordan 1993: 84–87 for more discussion.

61. Ram 1998.

62. Ibid.: 136.

63. Davis-Floyd 1992: 96–97.

64. Kitzinger 1991: 301.

65. Ibid.: 300; Boston Women's Health Collective 1992: 456.

66. Kitzinger 1991: 304.

67. Davis-Floyd 1992: 97.

68. Mukhopadhyay 1992: 68–76.

69. Illich 1976: 9.

70. For excellent critiques of romanticized notions of "traditional" birth, see Lukere & Jolly, eds. 2002 and Rozario 1998.

CHAPTER 5. MOVING TARGETS

A version of this chapter was previously published under the title "Moving Targets: Routine IUD Insertion in Maternity Wards in Tamil Nadu, India," *Reproductive Health Matters* 6, no. 11 (May 1997): 98–106.

1. Foucault 1977b: 171.

2. Horn 1994, ch. 3.

3. Ibid.: 49–50.

4. For some recent examples, see Anagnost 1995 on China; Morsy 1995 on Egypt; and Barroso & Corrêa 1995 on Brazil.

5. Ravindran 1994.

6. The neo-Malthusian population-control movement began in Britain in the 1870s and soon spread to the United States. This movement adopted the theoretical assumptions of Malthus but, whereas Malthus was opposed to international efforts to control population growth, the neo-Malthusians saw this as

their primary mission (Clarke 1990: 24). For an example of how neo-Malthusian arguments were applied to economic development policies in India, see Myrdal 1968.

7. Scheper-Hughes & Lock 1987: 27–28.

8. See for example Ravindran 1994; Qadeer 1994; Anandhi 1994; Mamdani 1972.

9. Qadeer 1994.

10. For example, railroad ticket inspectors began to clamp down on (previously ignored) ticketless travelers and negotiated with these passengers, agreeing to waive the exorbitant penalty fees if the passenger agreed to be sterilized.

11. Gwatkin 1979.

12. Nortman 1978; Gwatkin 1979; Kocher 1980.

13. From "Are Women No More?" *The (Madras) Hindu,* June 26, 1994.

14. *The Family Welfare Program in Tamilnadu: Year Book 1989–90,* p. 47, states that the amount given per bed was Rs. 3,000 and seventy-five tubectomies had to be conducted per bed. Voluntary organizations which ran their own hospitals could also receive this amount if they performed sixty tubectomies per bed each year. See Government of Tamil Nadu 1991.

15. Ibid.: 44.

16. Ibid.: 28.

17. Ibid.: 46.

18. Demographer, Tamil Nadu Department of Family Welfare, Madras, personal communication, February 12, 1995.

19. From Kalpana Sharma, "Population and Politicians," *The (Madras) Hindu,* January 17, 1995.

20. From M. D. Riti, "Busting the Baby Boom," *The Week,* April 2, 1995, pp. 10–16.

21. From Gargi Parsai, "Tamilnadu Family Planning Drive 'a Success,'" *The (Madras) Hindu,* May 4, 1995.

22. The "couple protection" rate is the number of married couples with a woman between fifteen and forty-four years of age that are using some form of birth control.

23. From Government of Tamil Nadu 1991.

24. From Government of Tamil Nadu 1995b.

25. Government of Tamil Nadu 1991: 116.

26. Ibid.: 120.

27. See Cre-A Tamil-English dictionary.

28. For the view that the family-planning campaign in Tamil Nadu is cooperative, see A. Sen, "Population Policy: Authoritarianism versus Cooperation," paper presented at The John and Catherine T. MacArthur Foundation Lecture Series on Population Issues, New Delhi, August 17, 1995 (cited in Swaminathan 1996).

29. Swaminathan 1996.

30. This figure was provided by the Department of Demography, Tamil Nadu Department of Medical Service, Madras, 1995.

31. Government of Tamil Nadu 1991: 26.

32. Cited in Ravindran 1995b.

33. From *A Short Account on the Status of IUD Users and Service Delivery System in Tamil Nadu* (Working Women's Forum 1996).

34. Personal communication with Marge Berer and T. K. Sundari Ravindran, editors of the journal *Reproductive Health Matters,* September 30, 1997.

35. Bhatia 1988; Ravindran 1994.

36. For more information on the medical risks of IUD use and on the history of IUD use in the United States, see the Boston Women's Health Collective 1992 edition of *Our Bodies Ourselves.*

37. For a discussion on South Asian cultural notions about how and why IUDs prevent conception, see Nichter 1989: 71–72.

38. In Ayurveda these are known as *vayu, pitta,* and *kapha* respectively.

39. Personal communication with Dr. Kalyanasundaram, Anna Hospital, Arumbakkam, Madras, May 9, 1997.

40. Basham 1976: 22–23; Beals 1976: 189–190.

41. Obeyesekere 1976: 202.

42. Srinivasmurthi 1923, cited in Nandy & Visvanathan 1990: 178.

43. Daniel 1984: 70.

44. Information about these two meetings was provided by WWF organizers, December 12, 1995.

45. For brief discussion of feminist critiques of injectible-contraception trials in India, see contributions in *Population Policy and Reproductive Rights* (Anandhi, ed. 1994).

46. From "Birthrate: Southern States Complimented," *The (Madras) Hindu,* March 9, 1995.

47. From "Incentives for Population Programme to Go," *The (Madras) Hindu,* December 24, 1995.

CHAPTER 6. "BABY FRIENDLY" HOSPITALS AND BAD MOTHERS

A version of this chapter appeared in *The Daughters of Hariti: Birth and Female Healers in South and Southeast Asia* (London: Routledge, 2002): 163–181. I would like to thank Akhil Gupta, Stacy Pigg, Jenny Springer, and Rebecca Klenk for their fruitful discussions on my theoretical engagements on this topic in our panel entitled "Maneuvering Development in South Asia," presented at the American Anthropological Association Annual Meeting, Washington, D.C., November 1997.

1. Escobar 1995.

2. Ferguson 1994: xiii.

3. Rostow's well-known economic theory of the stages which a Third World country must go through in order to "take off" into the hallowed realm of the "developed" nations is exemplary of post–World War II discourse (Rostow 1991).

4. Escobar 1995: 6–7.

5. Gupta 1998: 6.

6. In this case the reference was to thermal temperature, whereas in many other instances "hot" and "cold" foods referred instead to the effects of the food on the body.

7. Episiotomies are done routinely in many of the public and private hospitals in Tamil Nadu. Some women who conduct home deliveries also know how to suture tears but do not perform episiotomies.

8. "*Māntam*" is a local, non-allopathic term which usually refers to a severe kind of diarrhea which is thought to be unique to children from birth until age three. One Siddha doctor, however, told me that although digestion problems are often symptoms of *māntam,* they are not necessarily present. Rather, he explained, the main symptom is a kind of mental and physical dullness and lack of responsiveness in the child.

9. *Racam* is a watery soup made with peppers and cumin. It is commonly taken with rice (which is sometimes called *cātam*) after the main vegetable or meat dishes and before the curds.

10. Mohanty 1991.

11. *Pattiyam* means a prescribed diet, and "*cāppāḍu*" is a word used to mean "food" or "meal" in a general sense, but only rice-based meals are considered to be real *cāppāḍu.*

12. Daniel 1984.

13. Chili powder in particular should be avoided but black pepper may sometimes be used since it is thought to be beneficial for healing wounds.

14. This is also known as *sitala.* In many parts of North India, the goddess of smallpox is known as Sitala Devi. Since smallpox is associated with intense heat, the goddess Sitala is known as one who desires cooling offerings (see Winslow 1979 (1862); see also Marglin 1990).

15. "Cold" foods include such vegetables as cabbage, Bangalore *brinjal,* and cucumber, as well as fruits like bananas, *sapotas,* and jackfruit. For more discussion on cultural conceptions of "hot" and "cold" foods and their relation to pregnancy and the postpartum period in Tamil Nadu, see S. B. Mani 1981.

16. See Verderese & Turnbull 1975: 38.

17. Laderman 1983: 186.

18. For a critique of the construction of such categories as "pregnant" and "lactating" women in development discourse, see Escobar 1995.

19. Siddha and Ayurvedic medical knowledge categorize medicines according to the different ways that they are manufactured. *Lēkiyam* refers to those medicines which are confectioneries; that is, they are made from a sweet base with things like white and brown sugar and jaggery. The other ingredients are mixed with the sweet base, and ghee is often added as a preserving agent. The final product is rolled into small balls which harden and can be kept in a jar for up to a year.

20. The ingredients listed on a bottle of *piracava maruntu lēkiyam* that I purchased from a Siddha/Ayurveda medical shop were as follows: dried ginger, 13.3 g.; *sadakuppai,* 8.3 g.; coriander seeds, 5 g.; *waivilangam,* 1.6 g.; *sirunagapoo,* 1.6 g.; black cumin seeds, 1.6 g.; pepper, 1.6 g.; cumin, 1.6 g.; yelam/cardamom, 1.6 g.; *thippili,* 1.6 g.; *lavangampattai* (clove),1.6 g.; *lavangampattiri* (clove leaves), 1.6 g.; *koraikirangu,* 1.6 g.; jaggery, 187.5 g.; ghee, 20 g.

21. The Tamil term "*iḍuppu*" in this case refers to the hips as well as the entire abdominal area enlarged during pregnancy. Thus, labor pains are sometimes referred to as *iḍuppu vali.*

22. Nandy & Visvanathan 1990: 147.

23. For discussion on the widespread cross-cultural restrictions on colostrum, see Baumslag & Michels 1995: 23–25.

24. Zeitlyn & Rowshan 1997: 61.

25. See Radhika & Balasubramanian 1990, part 2: 45–48. According to Janet Chawla, the problem with this debate is that Ayurvedic texts suggest that colostrum may be considered inappropriate for a baby because the qualities of the colostrum are judged by the same criteria as breast milk. As Chawla points out, colostrum and milk are not the same thing and therefore their qualities should be judged using different criteria (Janet Chawla, personal communication, May 1997).

26. Concerns over the decline in breastfeeding existed prior to the 1970s and were attached to different kinds of social movements. In India, for example, this concern was voiced as early as 1917 in the context of nationalist critiques of the effects of industrialization on cultural notions of femininity (see Srinivasmurthi [1923] cited in Nandy & Visvanathan 1990: 159). The point here is that it was in the early 1970s that this concern became a part of the *development* agenda.

27. See Baumslag & Michels 1995, sec. 3; and Raphael, ed. 1979 for more discussion.

28. Gaynes & Hale 1979: 115. At the time Gaynes was working for Morgan, Kennedy, Olmstead, and Gardner of San Francisco, and Hale was working with the Human Lactation Center.

29. Escobar 1995: 101.

30. The ten steps are as follows: 1. have a written breastfeeding policy; 2. train all health staff to implement this policy; 3. inform all pregnant women about the benefits of breastfeeding; 4. help mothers initiate breastfeeding within half an hour of birth; 5. show mothers the best way to breastfeed; 6. give newborn infants no food or drink other than breast milk, unless medically indicated; 7. practice "rooming in" by allowing mothers and babies to remain together twenty-four hours a day; 8. encourage breastfeeding on demand; 9. give no artificial teats, pacifiers, dummies, or soothers; 10. help start breastfeeding support groups and refer mothers to them.

31. Personal communication with Dr. Srilata (real name), UNICEF, Madras, May 1997.

32. The *poḍḍu* is the dot which Hindu women wear on their foreheads.

33. In her work in Malaysia, Laderman notes a similar kind of tension between practices to detract the sexual attention of the husband during the postpartum period and the need to agree to the husband's sexual demands at this time in order to avoid the possibility of divorce (Laderman 1983: 204).

34. A *pālāḍai* is a small, shallow metal cup which sits in the palm of the hand. It is shaped like a teardrop and is commonly used to feed small children.

35. See Government of India 1960.

36. For more in-depth discussion of the construction of insufficient milk syndrome within the context of international health programs, see Van Esterik 1988; Zeitlyn & Rowshan 1997. In her study of women in northeast Brazil, Scheper-Hughes writes, "When they refer to their own milk as scanty, curdled, bitter, or sour, breast milk is a powerful metaphor speaking to the scarcity and

bitterness of their lives as women" (1992: 326). This is a very apt way of understanding similar expressions made about the low quality and quantity of breast milk among poor women in Tamil Nadu.

37. Although most of the people I met in most regions of Tamil Nadu which I visited were explicit about the fact that they give the real milk of donkeys to infants, several women in Tanjavur District told me that although this substance is called "donkey's milk," it is in fact a mixture of water and donkey's blood taken from the donkey's ear.

38. One woman told me that she knows people who give their babies mercury to cure *karuppu*. Some Siddha medicines are made with a small amount of mercury, so it is probable that she was referring to a Siddha medicine.

39. Botanical name: *Thespesia populnea.*

40. Botanical name: *Sarcostemma brevistigma.*

41. Botanical name: *Boer haavia diffusa.*

42. In their restudy of the status of health in the village of Thaiyur (also in Chingelput District), Djurfeldt, Lindberg, and Rajagopal (1997) translate *karuppu* as neonatal tetanus (187). In my discussions, however, people referred to neonatal tetanus as *rana janni,* associated with severe fever and "fits," and distinguished it from *karuppu,* which was associated with skin blemishes and listlessness.

43. It is of course possible that people used the category of *"karuppu"* to explain the death of an infant who was in fact killed, but that is different from claiming that the disease itself was invented for this purpose.

44. Foucault 1977a.

45. A "joint family" is a household unit that consists of brothers, their inmarrying wives, their unmarried sisters, and their parents.

46. The *annapirāsanam* is a Vedic ceremony performed by Brahmins in which a baby is given its first solid foods, usually a rice-based food which is served to the baby on a silver plate or coin. (For more information on this, see Stevenson 1971 [1920]: 19–20).

47. For example see "Born To Die," *India Today,* June 1986, cited in Elizabeth Bumiller 1990: 104–105; Jaya Arunachalam, "Infant Killers of Dharmapuri," *The Hindustan Times,* September 29, 1994, C1; "Born to Die: Tragedy of the Doomed Daughter," *The (Madras) Hindu,* November 20, 1994, section M; Usha Rai, "Where There Is No Place for Baby Girls," *The Indian Express,* September 26, 1995; Carol Aloysius, "She's Also Made of Flesh And Blood: Why Destroy the Girl Child?" *The Sunday Observer,* June 29, 1997, p. 2. Elizabeth Bumiller's journalistic report on female infanticide in Tamil Nadu in her widely distributed book *May You Be the Mother of a Hundred Sons* (1990) helped to bring international attention to this story. Most reports of female infanticide in Tamil Nadu originate in Dharmapuri in Salem District and Usilampatti in Madurai District.

48. As the then–chief minister of Tamil Nadu, Jayaram Jayalalitha said in her speech inaugurating the government of Tamil Nadu's new State Plan of Action for the Child in 1993: "The child in the Indian tradition is not viewed in isolation but was and is considered as part of a larger matrix in which the mother-child unit is the very foundation. Measures to promote the child *[sic]* growth or

to alleviate its distress are required to be directed toward this unit with the centre of protection shifting gradually from the mother to the child."

49. Some Muslims call this day *chilla;* most simply call it the "fortieth day" *(nakpadāvadu nāḷ)*. The new Muslim mother and her husband are expected to abstain from sexual relations during the first forty days following the delivery, and they are usually separated during this time. The "fortieth day" marks the time when the couple is expected to be reunited and to resume sexual activity.

50. For details of these debates, see Dumont 1980; Das 1977; Carman 1983; Marglin 1985; Parry 1991; and Madan 1991.

51. Bean 1981.

52. Jeffery et al. 1989.

53. Ram 1994: 23.

54. Ferro-Luzzi 1974.

55. This does not mean that people do not also use terms like "*rattam*" and "*utiram*" to refer to postpartum and menstrual blood, but simply that *tīḍḍu* has this specialized meaning.

56. *Cīyakkāy* powder is made from soap pods which are dried, powdered, and mixed with fenugreek.

57. Some *maruttuvaccis,* however, told me that oil should *not* be used until the baby is three months old, because as a "cooling" agent the oil may cause the baby to get *caḷi*. Instead of oil, during the first three months they rub egg whites on the baby's body to remove the dryness of the skin before washing it off with baby soap.

58. Raheja 1988; Parry 1994.

59. Not all families, however, give their clothes to the *vaṇṇātti*. In many cases the new mother's own mother will wash the soiled clothes. When a girl goes through puberty her own mother should not see her menstrual blood. After that, it is not only acceptable but appropriate for the mother to wash her daughter's *tīḍḍu* clothes, whereas it is sometimes considered taboo for the mother-in-law to touch her daughter-in-law's *tīḍḍu* clothes. I was even told on a few occasions that it is because of the taboo against the mother-in-law's touching the postpartum blood that the new mother will return to her own mother's house for the delivery and postpartum period.

60. Raheja 1988: 45.

61. See Jeffery et al. 1989.

62. Personal communication with P. Jeffery, July 28, 1999.

63. Jeffery et al. 1989: 67.

64. See the Government of India's *Second Five Year Plan* (1956), p. 540.

65. Jeffery et al. 1989: 12.

66. Sheila Kitzinger defines "vernix" as "a creamy substance which protects [the baby's] skin inside the uterus and prevents it from becoming waterlogged. This vernix sticks to hairy parts and many babies are born still coated with it" (Kitzinger 1991: 68).

67. S. Venkatesh, who as a member of PPST in Madras is an advocate of revitalizing "traditional" medicine, made an interesting point with respect to the relative benefits of oil baths for infants. She agreed that infant oil baths definitely cause infection. Yet she argued that this is due to the modern methods used to

produce and manufacture the oil. In the past, she said, when oil was individually produced by a "traditional" medical practitioner or by members of the family in the home, there was more control of the nature of production, and the oils made then were beneficial to the baby's health. Today, however, when oils are mass-produced and sold in stores they are often mixed with other substances and may be exposed to germs along the way and thus result in infection (personal communication, May 13, 1997).

68. Pigg 1992: 511.

69. Ferguson 1994.

CONCLUSION

1. R. Chakrapani, "Discord at Meet on Draft for Beijing," *The (Madras) Hindu,* April 13, 1995, p. 11; Kalpana Sharma, "Meet Inching towards Consensus," *The (Madras) Hindu,* September 15, 1995; Kalpana Sharma, "NGOs Step up Efforts to Bring Accord in Document," *The (Madras) Hindu,* September 13, 1995.

2. Kalpana Sharma, "India to Co-chair Drafting Panel," *The (Madras) Hindu,* September 12, 1995, p. 14; editorial, "The Beijing Spirit," *The (Madras) Hindu,* September 19, 1995, p. 12.

3. S. Swaminathan, "Women in Development—Globalisation in Lieu of Localisation?" *The (Madras) Hindu,* September 6, 1995.

4. Ratna Kapur, "Feminist Reflections, Myths, and Fears," *The (Madras) Hindu,* March 8, 1992, p. 1.

5. Ginsburg & Rapp 1995: 9.

6. Messer 1993.

7. See Chapter Four of this book, note 58, on the lithotomy position.

Bibliography

Agarwal, Bina. 1994. *A Field of One's Own: Gender and Land Rights in South Asia.* Cambridge: Cambridge University Press.

Anagnost, Ann. 1995. "A Surfeit of Bodies: Population and the Rationality of the State in Post-Mao China." In *Conceiving the New World Order,* edited by F. Ginsburg and R. Rapp, 1–41. Berkeley: University of California Press.

Anandhi, S. 1994. "Population Policy and the Politics of Reproductive Rights." In *Population Policy and Reproductive Rights,* edited by S. Anandhi, 1–12. Madras: Initiatives: Women in Development.

Anderson, Sandra V., and Eleanor Bauwens. 1982. "An Ethnography of Home Birth." In *Anthropology of Human Birth,* edited by M. Kay, 289–303. Philadelphia: F. A. Davis.

Appadurai, Arjun. 1996. *Modernity at Large: Cultural Dimensions of Globalization.* Public Worlds, vol. 1. Minneapolis: University of Minnesota Press.

Appadurai, Arjun, and Carol Breckenridge. 1995. "Public Modernity in India." In *Consuming Modernity: Public Culture in a South Asian World,* edited by C. Breckenridge, 1–20. Minneapolis: University of Minnesota Press.

Apple, Rima D., ed. 1990. *Women, Health, and Medicine in America: A Historical Handbook.* New York: Garland.

Arnold, David. 1993. *Colonizing the Body: State Medicine and Epidemic Disease in Nineteenth-Century India.* Berkeley: University of California Press.

———. 1988. "Introduction: Disease, Medicine and Empire." In *Imperial Medicine and Indigenous Societies,* edited by D. Arnold, 1–26. Manchester: Manchester University Press.

Bala, Poonam. 1991. *Imperialism and Medicine in Bengal: A Socio-historical Perspective.* New Delhi: Sage.

Barroso, Carmen, and Sônia Corrêa. 1995. "Public Servants, Professionals, and Feminists: The Politics of Contraceptive Research in Brazil." In *Conceiving the New World Order,* edited by F. Ginsburg and R. Rapp, 292–306. Berkeley: University of California Press.

Basham, A. L. 1976. "The Practice of Medicine in Ancient and Medieval India." In *Asian Medical Systems: A Comparative Study,* edited by Charles Leslie, 18–43. Berkeley: University of California Press.

Baumslag, Naomi, and Dia L. Michels. 1995. *Milk, Money, and Madness: The Culture and Politics of Breastfeeding.* Westport, Conn.: Bergin & Garvey.

Beals, Alan R. 1976. "Strategies of Resort to Curers in South India." In *Asian Medical Systems: A Comparative Study,* edited by Charles Leslie, 184–200. Berkeley: University of California Press.

Bean, Susan S. 1981. "Toward a Semiotics of 'Purity' and 'Pollution' in India." *American Ethnologist,* Special Issue on Symbolism and Cognition, 8, no. 3: 575–595.

Becker, Gay. 2000. *The Elusive Embryo: How Women and Men Approach New Reproductive Technologies.* Berkeley: University of California Press.

Bhat, P. N. Mari, K. Navaneethan, and S. Irudaya Rajan. 1995. "Maternal Mortality: Estimates from an Econometric Model." In *Women's Health in India: Risk and Vulnerability,* edited by M. Das Gupta et al., 97–121. Madras: Oxford University Press.

Bhatia, J. C. 1988. *A Study of Maternal Mortality in Anantapur District, Andhra Pradesh, India.* Bangalore: Indian Institute of Management.

Boddy, Janice. 1998. "Remembering Amal: Birth in Northern Sudan." In *Pragmatic Women and Body Politics,* edited by Margaret Lock and Patricia Kaufert, 28–57. Cambridge: Cambridge University Press.

Borthwick, Meredith. 1984. *The Changing Role of Women in Bengal, 1849–1905.* Princeton: Princeton University Press.

Boston Women's Health Collective. 1992. *The New Our Bodies, Ourselves: Updated and Expanded for the '90s.* New York: Simon & Schuster.

Breckenridge, Carol A., ed. 1995. *Consuming Modernity: Public Culture in a South Asian World.* Minneapolis: University of Minnesota Press.

Browner, Carole, and Nancy Ann Press. 1995. "The Normalization of Prenatal Diagnostic Screening." In *Conceiving the New World Order: The Global Politics of Reproduction,* edited by F. Ginsburg and R. Rapp, 307–322. Berkeley: University of California Press.

Browner, Carole, and Carolyn Sargent. 1990. "Anthropology and Studies of Human Reproduction." In *Medical Anthropology: Contemporary Theory and Method,* edited by T. Johnson and C. Sargent, 215–229. New York: Praeger.

Bumiller, Elisabeth. 1990. *May You Be the Mother of a Hundred Sons: A Journey among the Women of India.* New Delhi: Penguin.

Chatterjee, Partha. 1990. "The Nationalist Resolution of the Women's Question." In *Recasting Women: Essays in Indian Colonial History,* edited by Kumkum Sangari and Sudesh Vaid, 233–253. New Brunswick, N.J.: Rutgers University Press.

Chawla, Janet. 1994. *Child-Bearing and Culture: Women Centered Revisioning of the Traditional Midwife, the Dai as a Ritual Practitioner.* New Delhi: Indian Social Institute.

Clarke, Adele. 1990. "Controversy in the Development of Reproductive Sciences." *Social Problems* 37, no. 1: 18–37.

Clifford, James, and George Marcus, eds. 1986. *Writing Culture: The Poetics and Politics of Ethnography.* Berkeley: University of California Press.

Cohen, Lawrence. 1998. *No Aging in India: Alzheimer's, the Bad Family, and Other Modern Things.* Berkeley: University of California Press.

Comaroff, Jean, and John Comaroff. 1991. *Of Revelation and Revolution: Christianity, Colonialism, and Consciousness in South Africa.* Chicago: University of Chicago Press.

Cominsky, Sheila. 1976. "Cross-Cultural Perspectives on Midwifery." In *Medical Anthropology,* edited by F. Grollig and H. Haley, 229–248. The Hague: Mouton Publishers.

Cre-A. 1992. *Dictionary of Contemporary Tamil (Tamil–Tamil–English).* Madras: Cre-A.

Daniel, Sheryl B. 1980. "Marriage in Tamil Culture: The Problem of Conflicting 'Models.'" In *The Powers of Tamil Women,* edited by Susan Wadley, 61–91. Syracuse, N.Y.: Syracuse University, Foreign and Comparative Studies Program.

Daniel, Valentine. 1984. *Fluid Signs: Being a Person the Tamil Way.* Berkeley: University of California Press.

Das, Veena. 1977. *Structure and Cognition: Aspects of Hindu Caste and Ritual.* Delhi: Oxford University Press.

Das Gupta, Monica, and Lincoln C. Chen. 1995. "Overview." In *Women's Health in India: Risk and Vulnerability,* edited by M. Das Gupta et al., 1–16. Madras: Oxford University Press.

Davis-Floyd, Robbie E. 1992. *Birth As an American Rite of Passage.* Berkeley: University of California Press.

Davis-Floyd, Robbie, and Carolyn F. Sargent. 1997. "Introduction: The Anthropology of Birth." In *Childbirth and Authoritative Knowledge: Cross-Cultural Perspectives,* edited by R. Davis-Floyd and C. Sargent, 1–51. Berkeley: University of California Press.

———, eds. 1997. *Childbirth and Authoritative Knowledge: Cross-Cultural Perspectives.* Berkeley: University of California Press.

Djurfeldt, Göran, and Staffan Lindberg. 1975. *Pills against Poverty: A Study of the Introduction of Western Medicine in a Tamil Village.* Scandinavian Institute of Asian Studies Monograph Series, no. 23. London: Curzon Press.

Djurfeldt, Göran, Staffan Lindberg, and A. Rajagopal. 1997. "Coming Back to Thaiyur: Health and Medicine in a Twenty-five Years Perspective." In *The Village in Asia Revisited,* edited by J. Breman, P. Klaas, and P. Saith, 175–198. Delhi: Oxford University Press.

Duden, Barbara. 1993. *Disembodying Women: Perspectives on Pregnancy and the Unborn.* Cambridge, Mass.: Harvard University Press.

Dumont, Louis. 1980. *Homo Hierarchicus: The Caste System and Its Implications.* Translated from the French by Mark Sainsbury, Louis Dumont, and Basia Gulati. Complete rev. English ed. Chicago: University of Chicago Press.

Dyson, T., and M. Moore. 1983. "On Kinship Structure, Female Autonomy and Demographic Behavior in India." *Population and Development Review* 9, no. 1: 35–60.

Egnor, Margaret [Margaret Trawick, married name]. 1980. "On the Meaning of Sakti to Women in Tamil Nadu." In *The Powers of Tamil Women,* edited by S. Wadley, 1–34. Syracuse, N.Y.: Syracuse University, Foreign and Comparative Studies Program.

Ehrenreich, Barbara, and Deirdre English. 1973. *Witches, Midwives & Nurses: A History of Women Healers.* Old Westbury, N.Y.: Feminist Press.

Engels, Friedrich. 1972 [1942]. *The Origin of the Family, Private Property, and the State, in the Light of the Researches of Lewis H. Morgan.* With an introduction and notes by Eleanor Burke Leacock. New York: International.

Epstein, Scarlett T. 1973. *South India: Yesterday, Today and Tomorrow.* London: Macmillan.

Escobar, Arturo. 1995. *Encountering Development: The Making and Unmaking of the Third World.* Princeton: Princeton University Press.

Ferguson, James. 1994. *The Anti-Politics Machine: "Development," Depoliticization, and Bureaucratic Power in Lesotho.* Minneapolis: University of Minnesota Press.

Ferro-Luzzi, Gabriella Eichinger. 1974. "Women's Pollution Periods in Tamilnad (India)." *Anthropos* 69: 113–161.

Fielder, Deborah Cordero. 1997. "Authoritative Knowledge and Birth Territories in Contemporary Japan." In *Childbirth and Authoritative Knowledge: Cross-Cultural Perspectives,* edited by R. Davis-Floyd and C. Sargent, 159–179. Berkeley: University of California Press.

First All India Obstetric and Gynaecological Congress. 1936. *Proceedings.* Dr. A. Lakshmanaswami Mudaliar, chair. Conference held in the Museum Theatre, Egmore, Madras.

Flint, Marcha. 1982. "Lockmi: An Indian Midwife." In *Anthropology of Human Birth,* edited by M. Kay, 211–219. Philadelphia: F. A. Davis Company.

Ford, Clellan Stearns. 1964. *A Comparative Study of Human Reproduction.* New Haven, Conn.: Human Relations Area Files Press.

Foucault, Michel. 1977a. *Discipline and Punish: The Birth of the Prison.* Translated from the French by Alan Sheridan. New York: Pantheon Books.

———. 1977b. *Power/Knowledge: Selected Interviews & Other Writings, 1972–1977.* Edited by Colin Gordon and translated from the French by Colin Gordon et al. New York: Pantheon Books.

———. 1973. *The Birth of the Clinic: An Archeology of Medical Perception.* Translated from the French by A. M. Sheridan Smith. New York: Pantheon Books. Original edition, Paris: Presses Universitaires de France, 1963.

Frank, Arthur W. 1992. "Twin Nightmares of the Medical Simulacrum: Jean Baudrillard and David Cronenberg." In *Jean Baudrillard: The Disappearance of Art & Politics,* edited by William Stearns and William Chaloupka, 82–97. New York: Saint Martins Press.

Franklin, Sarah, and Helen Ragoné, eds. 1998. *Reproducing Reproduction: Kinship, Power, and Technological Innovation.* Philadelphia: University of Pennsylvania Press.

Fraser, Gertrude J. 1995. "Modern Bodies, Modern Minds: Midwifery and Reproductive Change in an African American Community." In *Conceiving the New World Order: The Global Politics of Reproduction,* edited by F. Ginsburg and R. Rapp, 42–58. Berkeley: University of California Press.

Freed, Ruth S., and Stanley A. Freed. 1980. *Rites of Passage in Shanti Nagar.* The Anthropological Papers of the American Museum of Natural History, volume 56, part 3. New York: American Museum of Natural History.

Freedman, Lawrence Z., and Vera Masius Ferguson. 1950. "The Question of 'Painless Childbirth' in Primitive Cultures." *American Journal of Orthopsychiatry* 20, no. 2: 363–372.

Friedson, Eliot. 1970. *Professional Dominance: The Social Structure of Medical Care,* parts 1 and 2. New York: Atherton.

Fuller, Christopher. 1996. "Brahmin Temple Priests and Hindu Revivalism in Contemporary Tamilnadu." *South Indian Studies* 1, no. 1: 1–34.

———. 1989. "Misconceiving the Grain Heap: A Critique of the Concept of the Indian Jajmani System." In *Money and the Morality of Exchange,* edited by J. Parry and M. Bloch, 33–63. Cambridge: Cambridge University Press.

Gandotra, M. M., and Narayan Das. 1988. *Infant Mortality and Its Causes.* Delhi: Himalaya Publishing House.

Garro, Linda. 1998. "On the Rationality of Decision-Making Studies: Part I: Decision Models of Treatment Choice." *Medical Anthropology Quarterly* 12, no. 3: 319–340.

Gaynes, Ben, Jr., and Lucinda Douglas Hale. 1979. "Political-Economic Factors of Breastfeeding." In *Breastfeeding and Food Policy in a Hungry World,* edited by Dana Raphael, 115–118. San Francisco: Academic Press.

Geertz, Clifford. 1973. "Thick Description: Toward an Interpretive Theory of Culture." In *The Interpretation of Cultures,* edited by C. Geertz, 3–30. New York: Basic Books.

Gélis, Jacques. 1991. *History of Childbirth: Fertility and Birth in Early Modern Europe.* Translated from the French by Rosemary Morris. Boston: Northeastern University Press. Original edition, Cambridge, England: Polity Press, 1991.

Georges, Eugenia. 1997. "Fetal Ultrasound Imaging and the Production of Authoritative Knowledge in Greece." In *Childbirth and Authoritative Knowledge: Cross-Cultural Perspectives,* edited by R. Davis-Floyd and C. Sargent, 91–112. Berkeley: University of California Press.

Gideon, Helen. 1962. "A Baby Is Born in the Punjab." *American Anthropologist* 64: 1220–1234.

Ginsburg, Faye D., and Rayna Rapp. 1995. "Introduction: Conceiving the New World Order." In *Conceiving the New World Order: The Global Politics of Reproduction,* edited by F. Ginsburg and R. Rapp, 1–17. Berkeley: University of California Press.

———. 1991. "The Politics of Reproduction." *Annual Review of Anthropology* 20: 311–343.

———, eds. 1995. *Conceiving the New World Order: The Global Politics of Reproduction.* Berkeley: University of California Press.

Goffman, Erving. 1961. *Asylums.* New York: Doubleday-Anchor.

Government of India. 1960. "Maternity Benefit Bill," *Gazette of India,* Registered No. D.221.

———. 1956. *The Second Five-Year Plan.* Delhi: GOI Planning Commission.

———. 1946. *Report of the Health Survey and Development Committee* (chair, Sir J. Bhore). 4 vols. New Delhi: Superintendent of Government Printing.

———. 1928. "Maternal Mortality in Childbirth in India: A Summary of the Investigation Conducted under the Indian Research Fund Association: 1925–27." *Health Bulletin,* no. 5. Calcutta: Government of India Central Publication Branch.

Government of Madras Presidency. 1923. G.O. No. 1437, Public Health, August 28, "Maternity and child welfare relief—Memorandum by the Director of Public Health—Communicated to local bodies."

———. 1927. G.O. No. 2201, Public Health, November 5, "Rules-Madras Nurses and Midwives Act, 1926—Draft rules notified for information."

———. 1929. G.O. No. 302, Public Health, January 31, "Report-National Health and Baby Week, 1928-Reviewed."

———. 1938. G.O. No. 2001, May 31, Department of Education & Public Health. No Title.

———. 1939a. G.O. Ms. No. 3441, September 26, Education & Public Health, "Midwives—Government Victoria Caste & Gosha Hospital, Madras—Midwifery Pupils—creation of 10 stipends—reconsideration of previous orders—declined."

———. 1939b. G.O. Ms. No. 4050, November 3, Education & Public Health, "Midwives—Rules for the admission and training of candidates in midwifery in the languages of the Province and the form of agreement to be executed by them—Approved."

Government of Tamil Nadu. 1995a. *Health for All by 2000: India Population Project-V.* Madras: India Population Project-V.

———. 1995b. "IPP-V Santhome Zone Information Booklet, 1994–1995." Unpublished internal report.

———. 1994a. *Statistical Handbook of Tamil Nadu.* Madras: Directorate of Public Health and Preventative Medicine.

———. 1994b. *Child Survival and Safe Motherhood in Tamil Nadu.* Madras: Directorate of Public Health and Preventative Medicine.

———. 1993. *State Plan of Action for the Child in Tamil Nadu.* Madras: Departments of Social Welfare, Health, and Finance.

———. 1991. *The Family Welfare Program in Tamilnadu: Year Book 1989–90.* Madras: Directorate of Medical & Rural Health Services, State Family Welfare Bureau, Demographic & Evaluation Cell.

———. 1990. *Children & Women in Tamilnadu: A Situation Analysis 1990.* Madras.

Guha, Supriya. 1996. *A History of the Medicalization of Childbirth in Bengal in the Late Nineteenth and Early Twentieth Centuries.* Ph.D. dissertation, Department of History, University of Calcutta.

Gupta, Akhil. 1998. *Postcolonial Developments: Agriculture in the Making of Modern India.* Durham, N.C.: Duke University Press.

Gupta, Akhil, and James Ferguson, eds. 1997. *Anthropological Locations:*

Boundaries and Grounds of a Field Science. Berkeley: University of California Press.
Gwatkin, D. R. 1979. "Political Will and Family Planning: The Implications of India's Emergency Experience." *Population and Development Review* 5, no. 1: 29–59.
Hart, Donna V., Phy Anuman Rajadhon, and Richard J. Coughlin. 1965. *Southeast Asian Birth Customs: Three Studies in Human Reproduction.* New Haven, Conn.: Human Relations Area Files Press.
Hobsbawm, Eric. 1983. "Introduction: Inventing Traditions." In *The Invention of Tradition,* edited by E. Hobsbawm and T. Ranger, 1–14. Cambridge: Cambridge University Press.
Horn, David G. 1994. *Social Bodies: Science, Reproduction, and Italian Modernity.* Princeton, N.J.: Princeton University Press.
Illich, Ivan. 1976. *Medical Nemesis: The Expropriation of Health.* New York: Pantheon Books.
Irschick, Eugene. 1994. *Dialogue and History: Constructing South India, 1795–1895.* Berkeley: University of California Press.
Jain, Anrudh K., and Pravin Visaria, eds. 1988. *Infant Mortality in India: Differentials and Determinants.* New Delhi: Sage.
Jeffery, Patricia, Roger Jeffery, and Andrew Lyon. 1989. *Labour Pains and Labour Power: Women and Childbearing in India.* London: Zed Books.
Jeffery, Patricia, and Roger Jeffrey. 1993. "Traditional Birth Attendants in Rural North India: The Social Organization of Childbearing." In *Knowledge, Power, and Practice: The Anthropology of Medicine and Everyday Life,* edited by Shirley Lindenbaum and Margaret Lock, 7–31. Berkeley: University of California Press.
Jeffery, Roger. 1988. *The Politics of Health in India.* Berkeley: University of California Press.
Jejeebhoy, Shireen J., and Saumya Rama Rao. 1995. "Unsafe Motherhood: A Review of Reproductive Health." In *Women's Health in India: Risk and Vulnerability,* edited by M. Das Gupta et al., 122–152. Madras: Oxford University Press.
Jolly, Margaret. 2002. "Introduction: Birthing beyond the Confines of Tradition and Modernity?" In *Birthing in the Pacific: Beyond Tradition and Modernity?* Edited by Vicki Luckere and Margaret Jolly, 1–32. Honolulu: University of Hawai'i Press.
———. 1998a. "Introduction: Colonial and Postcolonial Plots in Histories of Maternities and Modernities." In *Maternities and Modernities: Colonial and Postcolonial Experiences in Asia and the Pacific,* edited by K. Ram and M. Jolly, 1–25. Cambridge: Cambridge University Press.
———. 1998b. "Other Mothers: Maternal '*Insouciance*' and the Depopulation Debate in Fiji and Vanuatu, 1890–1930." In *Maternities and Modernities: Colonial and Postcolonial Experiences in Asia and the Pacific,* edited by K. Ram and M. Jolly, 177–212. Cambridge: Cambridge University Press.
Jordan, Brigitte. 1993. *Birth in Four Cultures: A Crosscultural Investigation of Childbirth in Yucatan, Holland, Sweden, and the United States.* Fourth ed. Prospect Heights, Ill.: Waveland Press.

———. 1978. *Birth in Four Cultures: A Crosscultural Investigation of Childbirth in Yucatan, Holland, Sweden, and the United States.* First ed. Prospect Heights, Ill.: Waveland Press.

Kapadia, Karin. 1993. "Marrying Money: Changing Preference and Practice in Tamil Marriage." *Contributions to Indian Sociology* 27, no. 1: 25–51.

Kay, Margarita A., ed. 1982. *Anthropology of Human Birth.* Philadelphia: F. A. Davis Company.

Kishwar, Madhu. 1984. "Introduction: Indian Women—The Continuing Struggle." In *In Search of Answers: Indian Women's Voices From Manushi,* edited by M. Kishwar and R. Vanita, 1–49. New Delhi: Horizon India Books.

Kitzinger, Sheila. 1994. "The Social Context of Birth: Some Comparisons between Childbirth in Jamaica and Britain." In *Ethnography of Fertility and Birth,* edited by Carol P. MacCormack, 171–194. Prospect Heights, Ill.: Waveland Press.

———. 1991 [1980, 1989]. *The Complete Book of Pregnancy and Childbirth.* Revised American edition. New York: Alfred A. Knopf.

———. 1979. *Birth at Home.* New York: Oxford University Press.

———. 1978. *The Place of Birth.* New York: Oxford University Press.

Kleinman, Arthur. 1980. *Patients and Healers in the Context of Culture: An Exploration of the Borderland between Anthropology, Medicine, and Psychiatry.* Berkeley: University of California Press.

Kleinman, Arthur, and Joan Kleinman. 1996. "The Appeal of Experience; The Dismay of Images: Cultural Appropriations of Suffering in Our Times." *Daedalus* 125, no. 1 (winter 1996): 1–23.

Kocher, J. E. 1980. "Population Policy In India: Recent Developments and Current Prospects." *Population and Development Review* 6, no. 2: 299–310.

Kolenda, Pauline. 1997. "Maternal Birth Experiences in a U.P. Village: 1950s, 1980s, 1990s." Paper presented at the Twenty-sixth Annual Conference on South Asia, University of Wisconsin, Madison, October 18, 1997.

Kynch, Jocelyn. 1987. "Some State Responses to Male and Female Need in British India." In *Women, State, and Ideology: Studies from Africa and Asia,* edited by Haleh Afshar, 130–151. Albany: State University of New York Press.

Laderman, Carol. 1983. *Wives and Midwives: Childbirth and Nutrition in Rural Malaysia.* Berkeley: University of California Press.

Lal, Maneesha. 1994. "The Politics of Gender and Medicine in Colonial India: The Countess of Dufferin's Fund, 1885–1888." *Bulletin of the History of Medicine* 68, no. 1: 29–66.

Lazarus, Ellen. 1997. "What Do Women Want? Issues of Choice, Control, and Class in American Pregnancy and Childbirth." In *Childbirth and Authoritative Knowledge: Cross-Cultural Perspectives,* edited by R. Davis-Floyd and C. Sargent, 132–158. Berkeley: University of California Press.

Leavitt, Judith W. 1986. *Brought to Bed: Child-Bearing in America, 1750–1950.* New York: Oxford University Press.

Leslie, Charles. 1976. "The Ambiguities of Medical Revivalism in Modern India." In *Asian Medical Systems: A Comparative Study,* edited by C. Leslie, 356–367. Berkeley: University of California Press.

———, ed. 1976. *Asian Medical Systems: A Comparative Study.* Berkeley: University of California Press.

Leslie, Charles, and Allan Young, eds. 1992. *Paths to Asian Medical Knowledge.* Berkeley: University of California Press.

Lewis, Oscar. 1958. *Village Life in Northern India: Studies in a Delhi Village.* Urbana: University of Illinois Press.

Lock, Margaret, and Patricia Kaufert. 1998. "Introduction." In *Pragmatic Women and Body Politics,* edited by M. Lock and P. Kaufert, 1–27. Cambridge: Cambridge University Press.

———, eds. 1998. *Pragmatic Women and Body Politics.* Cambridge: Cambridge University Press.

Lukere, Vicki, and Margaret Jolly, eds. 2002. *Birthing in the Pacific: Beyond Tradition and Modernity?* Honolulu: University of Hawai'i Press.

MacCormack, Carol P. 1994. "Health, Fertility and Birth in Moyambu District, Sierra Leone." In *Ethnography of Fertility and Birth,* edited by C. MacCormack, 105–129. Prospect Heights, Ill.: Waveland Press.

Madan, T. N. 1991. "Auspiciousness and Purity: Some Reconsiderations." *Contributions to Indian Sociology* 25, no. 2: 287–294.

———. 1980. *Doctors and Society: Three Asian Case Studies—India, Malaysia, & Sri Lanka.* New Delhi: Vikas Publishing House.

Mahadevan, K., M. S. R. Murthy, P. R. Reddy, P. J. Reddy, V. Gowri, and S. Sivaraju. 1985. *Infant & Childhood Mortality in India: Bio-Social Determinants.* Delhi: Mittal Publications.

Mamdani, M. 1972. *The Myth of Population Control.* New York: Monthly Review Press.

Manderson, Lenore. 1998. "Shaping Reproduction: Maternity in Early Twentieth-Century Malaya." In *Maternities and Modernities: Colonial and Postcolonial Experiences in Asia and the Pacific,* edited by K. Ram and M. Jolly, 26–49. Cambridge: Cambridge University Press.

Mani, Lata. 1990. "Contentious Traditions: The Debate on Sati in Colonial India." In *Recasting Women: Essays in Indian Colonial History,* edited by K. Sangari and S. Vaid, 88–126. New Brunswick, N.J.: Rutgers University Press.

Mani, S. B. 1981. "From Marriage to Child Conception: An Ethnomedical Study in Rural Tamil Nadu." In *The Social and Cultural Context of Medicine in India,* edited by G. R. Gupta, 194–220. Part 4 of *Main Currents in Indian Sociology.* New Delhi: Vikas Publishing House.

Marglin, Frédérique Appfel. 1990. "Smallpox in Two Systems of Knowledge." In *Dominating Knowledge: Development, Culture, & Resistance,* edited by F. Marglin and S. Marglin, 102–144. Oxford: Clarendon Press.

———. 1985. *Wives of the God-King: The Rituals of the Devadasis of Puri.* Delhi: Oxford University Press.

Martin, Emily. 1987. *The Woman in the Body: A Cultural Analysis of Reproduction.* Boston: Beacon Press.

McClain, Carol S. 1982. "Toward a Comparative Framework for the Study of Childbirth: A Review of the Literature." In *The Anthropology of Human Birth,* edited by M. Kay, 25–61. Philadelphia: F. A. Davis.

Mead, Margaret, and Niles Newton. 1967. "Cultural Patterning of Perinatal Behavior." In *Childbearing: Its Social and Psychological Aspects,* edited by S. Richardson and A. Guttmacher, 142–244. Baltimore, Md.: Williams & Wilkins.

Meillassoux, Claude. 1981. *Maidens, Meals, and Money: Capitalism and the Domestic Community.* New York: Cambridge University Press.

Menezes, Francis. 1999. "Implications of Financial Liberalization in India." *Swords and Ploughshares: A Journal of International Affairs,* spring 1999, pp. 1–12. Online version: www.american.edu/academic.depts/sis/sword/spring99/INDIA.PDF.

Messer, Ellen. 1993. "Anthropology and Human Rights." *Annual Review of Anthropology* 22: 221–249.

Miller, Barbara. 1981. *The Endangered Sex.* Ithaca, N.Y.: Cornell University Press.

Miller, L. G. 1979. "Pain, Parturition, and the Profession: Twilight Sleep in America." In *Health Care in America: Essays in Social History,* edited by S. Reverby and D. Rosner, 19–37. Philadelphia: Temple University Press.

Mines, Mattison, and Vijayalakshmi Gourishankar. 1990. "Leadership and Individuality in South Asia: The Case of the South Indian Big-man." *Journal of Asian Studies* 49, no. 4: 761–786.

Mitford, Jessica. 1992. *The American Way of Birth.* New York: Dutton.

Mohanty, Chandra Talpade. 1991. "Under Western Eyes: Feminist Scholarship and Colonial Discourses." In *Third World Women and the Politics of Feminism,* edited by C. T. Mohanty et al., 51–80. Bloomington: Indiana University Press.

Morsy, Soheir A. 1995. "Deadly Reproduction among Egyptian Women: Maternal Mortality and the Medicalization of Population Control." In *Conceiving the New World Order,* edited by F. Ginsburg and R. Rapp, 162–176. Berkeley: University of California Press.

Mukhopadhyay, Alok. 1992. "Health Systems & Services." In *State of India's Health,* edited by Alok Mukhopadhyay, 53–85. New Delhi: Voluntary Health Association of India.

Myrdal, Gunner. 1968. *Asian Drama: An Inquiry into the Poverty of Nations.* New York: Twentieth Century Fund.

Nadel-Klein, Jane. 1991. "Reweaving the Fringe: Localism, Tradition, and Representation in British Ethnography." *American Ethnologist* 18, no. 3: 500–517.

Nagarajan, Vijaya. 1993. "Hosting the Divine: The *Kōlam* in Tamil Nadu." In *Mud, Mirror, and Thread: Folk Traditions in Rural India,* edited by N. Fisher, 192–204. Santa Fe: Museum of New Mexico.

Nandy, Ashis. 1983. *The Intimate Enemy: Loss and Recovery of Self under Colonialism.* Delhi: Oxford University Press.

Nandy, Ashis, and Shiv Visvanathan. 1990. "Modern Medicine and Its Non-Modern Critics: A Study in Discourse." In *Dominating Knowledge: Development, Culture, and Resistance,* edited by F. Marglin and S. Marglin, 145–184. Oxford: Clarendon Press.

Newman, Lucile F. 1972. "The Anthropology of Birth." *Sociological Symposium: A Behavioral Science Journal* 8: 51–63.

———. 1969. "Folklore of Pregnancy: Wives' Tales in Contra Costa County, California." *Western Folklore* 28, no. 2: 112–135.

Nichter, Mark. 1989. *Anthropology and International Health: South Asian Case Studies.* Boston: Kluwer Academic Publishers.

Nortman, D. L. 1978. "India's New Birth Rate Target: An Analysis." *Population and Development Review* 4, no. 2: 277–312.

Oakley, Ann. 1977. "Cross-Cultural Practices." In *Benefits and Hazards of the New Obstetrics,* edited by T. Chard and M. Richards. Philadelphia: J. P. Lippincott.

———. 1984. *The Captured Womb: A History of the Medical Care of Pregnant Women.* New York: Basil Blackwell.

Obeyesekere, Gananath. 1976. "The Impact of Ayurvedic Ideas on the Culture and the Individual in Sri Lanka." In *Asian Medical Systems: A Comparative Study,* edited by C. Leslie, 201–226. Berkeley: University of California Press.

O'Brien, Mary. 1981. *The Politics of Reproduction.* Boston: Routledge & Kegan Paul.

Oldenburg, Veena Talwar. 2002. *Dowry Murder: The Imperial Origins of a Cultural Crime.* New York: Oxford University Press.

O'Neil, John, and Patricia Kaufert. 1993. "Analysis of a Dialogue on Risks in Childbirth: Clinicians, Epidemiologists, and Inuit Women." In *Knowledge, Power, and Practice: The Anthropology of Medicine and Everyday Life,* edited by S. Lindenbaum and M. Lock, 32–54. Berkeley: University of California Press.

———. 1990. "The Politics of Obstetric Care: The Inuit Experience." In *Birth and Power: Social Change and the Politics of Reproduction,* edited by W. Penn Handwerker, 53–68. San Francisco: Westview Press.

Osherson, Samuel, and Lorna Amarasingham. 1981. "The Machine Metaphor in Medicine." In *Social Contexts of Health, Illness and Patient Care,* edited by E. Mishler, 218–249. Cambridge: Cambridge University Press.

Parry, Jonathan P. 1994. *Death in Banaras.* Cambridge: Cambridge University Press.

———. 1991. "The Hindu Lexicographer? A Note on Auspiciousness and Purity." *Contributions to Indian Sociology* 25, no. 2: 267–285.

Patel, Tulsi. 1994. *Fertility Behaviour: Population and Society in a Rajasthani Village.* Delhi: Oxford University Press.

Pigg, Stacy Leigh. 1997. "Authority in Translation: Finding, Knowing, Naming, and Training 'Traditional Birth Attendants' in Nepal." In *Childbirth and Authoritative Knowledge: Cross-Cultural Perspectives,* edited by R. Davis-Floyd and C. Sargent, 233–262. Berkeley: University of California Press.

———. 1992. "Inventing Social Categories through Place: Social Representations and Development in Nepal." *Comparative Studies in Society & History* 34, no. 3: 491–513.

Qadeer, Imrana. 1994. "Rethinking Population Policy." In *Population Policy and Reproductive Rights,* edited by S. Anandhi. Madras: Initiatives: Women in Development.

Radhika, Vaidya M., and A. V. Balasubramanian. 1990. *Mother and Child Care in Traditional Medicine.* 2 volumes. LSPSS Monograph Series, nos. 3 and 4. Madras: Lok Swasthya Parampara Samvardhan Samithi.

Raheja, Gloria. 1988. *The Poison in the Gift: Ritual Prestation, and the Dominant Caste in a North Indian Village.* Chicago: University of Chicago Press.

Ram, Kalpana. 2001a. "Implicit and Discursive Knowledge: Fieldwork among Midwives in South India." Paper presented to the Department of Anthropology, University of Notre Dame, April 23, 2001.

———. 2001b. "Rationalizing Fecund Bodies: Family Planning Policy and the Modern Indian Nation-State." In *Borders of Being: Citizenship, Fertility and Sexuality in Asia and the Pacific,* edited by Margaret Jolly and Kalpana Ram, 82–117. Ann Arbor: University of Michigan Press.

———. 1998. "Maternity and the Story of Enlightenment in the Colonies: Tamil Coastal Women, South India." In *Maternities and Modernities: Colonial and Postcolonial Experiences in Asia and the Pacific,* edited by K. Ram and M. Jolly, 114–143. Cambridge: Cambridge University Press.

———. 1994. "Medical Management and Giving Birth: Responses of Coastal Women in Tamil Nadu." *Reproductive Health Matters,* no. 4: 20–26.

Ram, Kalpana, and Margaret Jolly, eds. 1998. *Maternities and Modernities: Colonial and Postcolonial Experiences in Asia and the Pacific.* Cambridge: Cambridge University Press.

Ramusack, Barbara. 2000. "Modernizing Mothers, Displacing Mothers: Baby Weeks in Late Colonial South India." Paper presented at the International Workshop on Gender and Transmission of Value Systems and Cultural Heritage(s) in South and Southeast Asia, Institute for Multi-Cultural and Comparative Gender Studies, University of Amsterdam, May 23–24, 2000.

———. 1997. "Issues of Equity: Maternal Medical Facilities in Rural Mysore, 1880–1920." Paper presented at a panel on "Maternal Birth Experiences: Historical and Anthropological Perspectives," Twenty-sixth Annual Conference on South Asia, Center for South Asia, University of Wisconsin, Madison, October 18, 1997.

———. 1996. "Motherhood and Medical Intervention: Women's Bodies and Professionalism in India After World War I." Paper presented at a panel on "The Modernization of Health Care in India: Women as Practitioners and Patients," Twenty-fifth Annual Conference on South Asia, Center for South Asia, University of Wisconsin, Madison, October 18–20, 1996.

Raphael, Dana, ed. 1979. *Breastfeeding and Food Policy in a Hungry World.* San Francisco: Academic Press.

Rapp, Rayna. 2000. *Testing Women, Testing the Fetus: The Social Impact of Amniocentesis in America.* New York: Routledge.

———. 1993. "Accounting for Amniocentesis." In *Knowledge, Power, and Practice: The Anthropology of Medicine and Everyday Life,* edited by S. Lindenbaum and M. Lock, 55–76. Berkeley: University of California Press.

———. 1991. "Moral Pioneers: Women, Men, and Fetuses on a Frontier of Reproductive Technology." In *Gender at the Crossroads of Knowledge: Feminist Anthropology in the Postmodern Era,* edited by M. di Leonardo, 383–395. Berkeley: University of California Press.

Ravindran, T. K. Sundari. 1995a. "Women's Health in a Rural Poor Population in Tamil Nadu." In *Women's Health in India: Risk and Vulnerability,* edited by M. Das Gupta et al., 175–211. Madras: Oxford University Press.

———. 1995b. "Factors Impeding Quality of Care: Rural Poor Women's Experiences with MCH/FP Services in Tamil Nadu." Paper presented at Ford Foundation/Population Council Workshop on Quality of Care in the Indian Family Planning Program, Bangalore, May, 1995.

———. 1994. "Women and the Politics of Population and Development in India." In *Population Policy and Reproductive Rights,* edited by S. Anandhi. Madras: Initiative: Women in Development.

Reissman, Catherine K. 1983. "Women and Medicalization: A New Perspective." *Social Policy* 14, no. 1: 3–18.

Rostow, W. W. 1991 [1960]. *The Stages of Economic Growth: A Non-Communist Manifesto.* Third edition. New York: Cambridge University Press.

Rothman, Barbara Katz. 1982. *In Labor: Women and Power in the Birthplace.* New York: W. W. Norton.

Rozario, Santi. 1998. "The *Dai* and the Doctor: Discourses on Women's Reproductive Health in Rural Bangladesh." In *Maternities and Modernities: Colonial and Postcolonial Experiences in Asia and the Pacific,* edited by K. Ram and M. Jolly, 144–176. Cambridge: Cambridge University Press.

———. 1995. "*Dais* and Midwives: The Renegotiation of the Status of Birth Attendants in Contemporary Bangladesh." In *The Female Client and the Health Care Provider,* edited by J. H. Roberts and C. Vlassoff, 91–112. New Delhi: International Development Research Centre.

Russett, Cynthia Eagle. 1989. *Sexual Science: The Victorian Construction of Womanhood.* Cambridge, Mass.: Harvard University Press.

Sandhya, S. 1991. *Socio-Economic and Cultural Correlates of Infant Mortality: A Demographic Appraisal.* New Delhi: Concept Publishing Company.

Sargent, Carolyn F. 1982. *The Cultural Context of Therapeutic Choice: Obstetrical Care Decisions among the Bariba of Benin.* Boston: D. Reidel.

Sargent, Carolyn, and Joan Rawlins. 1992. "Transformations in Maternity Services in Jamaica." *Social Science and Medicine* 35, no. 10: 1225–1232.

Sargent, Carolyn, and Grace Bascope. 1997. "Ways of Knowing about Birth in Three Cultures." In *Childbirth and Authoritative Knowledge: Cross-Cultural Perspectives,* edited by R. Davis-Floyd and C. Sargent, 183–208. Berkeley: University of California Press.

Scheper-Hughes, Nancy. 1992. *Death without Weeping: The Violence of Everyday Life in Brazil.* Berkeley: University of California Press.

Scheper-Hughes, Nancy, and Margaret Lock. 1987. "The Mindful Body: A Prolegomenon to Future Work in Medical Anthropology." *Medical Anthropology Quarterly* 1, no. 1: 6–41.

Scott, James. 1985. *Weapons of the Weak: Everyday Forms of Peasant Resistance.* New Haven, Conn.: Yale University Press.

Selby, Martha. 1999. "Constant Cravings: Listening to the Voice of the *Garbha* in the *Caraka-* and *Susruta-samhitas.*" Paper presented at the Annual Meeting of the Association for Asian Studies, Boston, March 13, 1999.

Sen, Amartya. 1995. "Population Policy: Authoritarianism versus Cooperation." Paper presented at the John and Catherine T. MacArthur Foundation Lecture Series on Population Issues, New Delhi, August 17, 1995.

Shiva, Mira. 1992. "Women and Health." In *The State of India's Health,* edited by A. Mukhopadhyay, 265–301. New Delhi: Voluntary Health Association of India.

Spencer, Robert F. 1977 [1950]. "Embryology and Obstetrics in Preindustrial Societies." In *Culture, Disease and Healing: Studies in Medical Anthropology,* edited by D. Landy, 289–299. New York: Macmillan.

Srinivas, M. N. 1989. *The Cohesive Role of Sanskritization and Other Essays.* Delhi: Oxford University Press.

Srinivasa, D. K., K. A. Narayan, Asha Oumachigui, and Gautam Roy. 1997. *Prevalence of Maternal Morbidity in a South Indian Community.* Pondicherry: Jawaharlal Institute of Postgraduate Medical Education and Research.

Srinivasmurthi, G. 1923. "Secretary's Minute." In *Report of the Committee on Indigenous Systems of Medicine.* Madras: Government Printing Press.

Stevenson, Mrs. Sinclair. 1971 [1920]. *The Rites of the Twice Born.* New Delhi: Oriental Books Reprint Corporation.

Stoler, Ann Laura. 1991. "Carnal Knowledge and Imperial Power: Gender, Race, and Morality in Colonial Asia." In *Gender at the Crossroads of Knowledge: Feminist Anthropology in the Postmodern Era,* edited by M. di Leonardo, 51–101. Berkeley: University of California Press.

Swaminathan, Padmini. 1996. "The Failures of Success? An Analysis of Tamilnadu's Recent Demographic Experience." Working Paper no. 141, Madras Institute of Development Studies.

Trawick, Margaret [née Margaret Egnor]. 1992. *Notes on Love in a Tamil Family.* Berkeley: University of California Press.

——— [Margaret Egnor]. 1980. "On the Meaning of Sakti to Women in Tamil Nadu." *The Powers of Tamil Women,* edited by S. Wadley, 1–34. Syracuse, N.Y.: Syracuse University, Foreign and Comparative Studies Program.

UNICEF. 1990. *Children and Women in India: A Situation Analysis.* New Delhi: UNICEF.

Upadhya, Carol Boyack. 1990. "Dowry and Women's Property in Coastal Andhra Pradesh." *Contributions to Indian Sociology* 24, no. 1: 29–59.

Van Esterik, Penny. 1988. "The Insufficient Milk Syndrome: Biological Epidemic or Cultural Construction?" In *Women & Health,* edited by P. Whelehan, 97–109. Granby, Mass.: Bergin & Garvey.

Van Hollen, Cecilia. 2003. "Invoking *Vali*: Painful Technologies of Modern Birth in South India." *Medical Anthropology Quarterly* 17, no. 1 (March): 49–77.

———. 2002. "'Baby Friendly' Hospitals and Bad Mothers: Maneuvering Development in the Postpartum Period in Tamil Nadu, South India." In *Daughters of Hariti: Birth & Female Healers in South and Southeast Asia,* edited by S. Rozario and G. Samuel, 163–181. New York: Routledge.

———. 1998a. "Criminal Mothers and Superstitious Fathers: A Shift from the Mother to the Child in Tamil Nadu's Maternal and Child Health Program." Paper presented at the Twenty-eighth Annual Conference on South Asia, Center for South Asia, University of Wisconsin—Madison, October 1998.

———. 1998b. "Moving Targets: Routine IUD Insertion in Maternity Wards in Tamil Nadu, India." *Reproductive Health Matters* 6, no. 11 (May): 98–106.

———. 1994. "Perspectives on the Anthropology of Birth: A Review." *Culture, Medicine and Psychiatry* 18: 501–512.

Verderese, Maria DeLourdes, and Lily M. Turnbull, eds. 1975. *The Traditional Birth Attendant in Maternal and Child Health & Family Planning: A Guide to Her Training and Utilization.* Geneva: World Health Organization.

Victoria Hospital for Caste and Gosha Women. 1904. *Report.* Madras: Victoria Hospital for Caste and Gosha Women.

Victoria Memorial Scholarship Fund. 1918. "Improvement of the Condition of Childbirth in India." Memorandum.

Visaria, P. 1971. *The Sex Ratio of the Population of India.* Census Monograph no. 10. New Delhi: Officer of the Registrar General, India.

Wadley, Susan, ed. 1980. *The Powers of Tamil Women.* Syracuse, N.Y.: University of Syracuse, Foreign and Comparative Studies Program.

Winslow, Miron. 1979 [1862]. *Winslow's: A Comprehensive Tamil and English Dictionary.* Madras: Asian Educational Services.

Wiser, William H. 1936. *The Hindu Jajmani System: A Socio-Economic System Interrelating Members of a Hindu Village Community in Services.* Lucknow, U.P.: Lucknow Publishing House.

Working Women's Forum. 1996. *A Short Account on the Status of IUD Users and Service Delivery System in Tamil Nadu.* Madras: Working Women's Forum.

World Health Organization. 1996. *WHO South-East Asia Region: Regional Health Report.* New Delhi: World Health Organization.

Zeitlyn, Sushila, and Rabeya Rowshan. 1997. "Privileged Knowledge and Mothers' 'Perceptions': The Case of Breast-feeding and Insufficient Milk in Bangladesh." *Medical Anthropology Quarterly* 11, no. 1: 56–68.

Index

abortions: family-planning tactics after, 142, 146–47, 149, 155, 164; legalization of, 154; for sex selection, 193–94
ācai (desire, cravings, passion): and allopathic care, 110; consumption context of, 88–89, 98; during pregnancy, 87–88, 252nn33,35; ritual satisfaction of, 77, 80, 88–89, 93–94
aciṅkam (unseemly, gross, or dirty): advanced pregnancy as, 252n41; expressions of pain as, 131, 132; vernix coating as, 203
Āḍi (a Tamil month), 84, 251n23
Adiramapattinam (Tamil Nadu), 158–59
Agarwal, Bina, 99–100, 253n57
agricultural laborers, 23, 25
AIADMK (All India Anna Dravida Kazhagam) party, 21
Aichison, Dr., 248n43
alcoholism, 25
All India Anna Dravida Kazhagam (AIADMK) party, 21
All-India Hospitals Postpartum Programme, 145, 146–48, 257n14
All India Obstetrics and Gynaecological Congress (1936), 38
allopathic childbirth. *See* biomedical childbirth
allopathic drugs: economic constraints on, 127; in home deliveries, 134–35, 137, 138–39; for labor inducement, 112–13, 115, 116; modernity discourse on, 34, 122–23; with nonallopathic remedies, 126, 137–38; for painless childbirth, 114–15, 116
allopathic practitioners: as anesthesiologists, 127; on baby bathing, 202–3; on baby oil application, 203, 262–63n67; in colonial era, 37, 45–47, 248n39; falsifiability principle of, 179; interview questions to, 230–35; on IUD insertions, 155–56, 161–62; on *karuppu,* 187–88, 261nn42,43; on postpartum diet, 170–71, 259n9; reaction to pain by, 128–29, 130, 131, 132–34, 138, 255n43; shifting of models by, 171–72, 178–79; *tridosa* logic of, 161–62. See also *ayahs*
ambulance services, 67
American National Twilight Sleep Association, 114
ammikkal (pounding stone) ritual, 134, 256n56
amniocentesis, 110–11
ampaḍḍaccis (Muslim midwives), 41
analgesics, 114–15, 116, 122–23, 127

Indexer:	Patricia Deminna
Cartographer:	Bill Nelson
Compositor:	G&S Typesetters, Inc.
Text:	10/13 Sabon
Display:	Sabon
Printer and binder:	Malloy Lithographing, Inc.